T0339490

# Breaking out of the Expat Bubble

Moving abroad means having to settle into a new host country. This book enables expats and those who support them to create intercultural connections and friendships both within and outside the workplace.

Having left behind a large part of their social network, expats need to make local friends to really settle in. This book shows you how this works, and that breaking out of the expat bubble and making local friends helps you adjust and settle in the new place you call home. Organisations and societies should also support expats if they would like to retain this international talent. It is important to create the conditions for expats to build a social network, for example by connecting them with a local buddy. Learn more in this book about the advantages of such contact and how to set up and manage a buddy system to the benefit of both your expats and your organisation or community. The book is illustrated by many quotes from almost 20 years of research and features 11 real-world experiences of expats around the world. It also includes practical recommendations for expats, organisations and societies.

An invaluable resource on creating more intercultural connections and friendships in the workplace and the local community, this book will be well placed in the hand luggage of expats – especially those who go without much organisational support – as well as on the desks of managers and HR professionals who would like to better support expats on this great adventure.

**Marian van Bakel** is Associate Professor at the University of Southern Denmark, where she conducts research in international human resource management, with an emphasis on expatriate management. She is passionate about bridging the gap between theory and practice to make sure practitioners benefit from her research. She is from the Netherlands and lived in France and the United Kingdom. She has been living in Denmark for 10 years now.

# Breaking out of the Expat Bubble

How to Make Intercultural Connections and Friends

Marian van Bakel

Routledge
Taylor & Francis Group
NEW YORK AND LONDON

ISBN: 9781032160412 (hbk)
ISBN: 9781032160399 (pbk)
ISBN: 9781003246855 (ebk)

DOI: 10.4324/9781003246855

Typeset in Sabon
by Newgen Publishing UK

The Open Access version of chapter 2 was funded by University of Southern Denmark

# Contents

# Boxes

# Foreword

Without question, *Breaking out of the Expat Bubble* is a book whose time has come. Multi-national corporations and organisations are operating in a rapidly changing world. Never before in history has there been so much intercultural mixing and interchange as there is today for those who work internationally. How does this affect the goals of the organisation sending its employees to work in other countries? How does this affect the person being sent? How does this affect those who independently choose to look for jobs in other countries?

In earlier years, few asked these questions. Many expats interacted with local citizens during the work hours, often in some managerial role. During the off hours, however, most retreated to the clubs, restaurants or living situations they shared with fellow expats. Together they formed another world separate from the one most locals around them lived in. It was the accepted – and easiest? – thing to do.

In this ground-breaking book, Marian van Bakel emphasises a different approach and explains why this is important for both the individual and the organisation. She begins by acknowledging the reality that cross-cultural interactions are not always easy or comfortable, giving real-life examples of specific intercultural difficulties expats often face, in particular with regard to making new friends abroad. She goes on to give concrete, practical ways on how to turn that challenge into an opportunity to become more culturally competent.

After emphasising the importance of preparing each expat to deal well with the cultural and social differences they inevitably encounter, the second half of the book introduces and expands on a brilliant, but often overlooked topic: the importance of expats being mentored by someone from the host culture rather than a fellow expat only.

Contrary to earlier eras and models of expat assignments which primarily featured expats going from the home office to a new place expecting to impart their great wisdom to others, Marian writes about the importance of expats also *receiving* from the host nationals, or 'locals' in each country.

Why is this important? For many reasons. First, for the expats themselves. We all learn more from a posture of humility rather than arrogance. Particularly in cross-cultural encounters, it is important to come as a learner rather than a 'know it all.' Who can better teach an expat the reason behind the perceived differences they are encountering than someone who is from that culture?

Second, for the local person. People of any and all cultures are honoured when their knowledge, wisdom and insights are sought out. It is part of knowing we are seen – something each of us also wants. That combination of mentee–mentor begins to forge friendships which, in the end, helps to meet the need for socialisation and a sense of belonging in this new place.

Third, for the organisation. As these friendships develop and expats learn more about the nuances of the local culture, they become increasingly effective in their work. They are now more able to develop culturally relevant means and methods to reach the goals the organisation is hoping to attain. Happy, effective employees are also the ones most likely to stay, so the talent pool is more stable. Marian offers many specific ways organisations can help to foster these types of effective mentoring programmes, including encouraging the learning of the local language when possible.

Fourth, for the host country. Many countries are trying to attract relevant talent for specific areas where they have a shortage. When expats feel at home and develop strong social connections, they are more likely to stay in long term.

This book makes clear why local relationships are a major key for success for any expat. They are key to the emotional well-being of each expat in their new place. They are also part of a key strategy for increasing the likelihood of success for the organisation as business models effective in one place may need to be adjusted in another. Expats who have been mentored by locals are often the most able to do that. Because this book was written for both the expats who go and those who support them, there are riches to uncover for all who are involved in any aspect of international, cross-cultural living.

In the end, however, as powerful these thoughts are for the expats and the organisations who employ them, it offers another key for us all. In a world that seems to be polarising as the speed of intercultural interactions leads to challenges of identity and belonging, what Marian is writing about is how to make friends with the 'other.' How do we learn to see 'them' as the people they are and from whom we can learn so much and our lives be enriched together?

Enjoy reading it. I did!

Ruth E. Van Reken

Co-author, *Third Culture Kids: Growing Up Among Worlds*, 3rd ed.

Co-founder, Families in Global Transition

# Preface

The topic of *Breaking out of the Expat Bubble* is near to my heart. When I was studying International Business Communication at Radboud University Nijmegen, the Netherlands, I spent a year abroad in Tours, France, and readily signed up for a *famille d'accueil*, or local host family, because I wanted to get to know the French better and this was a great way to get connected. Naturally I spent a lot of time with other international students – they were in the same situation which meant they also had a lot of time on their hands (not going back home in the weekends) and an interest in seeing something of the country, so we were travelling quite a bit in France itself. So being put in touch with the family Jacob was a great way to get out of this expat bubble. We regularly met up for some lovely dinners and chats, mainly at their house just outside Tours, which was a great way to learn more about French culture and also improve my French. When I finished my masters and got a scholarship to do research on expats and diplomats at the University of Oxford for 5 months, I jumped at the opportunity of getting a local host family through the charity HostUK. This time it was about a one-time visit with a host family somewhere in the United Kingdom. I was put in touch with the Joneses in Devon, and went there for a weekend, seeing a whole new area of the country. With both families I kept in touch for years afterwards, and when I came back to the Netherlands, I started thinking: what if I organise this for expats? Wouldn't that help them settle in? This led to my PhD research *In touch with the Dutch* (see Chapters 7–9) and a continuing research interest in how I can help expats make the most of their stay abroad by connecting with locals, which is something that is very enriching and helpful but not always easy to do.

I became interested not only in the expat's social life but also in how connections with local colleagues can be very helpful in the workplace. In 2009, I joined the International Human Resource Management conference in Santa Fe, United States, and met Charles Vance and Torben Andersen who invited me in on their ongoing research on the Host Country Liaison model, which is about the roles that locals can play in knowledge management. With this research they are trying to increase the focus on the local colleagues who have to work with the expats, since they are often neglected. We've been working together on validating this model in Malaysia, Mexico and the United States (see Chapter 5) and on the related topic of intercultural mentoring (see Chapter 6).

When moving to Denmark in 2013, I also started to be interested in how expats make new friends when abroad and discovered that not much was known about this process. I got curious when I read a conceptual article from 2010,[1] that made the choosing of friends sound like a very deliberate process, according to whether the person in question has 'host country expertise' or 'adjustment empathy', so I started interviewing expats to try to find out why they had 'selected' their friends. This turned out to be something the expats hadn't thought that much about, which made me think the process was much less deliberate than currently suggested in the literature. This ultimately led to the 72 interviews that much of this book is based on (see especially Chapter 2).

This book is where I collect all the interesting research that can help expats and their families with settling in abroad. I am passionate about bridging theory and practice, and would like to make sure that what research discovers is also read by those who can do something with the knowledge. That is why I have written this book for a practitioner audience, while still basing it on the latest academic research. With this book, I hope that even more people will benefit from what I learned through my research over the past 20 years, and that it helps expats and their families to make the most out of their experience of living and working abroad.

Many people have contributed in one way or another to this book. Of course, the book would not be what it is without all the expats and partners who participated in my research, and I would like to thank them for giving their time and wanting to share their experiences. I have tried to use all this information to the best of my ability in this book, so that many other expats and partners can benefit from it. As you hopefully know, I try my best to share the findings of my research with you. If you ever have participated but have not heard about any findings, then please contact me!

The writing of the book has been supported by a Monograph Fellowship from the Carlsberg Foundation, which provided the time and impetus to make this book a reality. I would also like to thank my university and research group for a writing retreat and the support of student helpers. Many thanks go to Fabrice Mielke, Mary Jan Saeed, Anna-Lena Schwarz,

Lisa Schlichting, Katrina Hu, Signe Nottelmann Andersen and Myra-Mirabel Beduma Aboagye, who supported me in interviewing the 72 expats and with other tasks related to the book.

The book has also been supported by many people in my network. I would like to thank the people who have contributed a box to this book: Signe Biering, Sven Horak, Annelies Kastein, Hanne Lee, Jong Gyu Park and Reto Wegmann. I am also very grateful to Maartje Reijnders from Heldermaker for working with me to create the wonderful illustrations at the start of each chapter. I would also like to thank Gordon Watanabe for introducing me to the Personal Leadership (PL) method at the Summer Institute for Intercultural Communication in 2012, and for gracefully allowing me to include two exercises from the PL method in the book. The final stages of the book have been supported by several people who read (parts of) the book and gave me some valuable feedback. Many thanks to Ruth Van Reken, who also contributed the foreword, Marinel Gerritsen, Charles Vance, Chris Brewster, Signe Biering, Mariola Kajkowska, Kate Dahl and Vlad Vaiman.

Over the years I have talked about this topic with so many people – colleagues, friends, family – and I would sincerely like to thank everyone for contributing their own stories, experiences and suggestions, which certainly have shaped my thoughts and research. Last but not least, my own social network has been invaluable in supporting me with the writing of this book. I would like to thank my closest friends and family – especially Assia and Søren – for their support over the years.

Marian van Bakel

## Note

1   Farh, C., Bartol, K., Shapiro, D., & Shin, J. (2010). Networking abroad: A process model of how expatriates form support ties to facilitate adjustment. *Academy of Management Review,* 35(3), 434–454.

# Experience

A Dutch expat in China – "I asked them so many questions, I really wanted to understand"

*Thijs is a 28-year-old Dutch expat in China. He came to China as an exchange student because he had always been fascinated by China, and then returned to also work there. He lived in three different places in China, among which Beijing and Shanghai, and stayed for 6 years in total.*

## Were you interested in meeting locals when you came to China?

Oh, definitely, I was very curious about locals. So, you know, when I arrived in China, I came before the semester started, so I was really alone. So, I had to go outside and explore the country by my own and for me, this was a very strange experience because it was actually my first time being alone in a foreign country, first of all. And second of all, in a country that is very different from my country. So, everyone looks different. Everyone speaks a different language. I could not read the street signs. So, you know, for me as a young guy, this was a very interesting but also very challenging experience. But I think what really helped me is my family background [...] I come from a mixed background [...], we have a lot of different countries and a culture mix going on in our family. So, from that side, I basically feel that when I go to a new place, I basically have to be openminded and try to understand more. And the only way you can do that is to speak to people, ask questions and try out new things. And that's what I did. I tried to talk with people. I try to look at what people are doing. [...] And then when I met my first classmates who were Chinese, I asked them so many questions. Not to judge, but I really wanted to understand like, Hey, why do you do this and how is that and why do people do that? And

DOI: 10.4324/9781003246855-1

luckily for me, I had a great university buddy, she was a Chinese girl. And she was really friendly, and I became great friends with her. And she really brought me around in the city and she taught me a lot of stuff. So that was a great time for me to get familiar with Chinese culture.

## How did you start making contacts in China?

So, for me, the first time when I came to China, it was mostly through school. So, I had a lot of classmates, Chinese classmates that I got in touch with. [...] And, you know, I've learned over time, living in another country, people are not going to come to you. You have to go out and meet people and make that effort. Yes. So that was that. As a professional, it also means that I have to put away maybe my shyness and go out and say 'hi' to people. And maybe not everyone is as receptive, right? Not everyone wants to be your friend, but that's okay. Eventually you will meet people and you can get a great connection. So, I think it really is about going out there saying 'hi' to people, putting yourself out there, at work, going to activities, you know, sports clubs, they're all different ways to meet people, I think. [...]

## And how did that go when you started working?

I think from a professional perspective, it's a bit harder to become friends, I feel. Because what I've noticed is that my Chinese colleagues tend to be very competitive at work. A lot of people distrust each other. So, it's kind of hard to really create strong friendships. But I felt sometimes, as a foreigner working in China, that especially because maybe I'm different, that I sometimes have to prove myself extra to show why I am there, and not a local person. Maybe that's my own feeling, but I got that feeling sometimes. But nevertheless, there were always a few people around, that you have good relationships with and I felt... when you complete certain projects, especially difficult projects, and you managed to complete it together, that bond kind of grows and that trust grows. And having lunches together with your colleagues helps to get to know each other more. I think it's more just that people don't know each other well, and they're maybe afraid of the unknown. Though, I try to always reach out to people and if people are not receptive, you know, just say 'hi,' and that's it, right? But if people are receptive, I try to build that relationship. [...]

And I think, something that's really helped me as well is every time that I lived in China, I've always avoided becoming this kind of an expat that goes to only expat places. Because I know that there are foreigners in China, who only hang out with other foreigners, or they always stay in their comfort zone, that they go to different restaurants and things. Yeah, but from day one that I came to China, I was different in that sense because I really wanted to know about China. [...] We can be studying books, I can study as many books about China, I can read about China, I can ask as many things, but it's something you have to experience. And I think I've taken that with me during my professional career. That and also, sometimes people would say, 'Hey, let's try this traditional Chinese thing.' And maybe I would say, 'why would I do that?' But then I would think, 'hey, I should just try it. You know, maybe I will like it. And if I don't like it, at least I tried.'

# Introduction

Working and living abroad is for many a dream come true. It is an opportunity to meet other cultures, develop intercultural competence and get international experience that may help in one's career. It is also a great way to expand one's horizon and develop a global mindset. Of course, it is not without its challenges, such as having to re-establish one's life abroad, and dealing with other norms and values that might impact on the way in which people live and conduct business. This book is about people who move abroad for their work, and the challenge of building a new social network, especially with locals of the host country. Many expats see this as a challenge; the most common concern for expats and their families before they move abroad is re-establishing social life (41%) and missing friends and family (34%).[1] The key aspect is to manage these challenges well. As Professor Colleen Ward wrote in the seminal book on the *Psychology of Culture Shock*:[2]

> The challenge is to understand and manage contact between culturally diverse people and groups in order to reduce the stresses and difficulties that are a normal aspect of such encounters, as well as to enhance the positive effects that cross-cultural encounters can bestow on the participants.

The number of international migrants has greatly increased in the past 50 years. The World Migration Report[3] estimates that in 2020 around 281 million people lived in another country than that of their birth – this is three times more than in 1970, though still only a small percentage of the total world population (3.6%). Workplaces are internationalising and, increasingly, local employees will have to work with people from different cultural backgrounds. It is important to manage these intercultural interactions well for the employees themselves (both international and local), for the organisations that employ them and the societies in which they

DOI: 10.4324/9781003246855-2

live. With this book, I hope to help with the social aspect of relocating abroad – how do expats build a new social network abroad and how can they make friends with locals? And how can organisations support their expats in all this?

## What are expats and locals?

So, what is an expat? There are many definitions of an 'expatriate' or expat in short. Originally, an expatriate means someone who lives outside their home country – *ex patria*. The term started to be used in the field of International Human Resource Management to indicate employees of an internationally operating company who have been sent to a foreign country – so-called assigned/company-sent/organisational expats. Around the turn of the 20th century, it was acknowledged that many expats went abroad on their own initiative and were not sponsored by a company. These are called self-initiated expats, and they are more often female and younger than assigned expats.[4] In this book I focus on both groups of expats since they all have to settle into a new host country and make new friends.

Some might wonder what the difference is between expats and migrants. There is certainly much discussion in the academic literature about these terms.[5] Professor Maike Andresen with her colleagues from the University of Bamberg and Cranfield University did a very helpful analysis of existing definitions in the literature of assigned expats, self-initiated expats and migrants, and they argue that expats are a subgroup of migrants, being individuals who move to another country while changing the dominant place of residence and executing legal work abroad.[6] Working legally abroad distinguishes expats from other migrant groups who do not (yet) work (e.g. the partner of the expat or international students who do not work in the host country) or those who illegally work abroad. Another often-made distinction between expats and migrants has to do with whether someone is staying temporarily or on a more permanent basis.[7] People can also move between categories, for example, a self-initiated expat can become a migrant. Even though I use the term 'expat' in my book, much of what I write about is also relevant for other migrant groups such as the partner of the expat, and international students, since they also move to a new country and have to build a new social network abroad. Similarly, refugees or those who are supporting them, can also learn a lot that may help them with settling into the new host country. For example, a buddy system (see Chapters 7–9) could also be set up for refugees to help them better integrate into the host society (see Box 9.1 on p. 210). For ease and conciseness, I mainly use the term 'expat' here, even though much of what I write also applies to the partners of expats.

In this book I will also talk a lot about 'locals' of the host country. With this term I mean the people of the host country or host country nationals. While this sounds rather simple, also here there can be discussions, for example about how 'local' a local really is. One study looked at local employees in U.S. American multinational corporations in Romania and concluded that the Romanian locals were not the same as the other Romanians.[8] They could rather be described as 'foreign locals,' differing from other Romanians on various dimensions such as assertiveness, individualism and attitude towards time. You can also discuss whether some expats who have been in the host country for 20 years or more can also be counted as 'locals,' but in this book I mean host country nationals when I mention 'locals of the host country.'

## Making friends abroad

When expats move abroad, they leave behind a large part of their social network – their friends and family – in their home country, and they have to make new friends. Of course, nowadays it's easy to keep in touch with family and friends back home through various technologies, and this can indeed offer some good support for the expat and their family. The downside is that expats might get more homesick because they are reminded of home, and this negatively influences well-being.[9] When homesick, expats might cope by spending more time keeping up with the culture and traditions of the home country, and by connecting with fellow nationals abroad. This behaviour can work both positively in helping someone cope with the homesickness, and negatively if the person gets too caught up in the home culture and does not integrate into the host culture.

In the host country, the expat and their family have to make new friends, and not just with other expats because this has downsides in the long run. While support from other expats can be very helpful especially in the beginning of the stay, it might work counterproductively in the long run, especially if, over time, one's close contacts are still from the same nationality.[10] International students who had co-national contacts among their three most frequent contacts over time experienced more stress and were less culturally adjusted to the host country. So, it is important to make connections with locals. Such contacts can have many benefits, as we'll see in Chapter 4, but it is not always easy. One of the most frequent complaints of international students is that they would like to have more contact with local students.[11] Many universities assume that having international students on campus and in the classrooms is enough to have positive effects, but in fact, students often keep to their own group.[12] Mere exposure to another group is not enough.

Intercultural interaction needs to be encouraged for positive effects to show. This line of thinking started after WWII in the United States, culminating in the seminal book *The Nature of Prejudice* by Allport.[13] Intergroup contact theory proposes that, under certain conditions, interpersonal contact could be the most effective way to reduce prejudices and stereotyping between different cultural groups. A meta-analysis of more than 500 studies[14] has indeed found that intergroup contact reduces prejudices, and even more so if certain conditions have been met. Intergroup contact is more effective if the groups have equal status, if they work together to achieve common goals, and if there is institutional support – such as from an organisation or institution – for the interactions between the two groups. How does such intergroup contact help reduce prejudice? Research[15] suggests that regular contact with people from other cultural groups reduces the anxiety that many people have about meeting 'others.' It becomes normal, and this allows people to learn about the other group and see the world from the other group's perspective. This empathy reduces prejudice towards that group.

It is particularly intercultural friendships that are effective at enabling someone to take the other's perspective. A large study done in 1988 among people in France, Great Britain, the Netherlands and West Germany showed how those with friends of another nationality, race, culture, religion or social class scored significantly lower on several indicators of prejudice.[16] Those with intercultural friendships feel more sympathy and admiration for the other group. These feelings can actually be quite pivotal; non-Jews who risked their lives to save Jews during World War II reported more close friendships as children with other groups. Intercultural friendships also have a positive influence on those who learn about such friendships; their prejudice towards that cultural group then also decreases.[17] This shows how important it is that close relationships are created between individuals of different cultural groups.

Historian Rutger Bregman also concludes in his book *Humankind* that contact between different groups is the best medicine for hate, racism and prejudice. It does take some time, but it then has great effects, as the research he summarises shows.[18] For example, living in a more culturally diverse neighbourhood decreased the support for Trump and Brexit, and it made people offer more support during the Boston marathon bombing in 2013. In the Netherlands, people working in a culturally diverse workplace are less Islamophobic. Also, protests that were violent when a refugee centre was announced in a Dutch neighbourhood had morphed into mainly positive experiences a few years later, when the neighbourhood had gotten to know the people. Bregman emphasises that intercultural contact doesn't mean we cannot be ourselves. He compares our identity to a house, and if the house has a solid foundation, we can open the doors.

## What is culture?

When talking about living and working abroad, cultural differences play a role – also in the way people socialise and make friends. Culture is about the values, beliefs and norms that guide one's everyday behaviour, and which are passed on from generation to generation.[19] There is a plethora of definitions and frameworks that describe culture, and it is beyond the scope of this book to cover all this. Rather than discussing at length what culture is, I would like to highlight two important issues. First of all, many cultural differences are invisible. Culture is often likened to an iceberg, with the majority of it (norms, values) being beneath the surface, which can cause issues because people don't expect these cultural differences. Second, there is a risk of generalising too much when people talk about culture. Especially with value-based frameworks such as that of Hofstede and GLOBE,[20] people seem to take a mental shortcut and easily think that everyone from a specific country will have the same values and behave in the same way. The assumption is that countries are homogenous, which they seldom actually are. Even in small countries such as Denmark, when I ask my students whether there are subcultures, they all say 'yes' and then point to another part of the country which is rather different from them, in their opinion. This is important to keep in mind when talking to people from other cultural backgrounds. While it can be helpful to learn about another culture and what is considered as normal behaviour there, the person in front of you is an individual that might have quite different preferences and behaviours. And you yourself also might not be the 'average' person from your own country. For example, I myself certainly am not as direct as many of the Dutch can be. There are also often cultural differences between different organisations or professional groups, for example nurses and accountants. So, it is difficult or even impossible to have a definitive framework of salient cultural characteristics for managing intercultural interactions, as Professors Nancy Adler and Zeynep Aycan also concluded in their review of the cross-cultural literature in 2018.[21] For this reason, while it can be helpful to know more about different cultures and how people might behave, it is ultimately more important to ask the right questions which has a lot to do with intercultural competence. In Chapter 3, I dive deeper into the topic of intercultural competence and how you can develop it.

## For whom is this book?

I have written this book for expats and their families, and for those who support them with settling into the new host country, such as organisations and municipalities. For expats, making new friends in the host country is very important for feeling good there. This book shows how important this actually is, and how expats can go about building a new social network abroad. This is especially helpful for self-initiated expats who often are not supported by an organisation, and can also be valuable for international students who plan to study abroad. The insights and recommendations shared in this book may also be relevant for other migrant groups and the institutions supporting them (see for example Box 9.1 on p. 210 about a buddy system for refugees).

For organisations that employ expats, this book can help by suggesting different ways in which to support the social aspect of living and working in a host country. This is not only relevant for multinational corporations with many assigned expats but also for organisations in the public and third sector. Governments and non-government organisations (NGOs) such as *Médecins Sans Frontières* send out diplomats and other personnel, who need to work with locals to be successful. Even smaller- and medium-sized domestic organisations increasingly hire international talent, whom they will need to support as well to be able to retain them. Expats who have a strong local network of friends are less likely to leave the country, and supporting expats and their families with building social connections can be a great way of retaining this international talent in the organisation.

Attracting and retaining international talent can be of interest to governments and municipalities as well, because many countries face increasing labour shortages. Denmark is one example of a country that needs expats to help solve labour shortages, with the Confederation of Danish Industry highlighting the urgent need for attracting foreign talent many times over the past years. Denmark has also benefited greatly from the non-Danish employees; in 2021 they added 211 billion Danish crowns (almost 30 billion euros) to the Danish labour market.[22] They are also responsible for 40% of the growth of Denmark's gross domestic product (GDP) since 2008.[23] Denmark is not necessarily the easiest place to settle into though, having a history of clear anti-immigrant policies that focus on trying to 'remould' everyone who does settle in Denmark.[24] While the country is usually seen as a good place to live, many expats complain that it is very difficult to make local friends (see also Box 2.2 on p. 57). And this can lead expats to take the decision to leave the country. Local and national level government policies can greatly benefit from ideas presented in this book to better welcome international talent and strengthen the local labour pool.

### What can you find in the book?

The book is divided into three main parts. Part I focuses on how expats build a new social network abroad, starting with highlighting the importance of having social connections as one of three basic human needs (Chapter 1). I then explain how expats make new friends abroad because it is important to understand this process to know how to influence it (Chapter 2). One essential competence to have when interacting with people from other cultural backgrounds is intercultural competence, and Chapter 3 shows how one can develop this with the help of several practical exercises.

In Part II, I focus specifically on contacts with locals of the host country. In Chapter 4, I discuss the potential benefits of contact between expats and locals both in private life and in the workplace. In the workplace these locals can play several liaison roles that can help the expat and the organisation from a knowledge management perspective (Chapter 5). This can also be seen as a form of intercultural mentoring, and Chapter 6 focuses on how such intercultural mentoring can be set up for different groups of global talent within an organisation.

Part III focuses on a practical intervention to bridge the gap between expats and locals, namely a buddy system. In Chapter 7, I discuss the benefits of such a buddy or local host based on my own research (Chapter 7), and the role the quality of the contact plays (Chapter 8). Chapter 9 discusses how organisations can set up such a system. The book ends with recommendations for expats, organisations and societies.

Throughout the book, I have used quotes from my own research and sometimes other publications to illustrate what I am talking about. To show the reality of building a social network abroad and connecting with locals in the workplace, I include 11 stories of expats building a social network, developing their intercultural competence or participating in a buddy system. These experiences are included between the chapters and are all shortened accounts of interviews done in the context of my research.

## The research in this book

Much of this book is based on my own research, and specifically on interviews that I held with the help of several student helpers with a total of 72 expats around the globe. Many different types of expats participated in the study – both men and women, single and with partner and children, assigned by their company or moved abroad by their own initiative, and working in industries as varied as financial services, food, drink and tobacco, and the hospitality sector. Figure 0.1 shows the 35 nationalities that participated in this research, who were located in 23 different host countries in Europe, North and South America, Africa and Asia. Every expat got a pseudonym to be able to use their interviews anonymously. If you would like to read more in-depth findings from these 72 interviews or see more details on the sample, please check out www.intersango.dk.

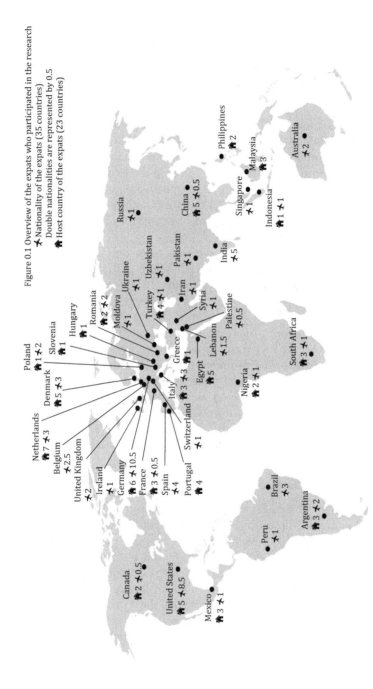

Figure 0.1 Overview of the expats who participated in the research
✈ Nationality of the expats (35 countries)
  Double nationalities are represented by 0.5
🏠 Host country of the expats (23 countries)

*Figure 0.1* The 35 nationalities of expats who participated in the research, and their 23 host countries.

In the book, I also regularly refer to published articles about my research. If you are interested in reading a particular article but don't have access, please do not hesitate to contact me so I can send it to you.

## Notes

1   The HSBC Expat Explorer Survey in 2010 (report Expat Experience) has focused on this topic and shows that women express even more worry about this than men (48% vs. 37%; and 44% vs. 29%, respectively). Furthermore, the HSBC survey in 2017 shows that the top challenges for expat children are missing family and friends back home (43%) and making new friends (33%).
2   Ward, C., Bochner, S., & Furnham, A. (2001). *The psychology of culture shock*. London and New York: Routledge, p. 18.
3   https://worldmigrationreport.iom.int/what-we-do/world-migration-report-2020 [Accessed on 26 August 2023].
4   Brewster, C., Suutari, V., & Waxin, M.-F. (2021). Two decades of research into SIEs and what do we know? A systematic review of the most influential literature and a proposed research agenda. *Journal of Global Mobility, 9*(3), 311–337.
5   This article sums up the discussion rather nicely: De Cieri, H., & Lazarova, M. (2021). "Your health and safety is of utmost importance to us": A review of research on the occupational health and safety of international employees. *Human Resource Management Review, 31*(4), 100790.
6   Andresen, M., Bergdolt, F., Margenfeld, J., & Dickmann, M. (2014). Addressing international mobility confusion - developing definitions and differentiations for self-initiated and assigned expatriates as well as migrants. *International Journal of Human Resource Management, 25*(16), 2295–2318.
7   McNulty, Y., & Brewster, C. (2016). Theorizing the meaning(s) of 'expatriate': Establishing boundary conditions for business expatriates. *International Journal of Human Resource Management, 28*(1), 27–61.
8   Caprar, D. V. (2011). Foreign locals: A cautionary tale on the culture of MNC local employees. *Journal of International Business Studies, 42*(5), 608–628.
9   Hofhuis, J., Hanke, K., & Rutten, T. (2019). Social network sites and acculturation of international sojourners in the Netherlands: The mediating role of psychological alienation and online social support. *International Journal of Intercultural Relations, 69*, 120–130.
10  Geeraert, N., Demoulin, S., & Demes, K. (2014). Choose your (international) contacts wisely: A multilevel analysis on the impact of intergroup contact while living abroad. *International Journal of Intercultural Relations, 38*, 86–96.
11  Gareis, E. (2012). Intercultural friendship: Effects of home and host region. *Journal of International and Intercultural Communication, 5*(4), 309–328.
12  Todd, P., & Nesdale, D. (1997). Promoting intercultural contact between Australian and international university students. *Journal of Higher Education Policy and Management, 19*(1), 61–76.
13  Allport, G. W. (1954). *The nature of prejudice*. Cambridge, MA: Perseus Books.

14 Pettigrew, T. F., & Tropp, L. R. (2006). A meta-analytic test of intergroup contact theory. *Journal of Personality and Social Psychology, 90*(5), 751–783.
15 Pettigrew, T. F., & Tropp, L. R. (2008). How does intergroup contact reduce prejudice? Meta-analytic tests of three mediators. *European Journal of Social Psychology, 38*(6), 922–934.
16 Pettigrew, T. F. (1998). Intergroup contact theory. *Annual Review of Psychology, 49*(1), 65–85.
17 Gareis, E., Goldman, J., & Merkin, R. (2019). Promoting intercultural friendship among college students. *Journal of International and Intercultural Communication, 12*(1), 1–22.
18 See Chapter 17 of Bregman, R. (2019). *Humankind. A hopeful history*. De Correspondent.
19 For a discussion of definitions of culture and theoretical developments in this area, see Adler, N. J., & Aycan, Z. (2018). Cross-cultural interaction: what we know and what we need to know. *Annual Review of Organizational Psychology and Organizational Behavior, 5*, 307–333.
20 GLOBE stands for Global Leadership and Organizational Behavior Effectiveness, https://globeproject.com/.
21 Adler and Aycan (2018).
22 www.danskindustri.dk/di-business/arkiv/nyheder/2022/4/udlandinge-skaber-vardi-for-over-200-mia.-kr/ (accessed on 23 August 2023).
23 https://cphpost.dk/2023-06-23/news/internationals-responsible-for-almost-half-of-denmarks-economic-growth-since-2008-report/ (accessed on 23 August 2023).
24 www.economist.com/europe/2021/12/18/why-have-danes-turned-against-immigration (accessed on 23 August 2023).

Part I

# Building a new social network abroad

# Experience

A South African expat in Portugal – "It gave us a glimpse into a true Portuguese family"

*Daniel is a South African expat who is now living in Portugal for about a year. He first moved to Spain for the same company, and then moved to Portugal when an opportunity opened up there. He lives with his wife and son.*

## Before you went to Portugal, what were your expectations in terms of making contacts with other people?

Well, for me, my expectation was purely professional because I knew that my job is going to keep me busy quite extensively. For my wife, I suspected that she would be able to make friends easier than me, because there's two dogs as well and she normally takes them to go walking and so on. And in Portugal, people are more open to expatriates than in Spain, and more people can speak English as well. So, the interaction would be a bit easier. And that is actually how she made initial friends and then more friends through that group.

## Who did you meet with in the first few months?

Well, previously when we were still in Spain, my current boss invited us to join them for Christmas in 2018 with him and his family. And we came to visit for Christmas up to New Year and through that we interacted with him and his entire family. And that was quite nice, because it gave us a glimpse into a true Portuguese family. All of them are obviously Portuguese, what their culture is and how they do things and how they interact with each other and the celebrations that they do. It was quite

DOI: 10.4324/9781003246855-4

nice. And last year, it was exactly the same. He told me again that we are now part of their culture, so we have to join them every year.

### Why did you start to connect particularly with these people?

I think mainly because it's easy. It's people that I work with and I interact with on a daily basis. So, one of my other colleagues that is in one of the other departments, he actually invited me along with another colleague from his department, and the three of us went for dinner, the one night. That's also a way that, again, it's going to grow. But again, it was colleagues. And I think now that summer is here, we will probably all get more involved with outdoor sports again, and probably through that I will make some more friends and contacts.

### Who do you think is a friend?

I think someone that you can ask for a favour. And then they can also, in turn, ask you for a favour. And it's on a friendly basis, it's not purely on a professional basis as with work. And it's someone that you would connect with outside of the professional basis. And someone that you would interact with not purely on a basis of having to gain something from them or they gain something from you. And obviously it needs to be a mutual thing.

### What do you appreciate in the contact with your new friends now in Portugal?

Well, number one is probably getting more insights from them, as to Portuguese culture. It's people that you can talk to, and most of the time vent some frustration with. And that I can explain why I'm frustrated with certain circumstances or certain situations. And then they would try to understand it from my point of view as well. But then also give me clarity to understanding it from another perspective. Probably being from the Portuguese perspective as well. [Also] we've had some difficulties with getting all the resources established for the house, for instance water and electricity. Then basically my boss's wife took over. She then made contact with the different departments that had to get things done. [...] In Portuguese law, for expatriates to do a rental, a person that is a registered citizen needs to sign basically on your behalf as a sponsor. [Laughing] It makes it quite interesting and a bit more difficult to find places. You need to be settled and registered and in Portugal before you can actually rent the place. And if you are not registered yet, then you need someone that is registered in Portugal. Most of the time a citizen needs to then sign as a sponsor, and my boss then signed for us.

### What would you recommend for new expats with regard to how to meet the Portuguese?

I would say number one is make an effort in learning Portuguese. I think in any country that you go to, the local people will appreciate it, and be more inclined to help you as well if they see that you are making an effort to try to at least learn their language. Obviously, learning a language at a very late age, or I would say after school, becomes more difficult. So, obviously, and I don't think anyone is realising that, if you are not from the country [people] would never expect you to be completely fluent in their language, but at least to try and make an effort to learn some basic phrases, so that you at least can greet people in the local language. That, I think, is the most important key. And then I would say, you need to start interacting in what your hobbies or your likes are that you tend to do. In any case, if you were in your home country […]. I think naturally through that you would then start building relationships with people that you either see regularly doing the same thing or that you would get to interact with at some point.

# Chapter 1

# A dive into the deep end of the social pool

## Introduction

It is hard to overestimate the importance of social relations for our well-being. Plenty of research has, by now, firmly established the importance of friendships. Robin Dunbar, emeritus professor of evolutionary psychology at the University of Oxford, concludes that friendship is the single most important factor for our health, well-being and happiness.[1] Aristotle already recognised this when he said friends are "the greatest of external goods" and that "the happy man needs friends,"[2] which is echoed by the Dalai Lama XIV: "We human beings are social beings. [...] For this reason, it is hardly surprising that most of our happiness arises in the context of our relationships with others." Let's have a closer look at friendships and well-being, and what a social network actually is.

## We are social beings

We need other people around us. You can see this need in many theories of human motivation, for example Maslow's pyramid where one of the needs is about giving and receiving love and includes social belonging and friendships.[3] Social psychologists studied the effect of social environments on people, and they have shown that people have three basic needs to help them flourish: competence, autonomy and relatedness.[4] People need to belong and have at least a certain minimum number of social relationships. The need-to-belong theory[5] suggests that this is one of the most powerful, universal and influential human drives, and much research has been done on how this need shapes how we feel, think and behave.

Social relationships are crucial for well-being, life satisfaction, happiness and health. A famous study is the Harvard Study of Adult Development, which has been following the lives of 268 Harvard-educated men from diverse socio-economic backgrounds since 1938. It merged with another study that followed 456 more disadvantaged young men from Boston

DOI: 10.4324/9781003246855-5

*Figure 1.1* A dive into the deep end of the social pool. Illustration by Heldermaker.

since the 1940s. The study has been tracking every aspect of their lives with regard to physical and emotional well-being, and a key finding is how important satisfying relationships with other people are for both aspects. The current director of the study, Robert J. Waldinger, M.D., gave a very interesting TedTalk in 2015 to highlight exactly this finding to the public.[6] His main takeaway is that the happiest and healthiest participants were the ones who maintained close, intimate relationships and were satisfied with them. This buffers some of the effects of getting old. Working on maintaining relationships with other people is what makes someone happy and healthy – more so than having a good income.[7]

Other studies have confirmed that social relations are very important for well-being. Loneliness is as bad for you as smoking, obesity and excessive drinking.[8] Not that one needs to have a large number of friends to feel the benefits of social relations[9]; it is the quality of the relationships that is the most important for physical and mental health. Having at least two high-quality relationships, for example with a spouse or with other friends, is associated with greater well-being,[10] especially later in life. People also have different friendship needs at different stages in their lives. A study that spanned 30 years showed that the quantity of social relations is more important when people are in their 20s, because having many different social connections allows them to learn about themselves and others, and to develop their social skills. In their 30s, the quality of the relationship becomes more important. By then, people are more looking for emotional closeness that is found in having a few very good friends.[11]

While good friends increase your well-being, interactions with strangers can also help. Having positive social interactions every day helps feeling good.[12] An interesting study in Chicago and London[13] shows how train commuters who talked to strangers had a more positive experience than those who did not. Yet, the authors found that commuters often avoid having conversations with strangers because they fear the other person is not interested in talking. Especially introverts underestimated the positive outcomes of such conversations. Talking to strangers not only feels good, but it might also lead to a friendship. All friendships have to start somewhere.

## How do friends improve well-being?

Apart from making you feel good about yourself and your life when you are embedded in a social network, social relations can also carry many benefits. You probably have experienced how a suggestion from a friend helped you find a new job, or how your family and friends pitched in when you needed help moving house. Family, friends and acquaintances can help with many things – these resources that one can mobilise through their social network are part of one's social capital.[14] There has been a lot of research on social capital and how important it is for, for example, finding work, climbing up the corporate ladder and having success as an entrepreneur. Strong ties have been distinguished from weak ties; while people who are close to you might be more willing to help you out, it is often acquaintances who might know of some new opportunities.[15]

Another stream of research relevant for the topic of making friends has focused on the importance of social support for well-being through buffering the effects of stress. The stress and coping framework highlights how life changes —— such as getting a job abroad – can be rather stressful, depending on how these changes are perceived or appraised, and the strategies one has to cope with the event.[16] Moving abroad for a job can be more stressful for one person than for the other; it depends on many factors such as whether the change is perceived as positive or negative, personality and cultural background and resources such as social support.

Social support is the psychological and material resources that spouses, family and friends can provide, and two main types are distinguished.[17] The first type is informational/instrumental support, which can be as simple as a tip about what restaurant you should try next time you want to go out, but also information that helps you solve a problem that you have. Another example is when someone is instrumental in helping you with a problem, for example by lending money, tools or a car, or spending their own time to help you, for example by babysitting so you have time to finish a project or to simply relax and regain energy. The second type of social support is socioemotional support, which includes having company for activities you like to do but also a listening ear when you need to vent. Reaching out to family and friends for help or a listening ear is an important way to cope with stressful situations; social support helps buffer the effect of stress.[18]

While there can be many benefits in social relationships, it is important to point out that those relationships can also be a source of stress, for example through the demands that the other makes of you.[19] Ultimately, it is about the balance between benefits and costs, which will be different for each individual.

## What is a social network?

The people we see on a regular basis – our family, friends and acquaintances – compose our social network. Most people have a personal network of (extended) family and one of friends, which are often rather isolated from each other but are influencing each other. People who have a large extended family have fewer friends, and those coming from a small family compensate with having more friends. We are not equally close to all our friends and don't spend our time and energy equally on all of them. Almost half of our social effort goes to just five of our most intimate friends, which is the innermost 'friendship circle' as defined by Dunbar.[20] This is also sometimes called our 'support network,' since those are the people who help out in times of extreme need. The next circle is composed of about ten more people we regularly meet socially and is sometimes called the 'sympathy group.' Dunbar proposes we have two more friendship circles with a limit of 50 and 150 people, where people support each other and exchange information. This limit of 150 is also known as Dunbar's number, indicating a cognitive limit to the amount of people one can have a face-to-face social relationship with.[21]

But what is a friend? When do you call someone a friend? Dunbar defines friends as

> the people who share our lives in a way that is more than just the casual meeting of strangers; they are the people whom we make an effort to maintain contact with, and to whom we feel an emotional bond.[22]

This definition of friendship also includes family and spouses because many people consider them friends or even best friends; one difference though is that friendships are more vulnerable to a lack of contact than family relations are. Professor Beverly Fehr[23] has been studying friendships since the 1990s and concluded that a friend is "a voluntary, personal relationship, typically providing intimacy and assistance, in which two parties like each other and seek each other's company."[24] Friendships are characterised by enjoyment, acceptance, trust, mutual assistance, confiding, understanding and spontaneity.[25] Fehr distinguishes acquaintances, friends, close friends and best friends, and studied how the interaction with acquaintances is different than that with friends – friends stand closer, touch each other more and smile and laugh more. Friends also tell each other more about themselves; sharing intimate information seems to signal that the relationship has developed into a friendship (and actually develops a relationship as well – see section 'How to make friends' on p. 31). Once a relationship is defined as a friendship rather than an acquaintance, an upward spiral in terms of intimacy, trust, support and loyalty can happen to make the friend a close friend or even a best friend.

Even though there are many definitions of friendship, it is still often vague what people mean when they say someone is their friend. One of the interviews for this book was with Becky, a U.S. American who lived in Denmark. At one point during the interview, she said laughing: "I feel like I have no friends" but when I asked her more specific questions, she had plenty of people I would call friends. Some of this might be explained by cultural differences in what one calls a friend. One study compared Japanese concepts of *shinyuu* (best friends) with a similar study done in the United States and found both culturally shared and culturally specific concepts of friendship.[26] For example, while U.S. Americans' friendship satisfaction was reached when the friend was active, energetic and creative, this was not present in the Japanese data. Instead, the Japanese emphasised a feeling of comfort, a person with whom one can spend a long time. Another example of a cultural difference is that the Japanese expected their friends to encourage them to overcome their problems, whereas U.S. Americans wanted their friends 'not to be a whiner,' which might be a reflection of a more individualistic culture where people are expected to solve problems themselves. Another explanation might be that U.S. Americans see their romantic partner as their closest relationship, as compared with Japanese who usually select a friend, and that U.S. Americans do accept 'whining' from their romantic partners, just not from their friends.[27] U.S. Americans also seem to have larger social networks than other countries,[28] which is probably rooted in their history of high residential mobility: people move around a lot in the United States, leaving behind their friends and having to make new ones.[29] We will return to this in Chapter 2 ('The context' on p. 56), when I discuss how expats build a new social network abroad. Coming back to Becky, she also speculates about a cultural difference when she says:

> But maybe I have the normal amount of friends for a European person. [...] I am used to having way more. No, I really do like it when you can just like go hang out with different people every night and things like that...

### Diving into the deep end of the social pool

Many people do not only move within their own country; they move to another country altogether. Expats have been around for ages; between 1602 and 1795 nearly a million mostly Dutch and German employees were sent to Asia,[30] and many more expats around the globe followed. Research only became interested in expats in the 1980s and 1990s, focusing on selection and training and determinants of expat adjustment. In the 1990s the idea also took hold that intercultural skills and being able to work with people from a different culture is very important for having success when working abroad.[31] I'll talk more about intercultural competence in Chapter 3.

The focus also slowly widened to include the environment of the expat. Some authors already pointed to the importance of social support for expats in the 1980s,[32] but attention for this topic only really boomed in the first two decades of the new century. It became increasingly clear that it is not just about selecting and training expats to make sure they succeed, but that social connections also play an important role. An expat's social network directly impacts their well-being on assignment,[33] and social support helps expat adjustment, performance, commitment and retention.[34] Many authors especially recommend considering how the people of the host country itself (host country nationals or locals) can help; social support of locals is positively associated with expat success and is very valuable to help expats succeed in their new host country (see Chapter 4). We also should not forget the accompanying family members of the expat who also have to adjust to a new country and are one of the three top reasons for the failure of an assignment.[35] When people move abroad, they need support of some kind.

## The expat bubble

When expats and their families move abroad, they leave behind a large part of their social network, and they need to build a new one in the new host country – and this is what worries many of them, as mentioned in the introduction. Expats can connect with other expats, of the same or a different nationality, or with locals from the host country, although it is not always easy to make connections with the latter group. Many expats feel socially isolated and have difficulty making friends with locals; such feelings are reported for most Northern/Western European countries as well as countries such as Kuwait, Saudi Arabia and South-Korea, and for Chinese expats in Australia and Europe.[36] Many expats stay within the so-called expat bubble where expats mainly meet other expats and miss out on the many benefits to be had from connecting with locals (see Chapter 4). Two major theoretical perspectives that explain how contact with locals can help expats in their assignment are the culture learning model and the stress and coping model. Contact with locals helps expats to learn about the new host culture, either by talking about it or by observing the local's behaviour. This can be more reliable information than one would get from other expats in the host country, as Ruth Van Reken, co-author of *Third Culture Kids: Growing Up Among Worlds*, experienced herself:

> Too often expats seem to teach fellow expats, but what they say is already filtered through their own lenses and I realised after several years in Liberia some of my assumptions learned from others like me wasn't necessarily how it was when I did stop to ask my Liberian friends!

Locals can also offer social support to deal with the stress of the cross-cultural transition; as mentioned earlier, this is an important way in which social relations in general can help well-being. As we will see in Chapter 4, contact with locals in general helps the expat adjust to the new host country, and contact with local colleagues is associated with improved performance. Locals can also help the expat learn about the organisation and the organisation can also benefit from good contact between their expats and the local workforce in terms of organisational knowledge sharing but also ease of implementing new management practices in a local subsidiary.

In many countries it is not easy to connect with locals, as is shown by many surveys among expats. One well-known survey is the ExpatInsider by the leading expat network InterNations, which is present in 420 cities around the world. This annual survey has been specifically asking about the ease of making local contacts for quite a few years now, ranking countries. It is interesting to study the bottom 10 of the list, since this shows the countries that expats consistently find difficult to make local friends. Many of them are European, such as Denmark, Norway, Sweden, Finland, the Netherlands, Belgium, Germany, Austria, Switzerland and Estonia, with other countries such as Kuwait, Saudi Arabia, Qatar and Japan, South Korea thrown in the mix (see Table 1.1). Certain nationalities also seem to have an easier time connecting with locals and building a new social network abroad; Spanish, French, Italian and Russian expats felt they did not have enough socialising opportunities or even a personal support network in their host country as compared with British, Austrian and U.S. American expats, who also had a larger share of local friends in their networks.[37]

It is not only expats who experience this bubble, also international students meet it often.[38] One international student described bubble formation at a U.S. university:[39] "[In university flats] Chinese students stick together with Chinese, Thai students with Thais.... when they go to the campus, they are together. I hardly see culturally mixed groups of people." International students also socialise more often with other international students, even though they would like more contact with local students. Local contacts help them feel less homesick and more satisfied with their study abroad stay,[40] and having more connections of the same nationality was more stressful and led to less cultural adjustment in the longer term.[41] This also goes for expats: even though fellow expats can offer much valuable support, staying within the expat bubble and having no connections with the local population can work negatively because it negatively impacts the expat's satisfaction with their stay.[42] The knowledge and support that locals can offer might not be available in expat-only networks, and having locals as friends also helps to feel embedded in the host country. It seems

Table 1.1 Most difficult countries to make local friends: hardest (1) to less hard (10)

|  | 2014 | 2015 | 2016 | 2017 | 2018 | 2019 | 2020 | 2021 | 2022 | 2023 |
|---|---|---|---|---|---|---|---|---|---|---|
| 1 | Kuwait | Kuwait | Denmark | Sweden | Kuwait | Denmark | Stockholm (Sweden) | Sweden | Kuwait | Denmark |
| 2 | Sweden | Denmark | Norway | Denmark | Sweden | Sweden | Salmiya (Kuwait) | Denmark | Sweden | Austria |
| 3 | Denmark | Saudi Arabia | Kuwait | Norway | Denmark | Kuwait | Copenhagen (Denmark) | Norway | Norway | Kuwait |
| 4 | Norway | Norway | Sweden | Switzerland | Switzerland | Switzerland | Stuttgart (Germany) | Kuwait | Luxembourg | Norway |
| 5 | Saudi Arabia | Finland | Switzerland | Kuwait | Saudi Arabia | Norway | Zürich (Switzerland) | Japan | Denmark | Germany |
| 6 | Qatar | Sweden | Qatar | Qatar | Germany | Germany | The Hague (Netherlands) | Switzerland | Finland | South Korea |
| 7 | Switzerland | Switzerland | Saudi Arabia | Qatar | Norway | Austria | Graz (Austria) | Austria | Germany | Switzerland |
| 8 | Austria | Germany | Netherlands | Germany | Finland | Finland | Tokyo (Japan) | Germany | Japan | Netherlands |
| 9 | Netherlands | Austria | Finland | Finland | Austria | Netherlands | Helsinki (Finland) | Netherland | Netherlands | Japan |
| 10 | Japan | Belgium | Germany | Saudi Arabia | Estonia | South Korea | Basel (Switzerland) | Finland | Switzerland | Sweden |

Source: The annual ExpatInsider survey done by InterNations.

like a balanced social network that consists both of other expats and of locals would be the perfect solution.[43]

### Reasons to stay in the expat bubble

So, why do both expats and international students often stay within a 'bubble' with other expats and international students? A very powerful explanation is what is called homophily or similarity. We are attracted to people who are similar to us, and that can be in many different respects. One aspect that has received the most research attention is attitudes, but it also goes for people who have the same abilities and opinions, economic status and personality.[44] Friends are also often similar in terms of gender, ethnicity, age, religion, education and social values.[45] Having something in common with someone else helps build the relationship, and expats who move abroad for their jobs are in the same boat; they are new in an often-unfamiliar country where they have to build up a new life and make new friends. They have a lot in common with each other, making it easier to connect with each other instead of with locals from the host country, who may also be quite dissimilar in terms of cultural values.

A second explanation for expat bubble formation is that we only have limited time and energy to devote to friendships. This has two effects relevant for the expat situation. First, according to human energy management theory in communication,[46] we all want to conserve our energy and make the most efficient choices, so we are less likely to reach out to people who are very dissimilar to us, because the unfamiliarity simply takes more energy. This reinforces the expat bubble because expats save energy when socialising with other expats who are more similar to themselves than locals. Second, locals have an existing social network in the host country and don't necessarily have extra time and energy to spend on building new social relationships. This reinforces the expat bubble even more, especially since many expats are only in the country for a few years and disappear again, which makes the time and energy investment the local makes in building such a friendship extra costly. As a Danish expat in Greenland said when interviewed by a magazine[47] about his stay in Nuuk, the capital of Greenland:

> It is easy to become a part of the Danish expat community, but it is more difficult to come close to the lives of the Greenlanders. That is understandable because there are many "revolving-door" Danes in Nuuk. And many Greenlanders have experienced that once they have gotten to know a Dane, they leave again. But I don't give up, and that's why I participate in events where also Greenlanders attend.

Finally, expats often also settle in areas where other expats already live,[48] for example because of the presence of international schools or because these neighbourhoods get recommended by other expats. There is plenty of information to be found online on 'best expat neighbourhoods' in cities around the world. This encourages bubble formation even more.

## How to make friends

At many times in our lives, we need to make new friends. First as a child in kindergarten and in school, then as an adult moving away from home, for example when moving to another city for studies. But apart from these obvious times when new friends are needed, we actually lose friends and make new ones all the time. Research in the Netherlands has shown that a large part of one's social network, about 70%, is renewed in 7 years.[49] Similarly, only 25% of the friends of U.S. American college students remained after 5 years.[50] Think back to who you were spending time with 10 years ago. Are they still the same people? Maybe you have moved house or gotten a new job – these life changes are important reasons for social networks to shift. In the case of expats, both are happening at the same time, and over a larger geographical distance, which increases the need for making new friends in the new location even more.

Even though it is very clear that social support is very important for expat success, we actually do not know much about how expats make new friends when abroad. This is how my own research interest started, after I read an article that did look at expat friendships and hypothesised how they were created, so I wanted to get into this topic and see if this was really the case. This led to 72 interviews among expats around the world, which is the basis of this book and led to a new process model which explains how expats actually build a new social network abroad (as will be explained in Chapter 2). To truly get a full picture of how expats build new friendships, it is important to also mention several key mechanisms that have emerged from research on the development of interpersonal relationships[51] because this is relevant for the expat situation as well.

First, it sounds very obvious, but you are more likely to develop friendships with people who live close to you, simply because you meet them more often. This is a very powerful effect, which is shown by several classic studies. The first one I would like to mention is done at a police academy back in the 1970s by Professor Mady Segal who was interested in interpersonal attraction.[52] She wanted to find out who the new cadets would make friends with, and discovered that their names – and specifically the first letter of their name – were what explained their new friendships the best. This actually explained more than religious background, age, whether they were married or not, ethnic background, hobbies and being a member of a group. Why would having the first letter of your last name in common with someone lead to friendship? The secret here is that the cadets were allocated a chair in the classroom based on their last name; so agent Johnson was sitting next to agent Jones, and agent Wilson was sitting close to agent Williams – and they were sitting far away from both Johnson and Jones. When the cadets were asked whom they had built a close relationship with, 90% of them mentioned the person sitting next to them. It was simple physical proximity that led to people becoming friends.

This effect has been shown in other studies as well, such as in a dorm. A group of students at the Massachusetts Institute of Technology were interviewed to make an overview of all the interpersonal connections between the students.[53] It turned out that those who lived at the end of the corridor were much less popular and had fewer contacts than those who lived in the middle of the floor. This could not be explained by any personal or physical characteristics, or even by a selection bias in that more extrovert students would choose rooms in the middle of the floor. The rooms were allocated by the administration, so it was completely random who lived where. When the students were asked who they had a good connection with, 40% mentioned their direct neighbour, and the chance to be friends with the neighbour of their neighbour was half as big. The farther the students lived from each other, the less likely they were to become friends. And for the students living at the end of the corridor, their physical location meant they had fewer neighbours to connect with, and this had a major impact on their social life. So, a very simple and powerful mechanism to make friends (and to keep them) is to make sure you are frequently in contact with people – and this can happen in a variety of social contexts, for example the neighbourhood, at school or at work, but also at a club or association, a café or bar or at a party of friends. Also, the internet is now a great place to meet new people.

A second key driver for building friendships is the cost and reward perspective. People only have a limited amount of time and energy to spend, as mentioned earlier. So, they have to make choices about whom to build friendships with, and one way to do this is to look at the benefits and the costs of a relationship. For example, the time and energy put into a relationship is a cost, and the reward is the social companionship or the support one gets out of it. This suggests a very rational approach to friendships, which is echoed in the existing literature on how expats develop new friendships. One model focuses purely on how expats can build new social ties that help them adjust to the new country. This article is what originally piqued my interest because I was really wondering whether it works that way – that, as an expat, you consciously select the people you feel can help you in adjusting to the host country, for example because they know a lot about the country or because they are in the same situation. As we will see in Chapter 2, the process of making friends abroad turns out to be less deliberate than that.

The third key driver for developing friendships is self-disclosure, when people gradually disclose more intimate information about themselves to the other person.[54] This is both about the range of topics (breadth of self-disclosure) and the extent to which these topics are private (depth of self-disclosure). As a relationship develops, more topics will be discussed, and the discussions will progress from superficial matters to more intimate topics, where people share private information about themselves. Self-disclosure is closely linked with liking:[55] we tend to tell more private information to people we already like. This link also sheds light on how self-disclosure actually helps the development of a friendship, in two ways: we start liking the person whom we have told private information to even more, and the other person also likes you more for disclosing more private information.

And this process is something you can encourage. In the 1990s a team of psychologists in the United States made an interesting experiment in order to create interpersonal closeness.[56] They made pairs of students who didn't know each other and had them sit together for 45 minutes to have a chat. Half of the students got questions that were more factual in nature, such as what countries they would like to visit or what film they liked best. The other half started out with such questions, but they then progressed to talk about more intimate matters, such as what friendship means to them, and how they feel about the relationship with their mother. And it became even more intimate than that. Towards the end, the students were asked to share an embarrassing memory, what they would save from their house in case there was a fire, and what – if they would die tonight – they would regret not telling someone. You can imagine that this last group will have shared much more than the first group, who only talked about more superficial topics. After 45 minutes of chatting, both groups were asked to score the closeness they felt with their conversation partner; it is no surprise that the students in the second group felt much closer to each other than those in the first group. And the interesting part is that this translated into more contact between the pairs during and after their classes – so this connection that was built in these 45 minutes didn't just disappear. It is clear that this self-disclosure – and making yourself vulnerable through sharing personal matters – helps build relationships, and this, in turn, helps your feeling of belonging. Hall and Davis[57] looked at the role of 'communication episodes,' such as meaningful conversation, laughing and joking around, gossip or small talk, in satisfying the need to belong – one of three basic human needs. They created a pyramid to show how much each of these different 'communication episodes' help make you feel like you belong in a social group. Instrumental talk, impersonal communication and small talk is at the base of the pyramid; these are rather frequently happening but not actually contributing all that much to the need to belong. This need only really gets satisfied when moving higher up in the pyramid with meaningful talk, self-disclosure and affection; for example, saying that you love someone or appreciate them as a friend. Through such communication we create the relationships that make us feel like we belong, which is essential for our well-being.

### Intercultural friendships

Researchers have also turned to international students and their friendships. A common observation of many of these studies is the fact that international students often would have liked more contact with the local students, and that this negatively influences their stay abroad.[58] This led to several studies looking into how international students make friends, and these studies echo many of the findings of the domestic friendship literature.[59] International students also prefer to make friends with those who are similar to them, and proximity (living in the same dorm or sharing classes) gives them the opportunity to build a friendship. Also, self-disclosure and the balance between costs and rewards of a relationship were found to help or hinder intercultural friendships. But there is more that influences making friends in an intercultural setting, namely cultural differences, and the attitude of both the international student and the local.

Professor Elisabeth Gareis from City University of New York has done a lot of work on the topic of intercultural friendship. For one study[60] she interviewed five German students in the United States, which showed that cultural differences influence friendship formation between people from different cultural backgrounds, starting with the word 'friend' itself. The German students used the word in a narrower meaning, indicating only close friends and not also casual friends or acquaintances.

Another cultural difference between Germany and the United States is with regard to public and private personality layers, as German-American psychologist Kurt Lewin already described in 1936.[61] Both cultures have the same number of personality layers, with public layers on the outside and a private centre at the core. The cultural difference between the United States and Germany is that most of the layers in the United States are open to the public and only the innermost layer is private; yet in Germany (and other European and Asian countries) it is the other way around. Only the outermost layer is public, the rest is private. This has consequences for making friends because while inviting someone to their house is part of the public layer in the United States, it is part of the private layers in Germany, and this leads Germans to think such an invitation is a sign of friendship. They then often feel that U.S. Americans are superficial when the expected friendship does not develop. One study found that Korean expats in the United States found U.S. Americans very friendly at a superficial level but quite unwilling to develop deeper friendships.[62] Conversely, U.S. Americans in Germany should realise that the friendliness and openness that meet you directly in the United States is there but hidden behind a first public personality layer that causes Germans often being seen as unfriendly, arrogant and formal. This is the case in other European countries as well. For example, foreign physicians in Sweden found the first step of getting in touch with Swedes quite difficult but once you know them, "it's happy life, really."[63] As Lewin observed:

> Compared with Germans, Americans seem to make quicker progress towards friendly relations in the beginning, and with many more persons. Yet this development often stops at a certain point; and the quickly acquired friends will, after years of relatively close relations, say goodbye as easily as after a few weeks of acquaintance.[64]

This suggests that culture is important for making friends; and this is something I will also touch on in my process model of how expats build a new social network abroad in Chapter 2 (Figure 2.1 on p. 46).

Not all international students had the same difficulty in making friends with U.S. Americans. Another of Gareis' studies took a quantitative approach with a survey among 454 international students in the United States,[65] so she could compare different home and host regions. She found that East Asian students had more difficulty forming friendships with U.S. Americans than English-speaking students or students coming from Northern and Central Europe. Gareis also probed the students themselves for reasons why they were less satisfied with their friendships, and they mentioned their own low language proficiency, limited social time and cultural differences. Many of them also suggested the main problem actually lay with the U.S. American hosts, in particular their lack of interest and, when a casual friendship was struck, an unwillingness in having this relationship become closer. This is where the aforementioned difference in personality layers may cause some difficulties because international students might interpret some actions of U.S. Americans as first step towards a close friendship. Cultural differences also play a role, and partly explain why East Asian students find it more difficult to make local friends. Friendships in the United States are more transient, less intensive and more short-lived than many international students are used to from their home environment. To make friends in the United States you need a specific set of social skills, for example the ability of making small talk, which might come less easy to those coming from more collectivistic cultures, where friends are more automatically made because of being a member of the same group. Language skills are also important. Not speaking English very well makes the students more nervous and anxious about talking to U.S. Americans, and it also lessens the interest of the U.S. Americans to talk to these international students. Not only the cultural background of the international student was relevant, also where in the United States they were located. Students in the South (Alabama, Georgia, North Carolina and Mississippi) found it easier to connect with locals compared to the Northeast (New York, Connecticut and New Jersey). Some of this may be due to cultural differences between these regions, with a Southern way of life often characterised by amiability and good manners, and a slower pace of life. Gareis also compared New York City to smaller cities (100,000 inhabitants or less) and found that friendships were more easily formed in the smaller ones. A possible explanation is that New York City is very diverse and offers the possibility of easily finding friends from the same nationality, as compared to the smaller cities. All this shows that the context in which you try to make friends matters as well – a point which is also made in my model as explained in Chapter 2 (pp. 49 and 56).

But culture does not always present a problem; it can also provide a starting point for a relationship as a respondent in another study on international students at a U.S. university[66] mentions:

> Actually, the cultural differences helped to start the friendship because, at least on my side, I was attracted to her because she was unique. She came from another country, an entire different culture, different language. I have always been impressed by people who come to this country. English is not their first language and they succeed as students or whatever they do. So I think the difference actually helped earlier and then as we got to know each other, we realized that we were fairly similar in a lot of ways.

This international student was very open to other cultures and would like to get to know the locals. This openness is key in intercultural interactions – and we will revisit this topic in Chapter 3 on intercultural competence. Intercultural competence is very important for making friends from a different cultural background.

Social connections are very important for well-being, especially so for expats who move abroad and leave behind most of their family and friends. Since it is not always easy to create new connections and friendships, the next chapter focuses on how expats build a new social network in the host country.

## Notes

1 Dunbar, R. I. M. (2018). The anatomy of friendship. *Trends in Cognitive Sciences, 22*(1), 32–51.
2 Aristotle, & Ross, W. (2013). *Nicomachean ethics.* Cambridge University Press; book VIII.
3 Maslow, A. H. (1943). A theory of human motivation. *Psychological Review, 50*(4), 370.
4 Deci, E. L., & Ryan, R. M. (2012). Self-determination theory. In *Handbook of theories of social psychology, Vol. 1* (pp. 416–436). Thousand Oaks, CA: Sage.
5 Baumeister, R. F. (2011). Need-to-belong theory. *Handbook of theories of social psychology, 2*, 121–140.
6 www.ted.com/talks/robert_waldinger_what_makes_a_good_life_lessons_from_the_longest_study_on_happiness [accessed on 12 August 2023].
7 Kahneman, D., & Deaton, A. (2010). High income improves evaluation of life but not emotional well-being. *Proceedings of the National Academy of Sciences, 107*(38), 16489–16493.
8 Holt-Lunstad, J., Smith, T. B., & Layton, J. B. (2010). Social relationships and mortality risk: A meta-analytic review. *PLoS Medicine, 7*(7), e1000316.
9 Cohen, S., & Wills, T. (1985). Stress, social support, and the buffering hypothesis. *Psychological Bulletin, 98*(2), 310–357.
10 Antonucci, T. C., Ajrouch, K. J., & Birditt, K. S. (2014). The convoy model: Explaining social relations from a multidisciplinary perspective. *The Gerontologist, 54*(1), 82–92.
11 Carmichael, C. L., Reis, H. T., & Duberstein, P. R. (2015). In your 20s it's quantity, in your 30s it's quality: The prognostic value of social activity across 30 years of adulthood. *Psychology and Aging, 30*(1), 95.
12 Antonucci et al. (2014).
13 Schroeder, J., Lyons, D., & Epley, N. (2022). Hello, stranger? Pleasant conversations are preceded by concerns about starting one. *Journal of Experimental Psychology: General, 151*(5), 1141–1153.
14 Portes, A. (1998). Social capital: Its origins and applications in modern sociology. *Annual Review of Sociology, 24*(1), 1–24.
15 Granovetter, M. (1983). The strength of weak ties: A network theory revisited. *Sociological Theory, 1*(1), 201–233.
16 Ward, C., Bochner, S., & Furnham, A. (2001). *The psychology of culture shock.* London and New York: Routledge.
17 Podsiadlowski, A., Vauclair, C.-M., Spiess, E., & Stroppa, C. (2013). Social support on international assignments: The relevance of socioemotional support from locals. *International Journal of Psychology, 48*(4), 563–573.
18 Cohen and Wills (1985).
19 Lazarus, R. S., & Folkman, S. (1984). *Stress, appraisal and coping.* New York: Springer.
20 Dunbar (2018).
21 Dunbar, R. (2010). *How many friends does one person need?: Dunbar's number and other evolutionary quirks.* London, UK: Faber & Faber.

22 Dunbar (2018).
23 Fehr, B. (1996). *Friendship processes.* Thousand Oaks, CA: Sage.
24 Fehr (1996), p. 7.
25 Hendrickson, B., Rosen, D., & Aune, R. K. (2011). An analysis of friendship networks, social connectedness, homesickness, and satisfaction levels of international students. *International Journal of Intercultural Relations, 35*(3), 281–295.
26 Maeda, E., & Ritchie, L. D. (2003). The concept of shinyuu in Japan: A replication of and comparison to Cole and Bradac's study on US friendship. *Journal of Social and Personal Relationships, 20*(5), 579–598.
27 Maeda and Ritchie (2003).
28 Adams, G., & Plaut, V. C. (2003). The cultural grounding of personal relationship: Friendship in North American and West African worlds. *Personal Relationships, 10*(3), 333–347.
29 Oishi, S., Kesebir, S., Miao, F. F., Talhelm, T., Endo, Y., Uchida, Y., ... Norasakkunkit, V. (2013). Residential mobility increases motivation to expand social network: But why? *Journal of Experimental Social Psychology, 49*(2), 217–223.
30 Van Gelder, R. (1997). *Het Oost-Indisch avontuur: Duitsers in dienst van de VOC (1600–1800) [The East Indian adventure: Germans employed by the United East-India Company].* Nijmegen, The Netherlands: SUN.
31 Gertsen, C. (1990). Intercultural competence and expatriates. *International Journal of Human Resource Management, 3*(3), 341–362.
32 Fontaine, G. (1986). Roles of social support systems in overseas relocation: Implications for intercultural training. *International Journal of Intercultural Relations, 10*(3), 361–378.
33 Wang, X., & Kanungo, R. N. (2004). Nationality, social network and psychological well-being: expatriates in China. *International Journal of Human Resource Management, 15*(4), 775–793.
34 van der Laken, P., van Engen, M., van Veldhoven, M., & Paauwe, J. (2019). Fostering expatriate success: A meta-analysis of the differential benefits of social support. *Human Resource Management Review, 29*(4), 100679.
35 Goede, J., & Berg, N. (2018). The family in the center of international assignments: A systematic review and future research agenda. *Management Review Quarterly, 68*, 77–102.
36 van Bakel, M., & Vance, C. M. (2023). Breaking out of the expatriate bubble in Denmark: Insights from the challenge of making connections with local Danes. *Journal of Global Mobility, 11*(1), 21–42.
37 InterNations (2018). *ExpatInsider 2018. The World Through Expat Eyes.*
38 Gareis, E. (2012). Intercultural friendship: Effects of home and host region. *Journal of International and Intercultural Communication, 5*(4), 309–328.
39 Kudo, K., & Simkin, K. A. (2003). Intercultural friendship formation: The case of Japanese students at an Australian university. *Journal of Intercultural Studies, 24*(2), 91–114.
40 Hendrickson et al. (2011).

41  Geeraert, N., Demoulin, S., & Demes, K. (2014). Choose your (international) contacts wisely: A multilevel analysis on the impact of intergroup contact while living abroad. *International Journal of Intercultural Relations, 38*, 86–96.

42  Podsiadlowski et al. (2013).

43  Wang and Kanungo (2004).

44  Byrne, D., Griffitt, W., & Stefaniak, D. (1967). Attraction and similarity of personality characteristics. *Journal of Personality and Social Psychology, 5*(1), 82–90.

45  Dunbar (2018).

46  Hall, J. A., & Davis, D. C. (2017). Proposing the communicate bond belong theory: Evolutionary intersections with episodic interpersonal communication. *Communication Theory, 27*(1), 21–47.

47  The interview was published in Djøfbladet on 11 February 2019: www.djoefbladet.dk/artikler/2019/2/t-ae-t-p-aa--magten-i-nuuk.aspx (accessed 11 August 2023).

48  Foged, M., Hansen, N. W., & Nigatu, N. S. (2019). *Expats and the firms they work in.* Report by University of Copenhagen, Employment Relations Research Centre.

49  Mollenhorst, G., Volker, B., & Flap, H. (2014). Changes in personal relationships: How social contexts affect the emergence and discontinuation of relationships. *Social Networks, 37*, 65–80.

50  McCabe, J. M. (2016). *Connecting in college.* Chicago, IL: University of Chicago Press, p. 142.

51  E.g., Altman, I., & Taylor, D. A. (1973). *Social penetration. The development of interpersonal relationships.* New York: Holt, Rinehart and Winston, Inc.

52  Segal, M. W. (1974). Alphabet and attraction: An unobtrusive measure of the effect of propinquity in a field setting. *Journal of Personality and Social Psychology, 30*(5), 654.

53  Festinger, L., Schachter, S., & Back, K. (1950). *Social pressures in informal groups: A study of human factors in housing.*

54  Altman and Taylor (1973).

55  Collins, N. L., & Miller, L. C. (1994). Self disclosure and liking: A meta-analytic review. *Psychological Bulletin, 116*(3), 457–475.

56  Aron, A., Melinat, E., Aron, E. N., Vallone, R. D., & Bator, R. J. (1997). The experimental generation of interpersonal closeness: A procedure and some preliminary findings. *Personality and Social Psychology Bulletin, 23*(4), 363–377.

57  Hall and Davis (2017).

58  Gareis (2012).

59  Kudo and Simkin (2003).

60  Gareis, E. (2000). Intercultural friendship: Five case studies of German students in the USA. *Journal of Intercultural Studies, 21*(1), 67–91.

61  Lewin, K. (1936). Some social-psychological differences between the United States and Germany. *Character & Personality: A Quarterly for Psychodiagnostic & Allied Studies, 4*, 265–293.

62  Toh, S. M., & DeNisi, A. (2005). A local perspective to expatriate success. *The Academy of Management Executive, 19*(1), 132–146.

63 Povrzanović Frykman, M., & Mozetič, K. (2019). The importance of friends: Social life challenges for foreign physicians in Southern Sweden. *Community, Work and Family*, 1–16.

64 Lewin (1936), p. 282.

65 Gareis (2012).

66 Sias, P. M., Drzewiecka, J. A., Meares, M., Bent, R., Konomi, Y., Ortega, M., & White, C. (2008). Intercultural friendship development. *Communication Reports, 21*(1), 1–13.

# Experience

**A Spanish expat in Denmark – "I am a bit tired of the social deprivation corona is putting us under"**

*Isabella is a 27-year-old Spanish expat who moved to Copenhagen for 3–5 years, together with her partner. She moved in early 2021, when the COVID-19 pandemic still caused lockdowns in Denmark.[1]*

## January 2021

I am a very social person, so I was looking forward to making some friends. However, the situation makes it very (VERY) difficult, what creates a bit of anxiety… For example, socialising with people at work is almost impossible, I would love to connect with them, maybe by grabbing a beer after work, but that is not possible – obviously, and at the moment it feels a bit too formal to invite them home for a dinner, so that will have to wait.

I am also in a couple of Facebook groups where some new people post asking if anyone wants to have a walk around the city, but the setup is quite awkward because of the social distancing and the limit of people allowed on meetups, also, the weather is not very inviting.

I've been an expat for a while now and the main 'source' of friends are the workplace and maybe gym classes? And this is something that can't happen now, so I might have to get outside of my comfort zone and use apps like Bumble BFF to meet friends?

When it comes to expectations, I didn't want to set any because of all I mentioned before, plus I knew from my previous experience in the Netherlands that it is not easy to have an established group of friends as soon as you arrive. Usually, the first people you meet are not the ones that you click with, but eventually you build a circle of friends that,

DOI: 10.4324/9781003246855-6

unfortunately, are also expats so they will end up leaving the country as well at some point. So, as I said at the beginning, expectations regarding socialising were low...

## March 2021

Made a few friends at work, but it is a bit awkward to invite them home directly, as I said in my previous email, in a different context it would be so easy – just grabbing a beer after work!

I used Bumble to meet friends – not dating profile, I met a nice girl, but the same case as above applies, feels a bit awkward to invite her home directly? So, we had a walk around the lakes and that was it. I feel a bit lazy meeting with her again, at my age it feels like a lot of effort to make new friendships. I met a couple of times with a girl from work that just moved to CPH, with her it feels easy to hang out because she's outgoing and an extrovert like me, so I don't feel like I have to put on a lot of effort as in with other new people I meet.

Overall, a bit on a negative note, I am a bit tired of the social deprivation corona is putting us under.

## May 2021

I felt an immense change since bars and restaurants open, I am able to engage in a nice scenario with my colleagues without having to invite them home. Also, elaborating on the above, there are people at work that I like more than others, but how awkward would it be if I just invite home the people I like? Or if I invited everyone and only the people I don't click with would have shown up? Also, I am not a great cook, if the first thing that these people are gonna get from me is a not-so-tasty meal, I am afraid that might influence in the idea they might get of me.

COVID aside, starting a new life in a different country is never easy, it requires to be constantly outside of your comfort zone, meeting new people and we don't always feel like being social, sometimes I just feel like asking my best friend to drop by to watch a movie, without any higher interaction than that – but you don't have that because you don't have anyone.

Because of COVID, group meetups (which are less awkward that a 1–1 engagement with someone new) were cancelled, and a very nice and relaxed way of meeting people is attending social events (i.e. a talk on sustainable start-ups), where if you want, you can stay and network with other people, and if you don't feel like it, you can always go home after a nice and fulfilling event. This point is a bit tricky to explain but I hope the message gets across, bottom line is that COVID is adding an extra step of difficulty and intensifies meeting with people in a way that they turn into awkward or very intense situations, when we are not always up for such an energy-consuming interaction.

## Note

1   These are excerpts of e-mails she sent to me for my research about how expats make friends during a pandemic.

# Chapter 2

# How do expats make new friends abroad?

## Introduction

How do expats build a social network when they are abroad? To get an idea of what shapes the expat social network 72 expats from many different nationalities and all around the world were interviewed. These expats were asked to think back to when they first arrived in the host country, and how they built their social network. This was sometimes hard because most expats didn't really think deliberately about who they contacted.[1] The Pakistani expat in the Experience section on p. 215 "never had a strategy" and Jennifer, a U.S. American expat in Egypt, said: "You don't choose your friends that much." These interviews resulted in a process model which is presented in Figure 2.1. The model starts with having the motivation to make new friends, getting in touch with potential friends and building a relationship with them. Each stage is influenced by many different factors, and it can be helpful to understand how it works, and also know where one can influence it.

## Stage 1: Wanting to make new friends

When expats and their families move abroad, they move away from a large part of their existing social network, and they will need to make new friends in the host country. Like Becky, a U.S. American expat in Denmark, said: "It's like you're starting from scratch. [...], it's like: 'okay, I have no friends.'" In this first stage of the process of making friends abroad, it is about how motivated expats are to make new friends. Partly, this is influenced by their personality, how extrovert they are. Some people want a lot of friends around them, others are perfectly happy with only a few. Extroverts generally have larger social networks than introverts.[2] Another aspect is how much time and energy expats have for making new friends (and keeping up their current friends, also those at home), for example due to long working hours or as one gets older.[3] This is also

DOI: 10.4324/9781003246855-7

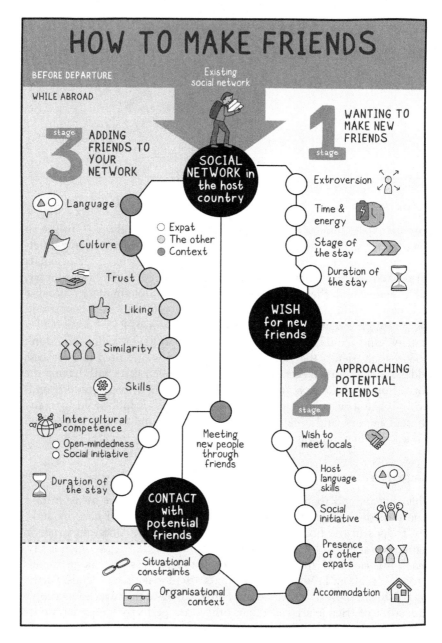

*Figure 2.1* How do expats make new friends abroad? Illustration by Heldermaker.

related to where the expat is in their stay: when they have only just arrived, they will be busy with settling in and don't really have time or a wish to meet new people.

> In the beginning, I just met like, probably like five, six people. And I said, like, that's enough for now. You know, and I settled down with my friends in the beginning, and I didn't really socialise anymore, up until the end of the year. Then I started socialising again and I met so many nice people.
>
> Ali, a Lebanese expat in Romania

How long the expat is planning to stay will also influence their motivation to make new friends in the host country. Jennifer, the U.S. American expat in Egypt, thought at one point that she was leaving Egypt, so she somewhat lost interest in making new friends because she didn't see the point if she was leaving anyway.

Many expats don't go abroad by themselves; they take a partner and possibly children with them. They may also already know some people in the host location too because they have been there before, for example, because they have been travelling there for work purposes before they were sent there on an assignment. This means they already have a beginning of a new social network in their host country. The advantage of going abroad as a couple is that expats and their partners have a readymade support system in place; someone who goes through the same challenges of moving to a new country and settling there. Networks of married people are often more centred around the family and the neighbourhood.[4] Ernst, a German expat in the United States, brought his family and enjoyed spending most of his time with them:

> I have my family, so... That was really nice when I came here that we were like a little group together and there was nobody... I wasn't hanging out with anybody else after work [...] So we got really close. That was a really nice time.

Bringing a family can also be a challenge, however, because both the expat and their partner will experience stress related to the move abroad, and they might be less able to support the other. Especially if the whole family is moving, much time will be spent in the beginning to settle in as a family, find a good place to live and choose a school. Single expats probably have a higher need to build a new social network and are usually more flexible in building relationships than, for example, expats who have (young) children. Jack, a British expat in the United States, was single when he arrived:

...from a expat perspective, it's probably the easier way and easier thing to happen, you don't have to worry about moving the whole family over here, but at the same time, you think of things being a little bit more lonely... The one thing I found was that the first few months are difficult, but at the same time it does really make you proactively try and find people to interact with outside of work.

This motivation of making new friends can change over time, as the new social network is being built. Once the expat is happy with the state of their social network, they will be less motivated to go out and make new friends. As Ali from Lebanon says: "Now, I socialise a lot with my current friends, but I don't, I'm not making any new friends like, oh, since the last two years. I, okay, I have a lot of friends and I think that's enough." And the motivation can increase again when people leave, or when the expat has more time and energy, for example after the first busy period of settling in has passed. The level of motivation is very important for the next step of getting in touch with potential friends.

## Stage 2: Getting in touch with potential friends

Once expats want to meet new friends, they have to create opportunities to meet new people. This can happen in a variety of contexts, like the neighbourhood, school, work, at a club or association, at home, via friends, at a public going-out place, on vacation, at church, at a party or on the internet.[5] Expats also meet people through their partner, their children (often at an international school) or during language learning activities (e.g. language school or tandem initiatives). Also, social network sites exist that are specifically targeted at expats, and help them meet other expats and sometimes also locals. InterNations is the largest global expat network with more than 4 million members, with many events that are ideal for meeting other expats. Adriana, a Brazilian expat in Italy, said: "InterNations was kind of a salvation for me, because I had friends now." Many expats also use Meetup, which is not specifically for expats, but offers opportunities to meet people in the new host country. For the British expat Jack, Meetup was a way to socialise with people in similar situations without necessarily having to join a social group. It can also be about joining some people on a trip or when they go out to a bar one night. The many expat groups on Facebook offer another opportunity to meet other expats, and expats also used WhatsApp, LinkedIn and dating apps to meet new people. Some social networks are specific for the host country, like WeChat in China, and it is good to figure out how these networks work in that (cultural) context. WeChat helped Daan, a Dutch expat in China, make a lot of new friends. It is very easy to connect with someone on WeChat; people are not very hesitant to add you on WeChat because it is not linked to their phone number, and they could block you again if they want to. Daan made friends through the 'People nearby' function, where he simply started chatting to those around him. "And out of the 10 people, 3 or 4 start talking back, you know, it's very easy to make friends and then say, okay, let's meet for drinks tonight." The app can also translate, so a language barrier is no problem. The question is sometimes whether someone really is interested in becoming a friend. Oliver, a British expat, sometimes felt like a 'token foreigner' for some Chinese who asked to connect with him on WeChat.

So, what influences who an expat meets and who might become a potential friend? Two categories of factors can be distinguished, namely those related to the expat, and those related to the context the expat finds themselves in. So, let's talk about the factors that are tied to the expat first. An important one is the attitude of the expat, and what motivates them. Many expats are very much interested in meeting locals, and they will put more effort in trying to meet host country nationals. Heike, a Swiss/German expat in Argentina, said: "I think naturally you'll have contacts to a lot of other expats just because of your own situation. But it's always the goal to meet locals and stay with the locals and have local friends" (see also Chapter 4 for the benefits of contact with locals of the host country). However, expats who do not speak the host country language may have difficulty connecting with locals of the host country. Lars, a Danish expat in Egypt, commented that one makes friends with those one can communicate with, which, for him, excluded Egyptians who did not speak English. Expats can also feel shy about using the host language in conversations when they are not very proficient. Emma, a U.S. American expat in Egypt, felt very nervous about speaking Arabic, so there were only a couple of people with whom she would speak it. Syed, on the other hand, the Pakistani expat in Turkey (see the Experience on p. 215), did manage to communicate with his Turkish neighbours: "We use our mobiles, hand gestures and try to explain. [...] We were understanding us very well." Another aspect is that expats need to take initiative to meet people. Being socially proactive is an important skill to create opportunities to socialise with others. As Thijs, a Dutch expat in China (see also the Experience on p. 1), notes: "You know, I've learned over time living in another country, people are not going to come to you, you have to go out and meet people and make that effort." This 'social initiative' is an important skill to make new connections in the host country and helps adjustment to the new culture.[6]

The second category of factors has to do with the context; the location the expat has moved to has certain characteristics that influence who the expat meets. For example, if the expat chooses to join one of the many expat associations (often organised per nationality) or live in a neighbourhood where many other expats have settled, they are more likely to meet those other expats in everyday life. And the other way around, like Peter, a Swiss/Belgian expat in China, said: "[...] because I'm alone here, I mean, I am the only Westerner, I never meet any other Westerners. I only speak to Chinese." A basic rule that has been confirmed in much research over the years is that the closer people live to one another, the more they interact.[7] Geographical proximity matters. The presence of other expats may lead to expats remaining in the so-called expat bubble. Jennifer, the U.S. American expat in Egypt, said: "When I first came, I came basically at the same time as a lot of other foreigners, and I think that [...] kept me in a small bubble."

The type of accommodation an expat chooses also shapes who they meet. Many younger expats mentioned that their form of 'communal' living led to new friendships, because they shared an apartment, or started in a hostel or Airbnb before they found something more permanent. On the other extreme, one expat in this study, Ernst, the German expat in the United States, lived on a property so big that he couldn't see his neighbours and didn't need to walk his dog anymore. Obviously, this also impacts the amount of contact he had with his neighbours. It is important to realise that the expat has a choice in this matter, and that choosing where to live is not just about the accommodation itself, or where it is located with regard to the workplace and the school of the children, but also has effects on who the expat will socialise with. For example, during my PhD I met one Shell expat in London who chose not to live on the "Shell street" which had 24 houses and a Dutch primary school, but instead lived half an hour away in an English neighbourhood and sent their children to a local school. You can imagine how this choice influenced their social network – instead of their daily life being around other Shell expats and their children playing with other Dutch people, they met English people. Emma, the U.S. American expat in Egypt, had the same motivation that made her choose to live outside of a compound in Egypt:

> If you are just moving here like as a single person thinking you want to know more about the culture, I cannot understand why you would live in a compound because it is like living in the U.S. I don't get it. Like why are you in Egypt, if you want to live in a house that looks just like an American house? I don't understand that at all.

Of course, though, in some countries there is not really a choice other than living in an expat compound, for example due to safety reasons (see

Box 2.1). It is important for expats and their organisations to consider the options in the host country and their priorities in terms of who they would like to socialise with when choosing an accommodation because having local friends in the host country is very important to feel good there.

---

### Box 2.1   Living in an expat compound

Dr. Reto Wegmann, Senior Advisor of Swiss Ibex LLC, Lecturer at the University of Lucerne

Making friends with locals is much more difficult when expats do not live among the local population, but rather in expat compounds. A compound is a gated residential community, which usually offers all kinds of amenities such as shops, pools and gyms. We generally see two reasons for this to happen or for this to even be the norm: security management and cultural norms.

The first reason, security considerations, applies to expat employers operating in high-risk contexts like Afghanistan, South Sudan or parts of the Sahel. In these regions, employers are faced with the dilemma that, while local integration might be desirable, they are also bound by their moral and legal duty of care towards their employees. Employees need to be protected from harm, both as a measure for occupational health and safety but also to keep operations running. The employers often impose several security management measures on the expat, such as limitations to freedom of movement, and living in a secured compound. This, obviously, makes it more difficult to integrate with local communities. While private companies might just withdraw if security considerations limit business and leisure activities too much, other employers (UN agencies and non-profits like NGOs, charities or faith-based organisations) tend to stay operational even in war zones and failed states. Their expats usually live in a self-contained compound.

The second reason, cultural isolation, applies whenever expat employers do not want to submit themselves, as an organisation or as agents for their individual employees, to certain local rules and laws. A widely known and frequent example of such a place would be Saudi Arabia, where organisations do not always want their employees to submit to all local rules (e.g. about alcohol, sexuality and role of the woman). Staff from Europe, Asia and from the Americas tend to stick to living in compounds, where no locals are offended and where authorities might turn a blind eye, when expats stick to their own customs and habits.

In the overlapping field of these two considerations, there is a grey zone of risks which is very difficult to handle for employers due to privacy issues. Personal characteristics of the deployed expats, like religion or sexual orientation, might pose a security risk for them. For example, the possession of the Bible on the Maldives is equally illegal as are male homosexual acts in Qatar. These security risks are tied to very private characteristics of the expat that the employer is often unaware of. In such cases, compound living also might be a reasonable alternative to full local immersion.

The workplace is another context that brings people together, and for expats who start a new job, this is the first place they will start looking. In some cultures, it is very normal to make friends at work, but other cultures have a stronger divide between work and private life. The Netherlands is one example, as an English expat from my PhD research commented:

[...] especially at the beginning, because the only people you know are the people you work with, and you never get invited out with them. That's just really... If you didn't know that was just part of the culture you would almost feel as 'they must not like me,' 'what I am doing wrong' or... This is really jarring.

Other aspects of the organisational context also influence who the expat meets, for example whether there are social events in the office that bring people together, and how many other expats work there. When I came to Denmark in 2013, I was the only expat in my department, so I mainly met other Danes at work, some of whom became friends, even if also Denmark has a divide between work and private life. An organisation can also arrange a buddy for newly arrived expats (Chapters 7–9 will dive deeper in this potential support option) and help out with all the practical matters that heap up when an expat arrives. This will free up time to socialise, and also reduce the expat's need to seek this support from their (new) friends. The job itself also influences who an expat meets. Thijs, the Dutch expat in China, had to build international relations for his job, so he met other expats more easily. On the other hand, Lars, the Danish expat in Egypt, felt that being a manager made it more difficult to make friends through work "because you cannot be friends with your employees, and they are the ones you spent most of your time with. At least for me I cannot." Carmen, an Italian expat in Portugal, was also hesitant to make friends at work because she works in human resources (HR), and sometimes she has to communicate bad news as well. And simply being an expat can also present a barrier to make friends with local colleagues. Chantal, a Belgian expat, experienced this in an NGO in Malaysia, where the local employees did not want to hang out with the expats who earn much more: "I understand that when you earn three times their salary, they're upset".

Finally, several situational constraints influenced who the expats were able to meet. One example is the opportunities expats have to socialise, such as events organised by a Chamber of Commerce but also the presence of clubs and associations, whether primarily for expats or locals. Safety can also be a concern that affects where one goes and whom one meets. Erika, a German expat in the United States, compared Portland, Oregon, where she was comfortable with talking to strangers sitting on the benches at the waterfront, to New Haven, Connecticut, where she never really felt safe. In Nigeria, Lakshmi, an Indian expat, was restricted by her husband's company guidelines, which prescribed that they always had to use a personal driver and not public transportation. She also felt unsafe visiting some of the local markets with her "expat face". Another situational element is the level of economic development of the country. For example, Anna-Lena, a German expat, went out much more than in Germany: "[...] in South Africa compared to Europe, and you have much bigger value for your money. So, you have more to just have fun". And in 2020, COVID-19 restrictions also influenced who expats were able to meet with, with most events being cancelled and relationships being built online instead. I will delve into this topic later in this chapter (p. 63).

Finally, expats often also meet new friends through an existing connection, for example their partner. Expats with children also often meet other parents through their children. This 'snowball' effect is a very easy way to meet new friends, because simply by being with friends they might meet new friends. Many expats say that they met a particular person and that their network grew from there. Of course, this depends on the extent to which the friend invites them for activities or events where they might meet new people, but the expat can also specifically ask to meet new people, like Heike, the Swiss/German expat in Argentina: "So many locals I met through referrals from other people I knew, because I was specifically asking to meet Argentines." In the model (Figure 2.1), this snowball effect is shown as a shortcut to Stage 3 because the expat doesn't have to do anything to meet those people.

## Stage 3: Adding friends to your network

Once an expat is in contact with a potential friend, many aspects influence whether that person becomes a friend and is added to the host country social network, or not. Those factors can be divided in three categories: those related to the expat, those related to the other person and those related to the context.

### The expat

We start with the factors related to the expat, and the first one is the often-limited duration of the expat's stay. I have already mentioned that this influences the expat's motivation to make friends in the host country, but it also means that new friends might be about to leave, and that people are less likely to want to become the expat's friend. Chantal, the Belgian expat in Malaysia, says:

> [...] the problem you have with the expat is the turnover. Even when you eventually have a friend, they leave. And that's also one of the reasons why locals socialise a bit less with us, I think for some they are, they just see us as we just pass, you know. Would they invest in someone that will go anyway?

The second expat-related factor is their intercultural competence, sometimes also called cultural intelligence, which is key to building new relationships across cultural borders, including friendships. It can be defined as "the knowledge, motivation, and skills to interact effectively and appropriately with members of different cultures"[8] – we will look more closely at intercultural competence and how to develop it in the next chapter. A starting point of intercultural competence is gathering knowledge about how things are done in the host country. Daan, the Dutch expat in China, comments how expats need to consider that locals have a different culture and background, and that it is important to know how they think and how they would react to you to be able to avoid issues and conflict. It also helps for expats to be open to people from other cultures and the different ways in which they may do things; such openmindedness is very important to build new social relations in the host country. Always say 'yes' to opportunities is advice often given to new expats. Emma, the U.S. American expat, says:

> [...] if my Egyptian friends want to do something, or they want to go somewhere, or they want me to meet other people, I ALWAYS say yes. Because I'm not just going to meet an Egyptian, I am not going to find my new best friend by walking down the street and say "excuse me sir, do you speak English, can we talk? Do you want to be friends?"

The third component of intercultural competence is skills. With regard to making new friends abroad, social initiative is a key intercultural skill. As mentioned earlier, social initiative is needed to actually meet new people who could become friends, but it also helps develop the relationship further by inviting the other to do something together.

Third, other skills such as social skills and host language proficiency help build an intercultural relationship. Ilse, a German expat in the Netherlands, made a particular effort to teach her son social skills:

> Everywhere I went I tried to start a conversation – also for my child so he could see: "you just have to try"! Try, and make mistakes and never mind if it is embarrassing – you just laugh and it's fine (laughter).

The expat's proficiency in the host language is particularly relevant if one wants to befriend people from the host country itself. Marjorie's (Hongkongese/U.S. American expat in Argentina) host language proficiency has developed over time; she now feels much more comfortable trying to speak Spanish while making new friends.

### The other person

When an expat is trying to build a relationship with someone, we also have to consider the other person. For example, the potential friend should also want to make a new connection. This is why it can sometimes be difficult to meet with locals, because they have their existing social network and are not necessarily looking for new friends – they might not have the time and energy for creating a new social relationship on top of maintaining the ones they already have.[9]

When the other person is also interested to build a relationship, it is the similarity between the expat and the other person that is a key factor for the development of the relationship. There is a wealth of research on the similarity-attraction hypothesis that shows that individuals with similar attitudes are more attracted to each other,[10] and that one needs some similarity in background, lifestyle, attitudes and values to develop the relationships to a higher quality.[11] Some common ground is important to build a relationship, and one way of meeting like-minded people is through activities and hobbies. Adriana, the Brazilian expat in Italy, recommended doing things one enjoys doing because it is a way to meet like-minded people. When meeting other expats, an important common ground is that they also have to adjust to life in a new host country. This is also called adjustment empathy.[12] Pablo, a Spanish expat in China, said: "… they were going through the same thing. And that was what made it fun. Because you were sharing the same frustrations. You were sharing the same excitement, you were sharing similar situations, right." Dissimilarity can slow down the development of a relationship, and one form of dissimilarity is a different cultural background. Cultural differences can be a barrier for the development of the contact[13]; for example, in my PhD research one expat was pregnant, and when the baby arrived, she felt her host should reach out to her. However, in the Netherlands, the custom is for the new parents to send out a *geboortekaartje* (a card to announce the birth) to all their friends and family, which also specifies how and when the new parents want to be contacted. The Dutch host was waiting for this to arrive, and this led to a breakdown of the contact, because both were waiting for the other to reach out. Another barrier can be the English language proficiency of the local if the expat doesn't speak the host language. Many locals feel 'shy' about using English or deem their English proficiency too low. Becky, the U.S. American expat in Denmark, said: "...my neighbour doesn't speak any English, so he doesn't ever try to talk to me because he knows, I just speak English."

Similarity is one of the ingredients that makes someone like the other person, and this liking is, obviously, also an important catalyst for the contact because you want to spend time with the other person. Shared fun and humour are important elements to push a relationship forward.[14] Dolores, a Spanish expat in Germany, when asked why she selected particularly those people, simply said: "Because I like them." And this works both ways – if someone feels the other person likes them, it is more likely that they will also like them in return. This reciprocity of liking[15] helps a relationship develop, through wanting to meet more often. It is important that this social initiative comes from both sides. Chantal, the Belgian expat in Malaysia, became somewhat frustrated with always being the one who was suggesting things, and concluded that they just didn't care so much for doing things together, otherwise they would have come up with something. Repeated social interactions will also build trust, which is a key factor to build a friendship with someone.[16] Ali, the Lebanese expat in Romania, says:

> And I wouldn't call anybody a friend just like that, it takes some trust, you know, like some actions that they've done or some situation that had happened, and if that person stood by me in those kinds of situations, I would consider that guy a friend.

### The context

Finally, contextual factors also influence whether someone becomes a friend. I will discuss two in more detail, namely culture and language. The culture of the host country provides the context in which the new friendships are made. I already mentioned that cultural differences

## Box 2.2   How to make friends in Denmark

Since 2014, Denmark is consistently ranked in the top five of countries where it is difficult to make local friends, as is shown in the
annual survey of InterNations, the global network for expats. As
The Local.dk headlines, Denmark "'world's worst' for making
friends,"[21] but why do expats find particularly Denmark difficult for
making local friends? In a chapter I wrote for a book about informal
networks in international business,[22] I dove into all the books I could
find about Denmark – written by historians, anthropologists and
other expats – to answer this question.

An important thing to know about Denmark is that it is a very
homogeneous nation with little past experience with immigration.
The historic losses of territory in the 19th century have led to the
Danes turning in on themselves, focusing on their own 'tribe' where
they find community and unshakeable trust, as the British ambas-
sador to Denmark Sir James Mellon observed in the 1980s. Historian
Jespersen describes Danish mentality as a circle of people sitting
around a campfire "shoulder to shoulder around it, with their backs
to the darkness outside the circle of light from the fire."[23] *Hygge*,
which is an emic Danish concept which reflects an "atmosphere
of security, warmth and inclusion,"[24] is an important part of this.
*Hygge*, however, also carries a pressure to conform to the point of
being coercive.[25] As one author states: "*Hygge* always has its backs
turned on the others. *Hygge* is for the members, not the strangers."[26]
This homogeneity and inward-looking mentality makes it more difficult for outsiders to be part of the social circle. Danes often have
an established social circle that dates back to their time in ground
school, since they spend the years from age 6 to 16 in the same class
with the same classmates. It is no wonder that many expats observe
that Danes all seem to have friends that go back to childhood.

Closely connected to homogeneity is the value that Danes place
on equality – the famous Law of Jante that states, among others,
that nobody is better than others. When everyone is the same, it
is easier to create the trust that is the backbone of Danish society.
Anthropologist Anne Knudsen adds: "The important part is the
inclusiveness: we want to include you, but that is only possible if you
are equal. It's what peasants do."[27] This value of equality can make
things difficult for newcomers because you can't 'get a seat at the
table,' where everyone is equal, unless you are invited in. Another

complication is the norm that Danes only talk to those they know and that introductions are usually not made, because this would only highlight your outsider status, and make you lose face.

A third important aspect that sheds light on why it can be difficult to make friends with Danes is the divide between public and private life. The Danes' private zone only covers family and friends, which can be interpreted as cold and difficult to access by those who come from a culture where there is less of a divide between work and private life and more spontaneity. Danes spend their time outside of work with family and friends, so expats should not expect their Danish colleague to become their friend outside of work. Danes also value privacy, which is why they do not appreciate unannounced visits to their home. The unfortunate thing for expats is that Danes also value the other's privacy, which means that they will not easily strike up conversations with an expat, since the expat is a stranger.

Language is another complicating factor. Even though Danes often are proficient in English, not all of them feel comfortable speaking it in front of other Danes. Together with the fact that the language is an important part of 'being Danish,', Danes often switch to their native language, especially outside the large cities. Social life, naturally, takes place in Danish, and Danes often are reluctant to include those who do not speak Danish. As one Dutch expat who participated in the corona study mentioned later in this chapter (p. 63) wrote:

> I need social contacts/people around me. To me well-being means having friends over/being invited. So far, I feel a bit lonely, the Danes are not super welcoming, and they don't make any effort in talking English to me. (Though I try to talk in Danish and they compliment me for that.)

The added difficulty for expats is that many Danes are not used to hearing their language spoken with an accent. Expats seem to have an easier time in large cities such as Copenhagen, but there an often-heard complaint is that Danes too easily switch to English which doesn't help the expat learning Danish.

So, what should you do if you find yourself in Denmark and you would like to make local friends? First of all, it is important to not take it personally and realise that Danes also don't reach out to fellow-Danes. They have an established social network and are not actively looking for new friends. This does not mean they might not want to meet you; but it does need an effort to participate in local life, learn (some of) the language, and join in some of the social rituals (there are many of them in Denmark!). Joining a club or association is a great way to make Danish friends; almost all Danes are member of one or other association, where their community spirit is expressed, and trust is built. A final recommendation is to learn to read between the lines of what the Danes say. An unfortunate consequence of valuing privacy is that Danes don't easily give invitations for fear of imposing. Don't sit around and wait for them to invite you!

can be a barrier for the contact itself, but culture also influences how people socialise, and what the best way is to meet new friends in that particular country. One already mentioned example is whether expats are likely to make friends in the workplace. One of the aims of my research is to raise awareness for these cultural differences as well as gather knowledge so expats know how to best go about to make new friends in their host country. The expats mention a great number of cultural differences that affect their socialising, which is valuable knowledge for new expats to have when trying to make friends in a particular culture.[17] In Box 2.2 I have more extensively written about the situation in Denmark, where certain cultural characteristics explain why many expats feel it is difficult to connect with the Danes. My colleagues Sven Horak and Jong Gyu Park have contributed Box 2.3 about making friends in South Korea. Countries also differ in terms of accessibility of the local population, or how open the locals are to becoming friends with expats. As mentioned, Denmark is a country where expats find it very difficult to make friends with Danes, and Danes are often described as cold and standoffish. Although part of this difficulty can be explained – and hopefully solved – by knowing more about the culture and how the Danes themselves socialise (see Box 2.2), some of it also seems to be rooted in the historical context in terms of residential mobility in a particular country. Residential mobility is the number of moves of an individual in a country, and the United States and Australia have high rates of residential mobility, where Japan and Denmark have low rates[18] – although there are regional and individual differences. This high residential mobility of the United States – one of

## Box 2.3  How to make friends in South Korea

Sven Horak, St. John's University, New York (USA) and Jong Gyu Park, College of Staten Island, The City University of New York, New York (USA)

South Korea (Korea hereafter) developed its economy over recent decades to one of the top 10 leading economies in the world.[28] Unsurprisingly, the number of foreigners in Korea also increased. Expats, however, paint an ambiguous picture of living and working in Korea. According to a survey conducted by InterNations in 2021,[29] expats praise the quality of the Korean healthcare system, its affordability and the country's transportation infrastructure. Also, almost all expats questioned say they feel safe in Korea. In contrast, when it comes to the "ease of settling in," InterNations' index ranked Korea among the worst destinations in the world for expats. Korea ranks low in the categories "feeling at home" and "making local friends." In the following, based on our research on informal networking and our own experience of living and working in Korea, we provide some clues why making friends in Korea may appear difficult and what expats can do to become better socially integrated.

Central for understanding how to socialise and make friends might be the fact that Korea is a homogenous culture, with a comparatively low level of immigration. Korea is a peninsula surrounded by water on three sides and a closed border to North Korea. Today the proportion of the population in Korea who are foreigners is approximately 4.4%, most of them from other Asian countries. Conventionally, Korea is described as a collectivist society that scores low in general trust (i.e. trust to foreigners) and high in particularistic trust. Traditional ideals characterizing Korean society are reflected in community orientation (i.e. in-group), conformity and social hierarchy based on the Confucian value and norm system. For understanding social relationships in Korea, it is important to understand social structures. While general trust and rather open social relationships are typical in Western societies, the distinction between in- and out-groups is important in Korea.

Analogous to *guanxi* networks in China, Korea can be best described as a network society. The most common informal networks in Korea are *yongo* and *inmaek* networks. *Yongo* consists of three traditional ties which are very difficult or even impossible for a foreigner to acquire: kinship and blood ties, ties to people from the same region or hometown and ties to people who have attended the same educational institution, high school, college or university. Given its members' backgrounds, *yongo* is rather homogenous, and it is closed and exclusive. *Yongo* can be seen as a determinant in distinguishing between in- and outgroups. It can happen that outgroup persons "are treated as 'non-persons' and there can be discrimination and even hostility."[30] Since *yongo* is important in business as well as in private life (a distinction not so important in Korea anyway), not having *yongo* is at times challenging for expats, as it is often instrumentalised for getting things done and to get ahead in life. *Inmaek*, which is closer to Chinese *guanxi* ties, refers to a network one develops in the course of life. *Inmaek* is used to help less-fortunate people secure a job or promotion, although this sometimes results in the employment of persons who lack suitable qualifications or skills. In principle, *inmaek* ties can be seen as positive and feature high levels of solidarity and goodwill. Compared to *yongo*, expats can develop *inmaek* ties in principle, and that is what we recommend expats to focus on, since forming *yongo* ties may simply not work.

However, these informal networks also are now to the advantage of foreigners. A new extension of traditional *yongo* ties are ties concluded at the workplace, so-called *jikyon* and *eobyon* ties. They refer to ties among people from the same company, industry or profession. These ties are based on similar values as *yongo*, and can be seen as *yongo* 2.0.[31] The main reason workplace ties are increasing in significance is that employees who only possess little or low-quality traditional *yongo* see the chance to get ahead in life and their careers in *jikyon* and *eobyon* networks. There are also dynamics observed in relation to *inmaek*. Today, Korean media more often use the term *global inmaek* when Korean celebrities and well-known businesspeople are shown in photographs with foreign celebrities, implying that there is a friendship-like relationship. The desire to have *global inmaek* can be seen as a new but significant form of networking for Korean professionals in the globalisation era. This is reflected in the desire to travel abroad and the increased preference for working abroad among Koreans.

In sum, the current development dynamics of traditional Korean social ties work to the advantage of expats, who can focus on developing friendships based upon workplace-related ties or *global inmaek*. What would that look like in practice? In Korea, co-workers frequently meet after work for dinner or on the weekend for leisure activities. It would be unwise to reject offers for these activities, especially when one wants to develop friendships further. Moreover, there are plenty of other opportunities to develop *global inmaek*. Cultural associations such as Alliance Française (France), the Goethe Institute (Germany) and others operate branches in Korea that can serve as a hub to make new friends. International service clubs (e.g. Rotary and Lions Clubs, etc.) and several business- and industry-specific associations (e.g. Chambers of Commerce) can support profession-oriented networking. Also, there are many foreign universities and academic institutions doing alumni work in Korea. For the religious expat, Korea has many religious communities one can get involved in. As there are plenty of opportunities for expats to socialise and make friends in Korea, the biggest challenge might be just to start, become proactive and from time to time get out of the expat bubble.

the most mobile nations in the world[19] – might explain the observations Kurt Lewin, a German-American psychologist, made already in 1936, about how U.S. Americans more quickly acquire friends to whom they can easily say goodbye (see p. 34 in the Introduction). With many people – friends – potentially moving away, U.S. Americans are motivated to make more friends, and are eager to talk to strangers. This can come across as strange to those who come from cultures where you don't really do that. I myself had such an experience during one of my first visits to the United States. I was walking along the beautiful Sunset Cliffs in San Diego, when a guy with a surfboard climbed down the cliffs to the otherwise deserted beach and started talking to me. I was surprised and wondered first if anything was wrong, and then what he wanted from me. It turned out he just wanted to chat and that was fun – I just wasn't used to having conversations for no apparent reason with complete strangers. I have also heard many people say that U.S. Americans are superficial, and this is why it is crucial to have this knowledge of cultural differences in socialising. For U.S. Americans it is very normal to invite people to a barbecue at their home, and expats could easily end up interpreting such an invitation with their own cultural lens, and then get disappointed when the expected friendship doesn't develop.

The second contextual factor influencing if an expat becomes friends particularly with locals of the host country is the language of the host country. If the expat doesn't speak the host language, it is important they have a language in common with locals to be able to become friends. Countries differ in terms of their English language proficiency,[20] so "in a country like Egypt where the English is very bad, I would need to learn it [Arabic] to make more local friends." [Lars, the Danish expat in Egypt]. Also, locals of the host country are not always willing to switch to English. Mihaela, a Romanian expat in France, comments how the French expect foreigners – or at least people who live in France – to speak good French. And even if locals of the host country are willing to switch to English, learning the host language can still help to make friends with locals because many "feel more comfortable speaking in their own language" [Alejandro, a Peruvian expat in Denmark] and "it will be more difficult for this person to integrate you in your life because his life is normally happening in German" [Dolores, the Spanish expat in Germany]. The Netherlands and Denmark are two examples of countries with a small host language, and a high English language proficiency. The enthusiasm with which many Dutch and Danes speak English to expats does not really make it easier for them to learn the language. In the Netherlands, you can buy a button which says '*Spreek Nederlands met mij*' (speak Dutch with me), which is a nice way to highlight to the locals that you are up for the challenge.

## Building a social network during a pandemic

Even though the COVID-19 pandemic put a stop to normal life in many respects, people were still moving abroad, leaving their social network behind. In spring 2021, I decided to follow several newly arrived expats in Denmark in their efforts of trying to build a new social network at a time when COVID-19 restrictions put a severe limitation on socialising opportunities. Fifteen expats shared their experiences with me for a few months in early 2021, until most of the restrictions in Denmark were lifted in by May 2021. Particularly the restrictions of cafes and restaurants being closed until 21 April 2021, the assembly bans (maximum five persons) and the recommendation to stay at home and only socialise with those you live with are relevant for their experiences.

A first observation reinforces what has been highlighted in the very first chapter of this book; how important social relations are for well-being (p. 21). Several expats comment on how they felt lonely or isolated. A Spanish expat (see also the Experience on p. 41) mentioned how she was getting tired of the "social deprivation" that the lockdown caused. Trying to make new connections – despite the circumstances – helped: an Italian expat went on some hikes and "it lightened my mood noticeably." Obviously, the COVID-19 pandemic impacted social life dramatically for a period, especially during lockdowns; many socialising opportunities were no longer possible or severely limited due to the restrictions. Many people were working from home for an extended period, and those who could go to the office faced restrictions such as a limited number of people one could have lunch with at the same time. The only social interaction an Italian expat got in her workplace were work-related chats in the corridors. People were also often hesitant to meet in person due to the risk of infection.

The pandemic not only added an extra layer of difficulty by presenting various barriers for socialising, it also changed the way in which people socialised. Contact often moved online, if people met physically it had to be in smaller groups or one-on-one, and the venue of many social interactions changed, for example from a restaurant or café to the home or outdoors. This presented its own challenges, for example, not everyone was ready to invite people to their home. The Spanish expat in the Experience on p. 41 also talked about how she would love to connect more with her colleagues. She would normally do this by grabbing a beer after work, but since that was not possible, she postponed it because she felt it was a bit too formal to invite them home for a dinner.

Outdoor meetings were also heavily influenced by the Danish weather; the lockdown started in winter and by the time spring arrived, restaurants and cafes were opening up again. A Polish expat said during lockdown: "The rain basically means no social life." A final, important, way in which the lockdown changed social life was that expats had to find new ways of making friends. A French expat comments: "I had to use another way; I had to get out of my comfort zone to actually get to meet people. I did things that I would never have done to try to make friends." Many resorted to Facebook and other social media to meet new people, since they couldn't meet them through work or a yoga class.

While some expats felt lonely, not everyone reacted the same to these limiting circumstances. As mentioned earlier, aspects such as extroversion and the stage of the assignment influence the need for social connections. A Spanish expat only wanted to get social again after the few first months after her arrival and, by then, restaurants and cafes were opening up again. Other expats didn't feel this need for social connections as much and were content with focusing on other things. One Swiss expat said: "[I] am not having difficulties being alone. Keeping myself busy with my own business, reading and trying to learn Danish as much as I can online."

An important factor that influenced how much expats wanted to socialise is their fear of infection. A U.S. American expat hadn't made any effort yet to meet people in person because she wanted to be cautious.

An Italian expat talks about how she tries to balance this anxiety and her need for social connections: "I feel like I need these activities to socialise a little and stop feeling very lonely before it gets too heavy for me, but at the same time I worry it is not a safe choice." In the later stages of the pandemic, this was mitigated for some due to the extensive testing in Denmark, which meant that people felt safer to socialise. The Italian expat said: "It's so easy to get tested that we do it beforehand, so we can meet responsibly. This really improved my perception of social interactions, as I feel less guilty and safer seeing people." If the need for social connections became too much, expats took initiative despite the lockdown. One Italian expat started actively searching on social media for a solution: "Luckily, I found a group that organised outdoor Corona-safe events."

In conclusion, many people had their social life 'on hold' during the pandemic. The limited opportunities for social interactions meant that many expats were not able to expand their network as they would have liked to, or only managed to establish weak new connections. A British/Dutch expat said: "It would be lovely to meet the locals and practise my Danish, but I keep telling myself that it doesn't have to be right now." Some expats made friends that were different from who they normally would make friends with, due to the circumstances. An Italian expat said: "I often feel like this is the social circle that I was able to find at this weird time, and I should stick to that, while I wait for other opportunities to expand my circle."

While the pandemic certainly made social life more difficult, some expats also saw some bright sides to the situation, for example that online socialising saves time and money. Another expat realised that social contacts take up a lot of energy, and that she could probably do with fewer contacts. A Dutch expat realised the importance of keeping up more distant contacts at home through the occasional video call. A French expat was pushed to be more open and creative in meeting new people, thereby surprising herself. She also made friends she normally wouldn't have and started to enjoy things she normally wouldn't do. She said: "If I had to resume how corona has influenced my social life in Denmark, I would say it had 'surprisingly' helped me to meet more people that I would have expected to."

The reopening of society was welcomed by all the expats in this study, as a return to a somewhat normal life. A Dutch expat felt freer after her first vaccination, because it meant she no longer had to be tested before going anywhere. She was also less anxious about the virus; she no longer was scared when someone came to close, and could go out for a night again, and have friends and family visit. A Singaporean expat said in May:

The last four weeks have been better in terms of social life. As the corona restrictions have lifted, this means that I can socialise with people outside or in restaurants. Furthermore, the group size has increased outdoors. This also meant that people are allowed to organise social events where I could meet people.

Many elements influence the process of making friends abroad, as is reflected in Figure 2.1. The process is dynamic and never ends; new people get added to the social network in the host country, people also leave again, and the motivation of the expat to make new friends also goes up and down. The model can guide expats in making friends abroad. While it isn't a topic many expats have really thought about before moving, there are certainly choices they can make that will facilitate them making the friends they would like to have in the host country. For example, decisions with regard to where to live and what school to choose for their children also have an impact on who the expat will meet and make friends with. In that sense, expats can also shape their own social network abroad. This model helps us understand the process of making friends abroad, which can also be supported by the organisation the expat works for (see Chapter 9 and the Recommendations for expats, organisations and societies), so that expats are better equipped to thrive socially in their new host country.

## Notes

1 You can read more about my study on expat social network building on my website www.intersango.dk.
2 Dunbar, R. I. M. (2018). The anatomy of friendship. *Trends in Cognitive Sciences, 22*(1), 32–51.
3 Dunbar (2018).
4 Mollenhorst, G., Volker, B., & Flap, H. (2014). Changes in personal relationships: How social contexts affect the emergence and discontinuation of relationships. *Social Networks, 37*, 65–80.
5 Mollenhorst et al. (2014).
6 Van Oudenhoven, J. P., & Van der Zee, K. I. (2002). Predicting multicultural effectiveness of international students: The Multicultural Personality Questionnaire. *International Journal of Intercultural Relations, 26*, 679–694.
7 Altman, I., & Taylor, D. A. (1973). *Social penetration. The development of interpersonal relationships.* New York: Holt, Rinehart and Winston, Inc.
8 Wiseman, R. (2002). Intercultural communication competence. In W. Gudykunst & B. Mody (Eds.), *Handbook of international and intercultural communication* (2nd ed., pp. 207–224). Thousand Oaks, CA: Sage.

9  Hall, J. A., & Davis, D. C. (2017). Proposing the communicate bond belong theory: Evolutionary intersections with episodic interpersonal communication. *Communication Theory, 27*(1), 21–47.

10  Byrne, D. (1971). *The attraction paradigm*. New York and London: Academic Press, Inc.

11  Sudweeks, S., Gudykunst, W. B., Ting-Toomey, S., & Nishida, T. (1990). Developmental themes in Japanese-North American interpersonal relationships. *International Journal of Intercultural Relations, 14*(2), 207–233.

12  Farh, C., Bartol, K., Shapiro, D., & Shin, J. (2010). Networking abroad: A process model of how expatriates form support ties to facilitate adjustment. *Academy of Management Review, 35*(3), 434–454.

13  van Bakel, M., van Oudenhoven, J. P., & Gerritsen, M. (2015). Developing a high quality intercultural relationship: Expatriates and their local host. *Journal of Global Mobility, 3*(1), 25–45.

14  Dunbar (2018).

15  Fehr, B. (2008). Friendship formation. In S. Sprecher, A. Wenzel, & J. Harvey (Eds.), *Handbook of relationship initiation* (pp. 29–54). New York, NY: Psychology Press.

16  Dunbar (2018).

17  On my website www.intersango.dk, I am compiling information about the best ways to socialise in specific countries, and I would love to get your input!

18  Oishi, S. (2010). The psychology of residential mobility: Implications for the self, social relationships, and well-being. *Perspectives on Psychological Science, 5*(1), 5–21.

19  Although, interestingly, this mobility has been decreasing - where three decades ago 20% of the U.S. population moved in one year, by now this is only 10%. (Frost, R. (2020). Are Americans stuck in place? Declining residential mobility in the US. Retrieved from www.jchs.harvard.edu/sites/default/files/harvard_jchs_are_americans_stuck_in_place_frost_2020.pdf (accessed on 12 August 2023).)

20  One country ranking is provided by the EF English Proficiency Index.

21  www.thelocal.dk/20160829/expats-name-denmark-worst-in-the-world-for-making-friends/ (accessed 12 August 2023).

22  van Bakel, M. (2022). Expatriate social network formation in Denmark: Challenges of developing informal ties locally. In S. Horak (Ed.), *Informal networks in international business*. Bingley, UK: Emerald.

23  Jespersen, K. J. V. (2011). *A history of Denmark*. London, UK: Palgrave Macmillan.

24  Jenkins, R. (2011). *Being Danish: Paradoxes of identity in everyday life*: Museum Tusculanum Press, p. 219.

25  Jenkins (2011), p. 41.

26  Østergård, U. (1990). *Peasants and Danes – Danish national identity and political culture*. Aarhus: Centre for Cultural Research, University of Aarhus, p. 25.

27  Booth, M. (2014). *The almost nearly perfect people: Behind the myth of the Scandinavian utopia*. New York: Picador.

28 By gross domestic product (GDP), nominal, 2020.

29 Internations (2021). Expat Insider 2021 – The Asian Tigers. *Source*: www. internations.org/expat-insider/2021/the-asian-tigers-40119 (accessed 26 August 2023).

30 Page 179, in Kim, Y.-H. (2000). Emergence of the network society: Trends, new challenges, and an implication for network capitalism. *Korea Journal*, *40*(3), 161–184.

31 Horak, S., & Park, J. G. (2022). Korea: Yongo 2.0, global Inmaek, and network multiplexity. In Horak, S. (Ed.). *Informal networks in international business*. Bingley, UK: Emerald Publishers.

# Experience

DOI: 10.4324/9781003246855-8

Danish students in Denmark – "Developing my openmindedness has been a great challenge for me"

*For a class on Global Competence Development, I gave 10 weeks of homework exercises to my students – many of which can be found in Chapter 3 – to help develop their intercultural competence. Here are some of their experiences, drawn from the self-reflection reports they handed in for the exam.*

One student said:

Developing my openmindedness competence has been a great challenge for me because I always believed that I was a very openminded person and that being openminded was a big part of my personality. I quickly found out, while doing one of the first exercises of attending to your judgements, that was not entirely true. The *Attend to judgement* exercise (see Box 3.1 on p. 78) revealed to me how judgemental I was towards other people and also towards myself sometimes. Although before the exercise I have been practising a little on my own of replacing negative judgements with positive ones, so I did not find it hard to do the exercise. However, being more aware of my judgements has made it easier for me to be more positive in my judgements instead of negative and also it has helped me reflect more on my judgements in order to understand or at least 'try' to understand why I have these judgments and where they might be coming from.

Furthermore, the exercises *Stand in someone else's shoes* (Box 3.7 on p. 89), *Let someone else decide* (Box 3.9 on p. 92) and *The road less travelled* (Box 3.5 on p. 86) were very fun exercises to do but at the same time they were also very challenging. The exercise *Stand in someone else's shoes*, which had its emphasis on cultural empathy; I interviewed my next-door neighbour. She was a girl with lots of things to do and relaxing was almost a word she did not know of. Putting myself in 'her shoes,' I found myself feeling very stressed out and not being able to focus as much on what is in front of me. At this point in my life, I find it very hard to relate to her because I appreciate too much my 'quiet space' by myself, as this is a way for me to recuperate and deal with stress or potential stress. But had I met her seven years ago, I would probably be more able to relate to her, as my life at that time was pretty much the same as hers; working more than one job, juggling with schoolwork and my social life and activities. It was a very stressful time in my life, and I was not a very happy person. So, when I finished high school, I decided to change my ways very dramatically and it has resulted in a calmer and happier person that I am today. Still working hard, but also finding time to relax and just being.

The exercise *Let someone else decide*, which had its emphasis on flexibility, I went for a walk with a classmate in a part of Slagelse that we both had never been before. The weather was very unstable that day and I was hoping we could cut the walk short, but he had other plans. Just to make the story short, we ended up walking seven kilometres where we took turns deciding the path to walk. It was fun in that sense that I kept choosing paths that led us back and he kept choosing paths that led us to walk further away. Eventually our paths led us back to where we started and at that point we both decided to go back home. The challenging part of this exercise was that I found out that I did not like the loss of control, especially because I kept on thinking that it would start to rain again and I did not like that thought at all. Although it did not start to rain but, better yet, the sun started to shine and the rest of our walk was nice. So, I was glad that he made the decision to 'stick with it' but losing my control is definitely something that I have to work more with.

The exercise *The road less travelled*, which had its emphasis on flexibility but also openmindedness, I went to Sct. Michael's church on a Sunday morning with the same classmate. It was a very traditional experience. Both him and I found it a little boring but it was nice to have finally experience the church from the inside, as I live right across from it and have always been curious of how it looked from the inside. I really practised my openmindedness on this exercise, as I am not usually very good on tradition and especially not in a religious context. However, the fun part of this exercise was the discussion I had with my classmate about the cultural differences between the Greek church traditions and the Danish church traditions. After our discussion we decided that it is actually a good idea, when visiting a foreign country, to go to church (or other places of worship depending on the religious beliefs of the country) and experience the religious traditions as a part of getting to know the foreign country and culture.

Another student concluded in her report:

During this semester I have learned a lot, things that I normally would not do, I did. I used a lot of time every week to think about how I could develop my competence. It has been really interesting to work and develop myself and to learn how, through different exercises, it is possible to change your thoughts and behaviour when encountering different situations and people. I have never worked on myself and think that is really helpful to overcome daily challenges, not just in a global setting but everywhere else as well. The self-development process has been challenging because of the weekly exercises and the time used on reflection, but it has been necessary in order for me to actually force myself out there and just do it.

# Chapter 3

# Developing competences for making intercultural friends

## Introduction

In the previous chapter I highlighted intercultural competence as essential to build a new social network abroad. Knowing about the norms and behaviours that are appropriate in other cultures, being open towards them and having the skills to navigate these situations can help to make friends abroad. But what is intercultural competence, why is it important and crucially, how can one develop intercultural competence to make the most out of going abroad?

### What is intercultural competence?

To be successful in intercultural contexts, you need intercultural competence[1] or cultural intelligence as it is sometimes also known,[2] which can be seen as the ability or capacity "to interact effectively and appropriately with members of different cultures."[3] The emphasis here lies not only with the extent to which one reaches their goals (effectiveness) but also the way in which one does this (appropriateness). It is important to emphasise that it is about both being effective and appropriate – it is not about reaching the goal no matter what the effect is on the other person. Someone with a high level of intercultural competence might have a great deal of knowledge of the local culture and language, an open attitude towards people from other cultural backgrounds and the skills to effectively communicate with them. Intercultural competence consists of these three components – knowledge, attitude and skills – but scoring high on one component does not necessarily mean that one would also score high on the other two components. For example, someone might have very good social skills, but they might not be very motivated to interact with people from different cultural backgrounds, or they might lack knowledge of the specific culture they are dealing with. That's why it is important to look at the separate components, and not try to assess it as a whole.[4]

DOI: 10.4324/9781003246855-9

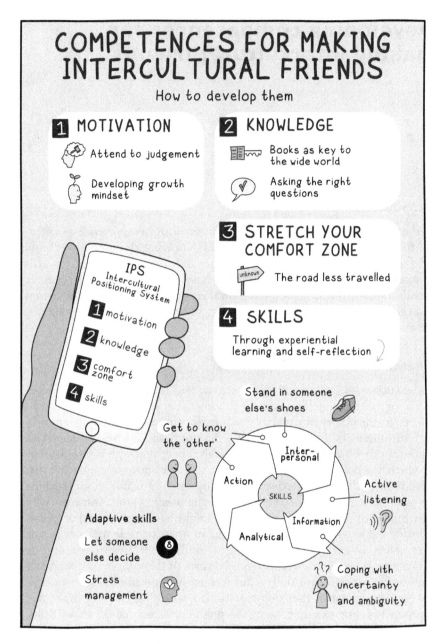

*Figure 3.1* Developing competences for making intercultural friends. Illustration by Heldermaker.

## *Why intercultural competence?*

Intercultural competence is not only important when you live and work abroad, but also in your home country where you might have international colleagues. With 281 million people living in another country than the one in which they were born, workplaces are internationalising, and more and more people have to deal with colleagues, customers and suppliers from another culture. Also, cultural differences exist within national cultures and also between organisations or professions. Intercultural competence helps to function effectively and appropriately when communicating with people from different cultural backgrounds. Research has shown that intercultural competence is positively related to job and team performance, and the intention to move abroad for work.[5] Many studies have been done on expats,[6] and show how intercultural competence – in particular the motivation for learning about intercultural situations and how to best behave in such situations – helps adjustment which then influences performance. Intercultural competence also helps leaders to be effective in intercultural contexts, and it positively influences intercultural cooperation and negotiations.

## Developing intercultural competence

When someone is sent abroad on an international assignment, the organisation often offers intercultural training to prepare for living and working in another culture. But organisations don't always offer intercultural training; for example when one is sent to a relatively nearby country, it is deemed not necessary.[7] And then there are the many expats who found a job abroad by themselves, the so-called self-initiated expat who often receive very little support from their employer with settling into the host country. How can they make sure they thrive in this new context? One way is through contact with people from other cultures and other activities. In this chapter I would like to challenge you to develop your own intercultural competence through various activities, which are based on the intercultural positioning system (IPS) of Dr Janet M. Bennett[8] as well as Yamazaki and Kayes' overview of cross-cultural learning competencies for expats.[9]

The IPS is an approach to building intercultural competence to help people work and live with culturally different others. Developing intercultural competence can be seen as a process similar to the triangulation of a global positioning system (GPS), where we collect perspectives from culturally different others, so we have the right information and knowledge to act upon. But first, we locate ourselves, develop our own cultural self-awareness through understanding our own cultural patterns and only then look at where others are and what the gap is between them and us. We then build a bridge over this gap together with the other. Interculturalists see this as an additive process: you don't lose anything of yourself in interacting with others from another cultural background, but you gain new knowledge and skills. "We adapt when we hope to achieve shared meaning, complete an effective business transaction, teach across cultures or accomplish anything well that involves culturally different others."[10] Sometimes we might choose *not* to adapt, for example when something we deeply believe in is violated or when it is about our safety. And, very occasionally, it happens that both interaction partners adapt to the other's culture, and they adapt past each other. There is no need to worry too much about that – it is still quite rare and usually ends up as a funny anecdote anyway.

The IPS has four steps which are outlined next. First, we discover and foster attitudes that motivate us, and then we discover knowledge that informs us of our own and others' cultural position. The third step is about assessing the challenge and support factors that affect our adjustment. And, finally, we have to develop skills that enable us to interact effectively and appropriately.

### Experiential learning and self-reflection

The exercises are as much as possible based on experiential learning, making sure that you go out and experience something which you can then learn from. A well-known model of learning and development is the 70-20-10 model[11] which basically says that optimal learning only involves about 10% of classroom learning. Most learning occurs in interactions with others (20%) and, in particular, on the job itself (70%). Experiential learning theory was introduced by the U.S. American educational theorist David A. Kolb[12] to emphasise the importance of experience as a basis for learning. The theory is also the basis for Yamazaki and Kayes' cross-cultural learning competences for expats.[13]

One goes through a learning cycle with four separate phases. The first phase is a concrete learning experience that the learner encounters, something that is new in some way. For example, you are joining your first meeting in the host country, and it goes very differently than you expected. You then reflect on that experience in the light of the knowledge that you have, and note that there is a gap or inconsistencies. You might realise you don't know how meetings are held in this country. In the third phase, you adjust or add to your knowledge – this is where you learn from the experience. You learn how meetings are usually held in the host country. In the final, fourth phase, you try out the new ideas and see what happens.

This then might lead to another new concrete learning experience, and the cycle continues. Learning is only effective if all four phases are gone through, and not just one or two.

Reflection is an especially important aspect of learning, and that is why training activities are usually debriefed, to make sure reflection on these experiences happens. Reflection means more than just being aware of what happened; it includes thinking critically about the experience, about how one thought, felt and acted, and why one did so. For the activities suggested in this chapter, I recommend that you write down some thoughts after you have done the exercise, and maybe discuss it with a friend or a family member. This will help you get the most out of the experience. This is also what I do with my students: I debrief activities in class, and as part of the exam, they have to write a self-reflection report based on their experiences. This stimulates their self-reflection and learning.[14]

## Step 1 of IPS: Fostering attitudes that motivate us

What makes one reach out to people from other cultural backgrounds? Curiosity and openmindedness are important attitudes that determine whether one actually gets the opportunity to learn from others, and how much one will learn. You could see them as sort of gatekeepers. Another important attitudinal aspect when developing intercultural competence – in fact, when trying to learn anything – is growth mindset, which is the belief that intellectual ability can be developed.[15] Let's discuss curiosity, openmindedness and growth mindset in more detail.

### Curiosity and openmindedness

Why would we want to learn about others? Curiosity has been highlighted as the key factor in developing intercultural competence. Curiosity is a sense of wonder which shows "we have reached the limits of our present understanding, and that things might be different from how they look."[16] It is the fuel for finding out more, and for understanding what really is happening in a particular situation. It is equally important to be open to what you might meet. Being openminded means having an open and unprejudiced attitude towards people from other cultural groups and towards different cultural norms and values.[17]

Curiosity and openmindedness thrive when one suspends assumptions and judgements to leave one's mind open to multiple perspectives.[18] One way to become more aware of your own culture and personal values is by looking at your judgements. A great exercise is called *Attend to judgement* (see Box 3.1), and it is part of the Personal Leadership method.[19]

Judgements can show you what you find important – and thereby mirror your values. Judgements are often made in a split-second, and they have a major influence on your behaviour, so if you are able to suspend judgements, you give yourself some time to make different decisions based on better information of what really is happening. After she did this exercise one student wrote:

> I really liked the *Attend to judgement* exercise because you learn a lot about yourself when you are conscious of your thoughts. When you attend to judgement, I believe that it is possible to change your thoughts and behaviour a little bit and then you might acknowledge that what you thought and perceived might not be the truth, but your truth. To be aware about that everybody judges can help you to change your thoughts and not judge yourself as much when a negative thought arises in your mind.

The exercise can be quite challenging because it might show a different reality than you expect, as one student experienced. She had always believed she was quite openminded when it came to meeting new people, but it was tougher than she thought when she started to track her judgements and became aware that a lot of her initial judgements on the people she met at a party were quite negative. This also shows how important it is to actually try out the exercises in this chapter to test out whether you indeed behave according to your own expectations.

---

### Box 3.1    Attend to judgement

The goal of this exercise is to become aware of your judgements, which helps you to become more openminded. It is based on the Personal Leadership method, and Schaetti and her colleagues[20] argue that it is impossible NOT to judge, so the best way is to pay attention to your judgements, so we learn about ourselves. And, once you are aware of these judgements, you can choose to act differently. They designed this exercise specifically to train this.

### Tracking your judgements

- Choose a block of time – at least 15 or 20 minutes – while you are doing something that is important to you.
- Notice the judgements, both positive and negative, that come up as you do whatever you are doing. They may come quickly, one right after the other, so be sure to pay close attention.

- Write them down as you notice them, and then continue with whatever you're doing. You can make a grid of four blocks on a piece of paper to help you note them down.

An example could be when you meet a person from a different culture for the first time, and you can't catch his name. You might think 'I'm really not good at remembering names' which is a negative judgment about self (and a fixed mindset as well). Or the person makes excuses for being 2 minutes late and says 'thank you' many times. You might think that this person is very polite (positive judgement about others), or you might think he is a bit strange (negative judgement about others).

### Reflect on the experience

- Once you are done, sit down and reflect on your judgements:
- How many of the judgements you made were about others, how many about yourself? How many had a positive valuation, how many a negative?
- How many were about what you were actually doing right then and there?
- How many were about something that happened in the past or that you imagine will happen in the future?
- What patterns do you see in what you targeted with your judgements, in whether they were positive or negative, and in what effect those judgements had on you?

### *Growth mindset*

It is also important how you approach these new learning situations. Are you eager to learn? Or do you often think that you are simply not good at that particular thing, and you start avoiding those situations? This way of thinking is captured in growth versus fixed mindset. A growth mindset is about challenging yourself and about seeing failure as opportunities to practice and to learn. A fixed mindset is the opposite. With a fixed mindset one is convinced that intelligence and abilities don't change, no matter how hard one tries. One doesn't really want to try new things because one is afraid to fail. Growth mindset helps people to thrive in the face of difficulty and continue to improve; growth mindset is associated with academic achievement, especially among lower achieving students.[21] One famous example is Edison, who famously said: "I have not failed 10,000 times – I've successfully found 10,000 ways that will not work."[22]

The good news is that our brains are malleable, and someone who tends often to a fixed mindset can develop towards a growth mindset. These mindsets are about one's response to difficulties and setbacks, and whether one believes one can change their abilities. Mindsets are not all-or-nothing: everyone is on a continuum from fixed to growth mindset and one can be at different places on this continuum at different times. A first step is to become aware of these mindsets before you can develop them (see Box 3.2). For example, you are learning the language of the country you are living in, and you go to the baker to get some bread. But then she frowns and asks you to repeat yourself in English. How do you approach it? Are you ready to give up because you feel embarrassed and that you must be very bad at speaking the local language? Or do you keep trying to learn the language because you are sure you will eventually be able to order your bread in the local language, and maybe even have a conversation with the baker or a fellow customer? The latter approach indicates a growth mindset, where one is willing to make mistakes and learn from them. It is important to realise that this mindset change might not necessarily lead to great changes in one's ability. If you are not very good at speaking languages, then you should not expect to become easily fluent by believing you can change your ability. It is not a magic trick. But you might be able to learn more of the language than you had expected by keep trying to talk to the local baker and learn how to better pronounce the words.

You can develop a growth mindset by putting yourself in situations that are challenging, so you try out new things and observe how you react. To make the most of the learning, you should reflect on these experiences, and then try out even more new things. While you are doing these new activities, it can help to make sure you have enough time for it and to ask for help from others who can support you with this challenge. You should also coach yourself and observe whether you secretly think: 'What if I fail? What if the baker starts frowning again when I open my mouth, because she doesn't understand me?' This indicates a fixed mindset, but you have a choice whether you want to listen to that thought or not. You can also change that inner voice to reflect a growth mindset perspective, by thinking things like: 'If I don't try at all, it is a failure. By trying out this word several times, I will learn how to pronounce it, so they understand me.' And, in the spirit of Edison, always replace the word 'fail' by 'learn' since failing is just a new way of learning. Everyone fails many times in their life, starting with the first time you tried to walk or ride a bike, yet you learned how to do it. After all, practice makes perfect.

## Box 3.2   Developing growth mindset

### Step 1: Awareness of fixed and growth mindset

Think of one situation in which you tend more to a fixed mindset, for example something you believe you are not able to do, and of one situation where you tend more towards a growth mindset where you persisted because you felt you could learn this. This can be both in the workplace as well as in private life. Examples can be trying to speak the local language, making a complicated recipe, learning how to dance or making small talk with a stranger. Explore both situations:

- Shortly describe both situations. How did the mindset show, and how did this make you feel?
- Do you tend more to a fixed mindset or to a growth mindset when you encounter new, challenging situations? For example, when you get a new project or task that you are unfamiliar with, is your first reaction 'Great, I don't know how to do it, but I'm sure I'll learn along the way,' or are you thinking of ways to get out of doing it altogether because you might fail? And are you seeking out new opportunities to learn something, for example, a new language or a new skill or hobby?

### Step 2: Developing growth mindset

It is also important to practice your growth mindset. Find a task in which you think in a fixed mindset (this can be the situation you described at Step 1) and challenge yourself to get to a better but still realistic improvement with the growth mindset. This can be something easy as not being able to cook something properly or thinking that you are not good at sports or drawing.[23] Try to improve your skills a little bit – don't expect to become brilliant at something just because you changed your mindset. When you do this activity, keep in mind:

- Observe your inner voice and change it to a growth mindset by saying things like 'If I don't try at all, it is a failure' and 'Let's see how much I can improve today.'
- Ask for help from others who can support you with this challenge.

- Replace the word 'fail' by 'learn' and see failure as simply another opportunity for learning.

One of my students, preparing for a semester abroad in Georgia, took on this challenge, and here is his experience: "I set out to make a Georgian meal for lunch yesterday, as I am trying to experience the food of the place I will visit for my exchange. As I am a poor cook and have never cooked anything Georgian before, this was challenging. Throughout the process of preparing this meal, I simply followed the tips. When the khachapuri was slightly burned, I did not say 'what if its inedible' instead I scraped off the burned part and reassured myself that if I don't try then it is already a failure. The lunch was in fact edible, although poorly tasting as I only have Danish ingredients and I can't cook at all."

## Step 2 of IPS: Discovering knowledge

Once one is motivated to talk to people with other cultural backgrounds, the next step is to find relevant knowledge that can help make the right decision on how to act. The starting point for positioning oneself interculturally is knowing more about one's own culture. One is often not aware what is so specific about one's own culture – one of the exercises I regularly do in my Human Resource Management class in Denmark is to have the students compare HR practices such as annual leave and parental leave across a number of countries. Danish students are often surprised to hear that the United States is the only rich country that does not have a national paid parental leave programme.[24] Extensive parental leave is very normal in Denmark and the other Scandinavian countries. And I was surprised to notice in Denmark that very few people worked part time, in contrast to the Netherlands, which is world champion of part time work, especially the women. This also shows how important it is to know your own cultural background because many would not find this surprising, since Denmark (16.6%) still scores above the average for the European Union (14.8%) as well as the Organisation for Economic Co-operation and Development (OECD) as a whole (16.4%) in terms of how many people work part time. Just not as much as the Netherlands (36%).[25]

Learning about your own culture also happens while learning about the host culture. When you move abroad, you will notice differences between your home and host country, which can be starting points to learn more about these cultures. Many expats have written books about their experiences in a host country, which can be interesting to read both as an expat and as a local (Box 3.3). Even more interesting are analyses by anthropologists and historians because they describe the culture and its historic roots in more detail, going beyond superficial 'strange things.'. While these books can be a starting point to learn more about a certain culture, it is important to not get stuck in superficial lists of do's and don'ts. There is a wealth of information available on culture in general as well about specific cultures through studies such as GLOBE, Hofstede, World Values Survey and many more.[26] While this information can be very helpful, one has to be careful to not generalise too much (see also the Introduction). Nowadays, culture is seen as a dynamic concept, and one that is not aligned with national boundaries.[27] In their 2018 review of what we know about cross-cultural interaction, Professors Nancy Adler and Zeynep Aycan state that this makes it very difficult, or even impossible, to distil the salient characteristics for managing any particular interaction. Instead, they argue, one should ask the right questions (Box 3.4).

---

**Box 3.3    Books as key to the wide world**

The novelist Jane Hamilton said: "It is books that are the key to the wide world; if you can't do anything else, read all that you can." If you don't have the opportunity to travel, or if you want to prepare for or add to your travel, then there are a lot of books to read and films to see. Novels can help develop empathy and reduce prejudice because the reader takes the perspective of the protagonist, and sees through their eyes.[28] For Barack Obama, reading novels developed his empathy:

> the most important set of understandings that I bring to that position of citizen, the most important stuff I've learned I think I've learned from novels. It has to do with empathy. It has to do with being comfortable with the notion that the world is complicated and full of greys, but there's still truth there to be found, and that you have to strive for that and work for that.[29]

There are many books and films that can help you learn about different cultures. I keep a list on my website www.intersango.dk with suggestions – I would be happy to hear your additions!

---

**Box 3.4   Discovering knowledge and asking the right questions**

This exercise helps you to gather more knowledge that you can use in intercultural interactions and be openminded about what you encounter. First, get to know your own culture – what is particular there? Being aware of your own cultural background will increase your awareness about what is specific about your own way of being and interacting. Then, get to know the other culture. How might they do things differently than you are used to, and why do they do it this way? This can help you understand that different ways of doing things can be equally valid. A third step is about asking the right questions before, during and after you talk with someone from a different culture:[30]

- Before: How do I remain openminded? Will I be open to changing my knowledge about 'the other'?
- During: What was as expected in the interaction, and what was different? What can you learn from this?
- After: How can the insights and knowledge gained from this interaction be used in other intercultural situations?

---

**Step 3 of IPS: Stretch your comfort zone**

To get the most out of any learning experience, one has to find a balance between the challenges that someone faces in a new situation and the level of support that is needed to adjust effectively.[31] If you are not challenged enough, not much learning takes place. It is important to get out of your comfort zone and into a 'growth zone' because that is where you learn the most. On the other hand, if you are challenged too much, you will probably try to escape from the situation. So, it is important to find a balance – it is good to stretch yourself, but not too much.

The global leadership development literature emphasises the importance of the transformative potential of an experience.[32] From certain experiences one can learn more than from others, and it is important for the development of global leaders that they meet enough high-level challenges so that competence development can take place. One way to determine the transformative potential of an experience is through assessing the complexity, emotional affect, intensity and relevance (CAIR) of an experience.

*Complexity* is the degree to which the experience involves situations or issues that can be interpreted in many different ways, which may also be contradictory. An intercultural situation is by definition more complex than a domestic one due to the presence of more than one cultural frame of reference. Speaking in a different language than one's native language can also increase the complexity. *Affect* involves the extent to which emotion is present or stimulated by the experience. Experiences that are frustrating or stressful last longer and remain more vivid in one's memory, so one can continue to reflect on them and learn. *Intensity* is the degree to which the experience requires concentrated attention or effort, which means that one is more alert to context-specific information that could help the task, and, thereby, learn more. Finally, *Relevance* is about the extent to which the experience is perceived as relevant to an objective or value important to the individual. If one finds an experience relevant, then one is more likely to pay attention as well as gather more information, and learn from and understand the experience.

One of the best ways of developing global leaders is through expatriate assignments. Such experiences have a high transformative potential. The situations are complex, involving different cultures and often languages, and very relevant because it's one's daily life and career. Living and work-ing abroad is also very intense because it's not just a training of one day, but one is immersed in the new culture. It often also allows plenty of room for frustrating and stressful experiences, where the emotional affect is high. Several factors can, however, buffer the expat from exposure to the new culture, such as having a chauffeur or translator, or living in a compound (see also Box 2.1 on p. 51), which reduces how much the expat will learn from being abroad. There is the danger of just checking the box, where it sounds like someone learned a lot because they lived and worked abroad for several years, but if that person did not engage much with the local culture, not much actual competence development would have taken place.

With the activities in this chapter, I hope to get you out of your comfort zone. So, if you feel a bit hesitant or unsure when you read an exercise, then I suggest you certainly try it out and challenge yourself. That is where the most learning happens. One Portuguese student in Denmark pushed herself out of her comfort zone and attended to her judgements:

> I went to an event out of my comfort zone and before approaching anyone, I noticed that I was more willing to talk to someone "similar" to my appearance. While maybe someone that I noticed that is more "alternative" or that dresses in a different way than me, I would not feel so confident to approach. However, after confronting that and

trying not to judge so quickly, I started talking with people that have an amazing personality that I wasn't expecting. This helped me make new friends, completely different from the ones I normally "choose". This helped me as well to learn the things that they are interested in that I didn't even know exist, opening to the possibility of new experiences and hobbies.

Another good starting point for stretching your comfort zone is to do the exercise *The road less travelled* (Box 3.5).

---

**Box 3.5   The road less travelled**

This exercise is really simple: just do something you normally wouldn't do. Explore something new, and see how that makes you feel. It can be as easy as saying 'yes' if someone suggests an activity where you normally would have said 'no.' This exercise stretches your comfort zone, and also works with your openmindedness and flexibility.

> Two roads diverged in a wood, and I–
> I took the one less traveled by,
> And that has made all the difference.
>
> Robert Frost

---

## Step 4 of IPS: Developing skills

The final step of the IPS is to develop the skills needed to communicate with people from other cultural backgrounds. Yamazaki and Kayes[33] have made a taxonomy of skills needed for cross-cultural learning. Following the experiential learning cycle, four learning skills dimensions (interpersonal, information, analytical and action skills) are important to develop, as well as two adaptive competences that help deal with change. I will discuss specific exercises to develop the skills one needs to make friends abroad.

### Interpersonal skills

The first intercultural competence is about being able to develop and maintain relationships with others. This is a crucial 'gateway' skill because it allows one to get in touch with people from another cultural background, to get the concrete experiences that starts off a learning cycle. The exercise *Get to know the 'other'* (Box 3.6) is designed to push you to reach out to a stranger and develop a new relationship. This is at the core of being able to make new friends – one must be able to make that first connection, which is not always easy to do and might lead to a lot of anxiety. How to manage the uncertainty and anxiety that is often part of interacting with a stranger is included in the information skills and adaptive competences (see page 90).

The second intercultural competence is valuing people of different cultures. Cultural empathy is the ability to empathise with the feelings, thoughts and behaviours of members from different cultural groups.[34] Empathy has been highlighted as one of the key competences in research on intergroup contact theory (see also p. 8 in the Introduction) and can be developed by contact between groups with different cultural backgrounds.[35] Such contact, especially when a close relationship has been built up, enables one to take the perspective of the other and empathise with their concerns. The activity *Stand in someone else's shoes* (Box 3.7) helps one to do just that.

One student in my class thought these two exercises were very challenging:

> The biggest challenge I had was when we got the assignment to ask somebody we don't know from another culture for an "interview." Mentally I used a lot of time (weeks) just for preparing myself to ask someone. I'm a really private person so this really put me out of my comfort zone. The situation where you don't know the person that well and need to spend time with that person without any form of purpose besides getting to know one another really forces me out of my comfort zone. But I did it, I asked someone from work who has an Indian background. In the beginning of the "interview" I felt it was a little bit awkward but at the end it was really nice to hear about his culture and how he thought of himself being from India but having being born and raised in Denmark. After the "interview" I was really proud of myself that I did something that I otherwise would never have done, and it went really well. This exercise really confronted many global competencies. I was openminded about another person's culture and open for meeting new people and not to prejudge. This exercise also touched the competence flexibility because I needed to adjust my behaviour to a new and unknown situation and social initiative since I actively encountered a social situation and at last the emotional stability because during the conversation, I remained calm.

**Box 3.6 Get to know the 'other'**

This exercise helps develop your relationship-building skills and cultural empathy by meeting someone different from yourself. The goal is to establish a new social connection, for example someone from another country, or, if you live abroad, someone from the host country. This can be another parent you have seen at the school gates several times but haven't formally met, or a colleague you have seen at the coffee machine but never really spoke to. Please be aware that in certain countries you have better chance of creating a new social connection when you approach people outside the workplace because of the divide between work and private life.[36]

You can also challenge yourself and talk to someone you do not yet know at all. Many people fear such talks are uncomfortable because they think the other would be uninterested in talking, but research among train commuters in London and Chicago showed that such talks with strangers were pleasant and that those who talked to strangers did have a more positive experience than those who did not.[37] Try to also build up a relationship by meeting each other several times.

- Find someone to connect with, and take that first step.
- Make notes of your experiences: Who did you reach out to? How does it feel to reach out to someone you don't know yet? How did it go? Did you enjoy it?
- For a more challenging version, have a look at the TedTalk by Elizabeth Lesser "Take 'the other' to lunch,"[38] where she suggests a simple way to start a meaningful dialogue with someone who is 'other' than you. This 'otherness' can be about voting for a different political party, another religion, lifestyle or opinion. She suggests setting ground rules before you get together, for example that you agree not to try to persuade the other or defend your opinions. But instead, that you are curious and listen to each other.

---

**Box 3.7 Stand in someone else's shoes**

For this exercise you interview an 'other' about their life. This exercise develops your cultural empathy, which is your ability to see the world from a different viewpoint and understand where the other is coming from (without judgement).

- Find an 'other' to interview about their life, their culture and their choices. This person should be different from you in some way or other. This can be nationality, but it can also be a different profession or religion. It can be the person you met for the exercise *Get to know the 'other'* (Box 3.6).
- Put yourself in their shoes by writing a summary of 500 words from the perspective of this person (I am Marieke, I am from the Netherlands, and I work as ...). It is very powerful to adopt a first-person perspective when you write about the person because it helps you see the world through their eyes.[39]
- Make notes about your experiences: How was your interviewee different from you? What did you learn from the interview? How did it feel to write the piece from their point of view? What did you learn from this exercise?

---

### Information skills

The concrete experiences one creates through getting in touch with 'others' are the basis for observation and reflection, which is the second stage of the learning cycle. To understand a situation, it is very important to carefully listen and watch what is going on. This is similar to what is called mindfulness in the Personal Leadership method, which is about being 'awake' and paying attention.[40] Through paying attention – both to what is going on in the situation and what happens within ourselves – one can create an opportunity to reflect and then decide to act differently than one initially would have done when still on autopilot. *Active listening* is a skill that can be trained, especially through experiential learning,[41] and means truly listening to what someone else is saying, instead of thinking about the story you might want to share yourself. The goal of active listening is to clearly understand what the speaker is saying as well as showing interest in it.[42] Ways to do this is by making emphatic comments, asking appropriate questions and regularly checking with the speaker whether you have understood them correctly. Any intercultural contact as well as most of the exercises mentioned in this chapter offer scope for practicing one's listening and observation skills, but you can also try to listen actively the next time you are talking to a good friend or your partner. Hold back on your own thoughts, ask questions and check whether you understood them correctly.

---

**Box 3.8  Coping with uncertainty and ambiguity**

This exercise is adapted from the Personal Leadership method,[44] and focuses on your reactions to uncertainty and ambiguity.

- Put yourself in situations where you are not sure what might happen, for example by talking to a stranger. You can combine this with the exercises *The road less travelled* (Box 3.5 on p. 86) and *Let someone else decide* (Box 3.9 on p. 92) because these will help you find new situations. Also the exercise *Get to know the 'other'* (Box 3.6 on p. 88) is useful because it might confront you with a situation where you are not sure what the other person means (ambiguity).
- Observe how you react for about 15–20 minutes. How do you react to not knowing what will happen when you first start talking to a stranger, or when you let a die decide what you will do next Saturday? Do you tend to want to fill the space with a plan? How about when you are not sure what the other person means with a remark or a certain behaviour? What are the judgements, emotions and physical sensations you experience when you don't know what to do or say?
- Then try to switch your mindset, and see it in a positive light. Try to be in the moment and see what is happening and what you can learn. And can this uncertainty and ambiguity also result in something positive if you learn to tolerate it?
- Afterwards, please reflect on this exercise. How did you react? Do you normally react like this when you face uncertainty? How do you feel about uncertainty and ambiguity? Were you able to change your mindset, and take it moment by moment? Did anything positive come out of this experience?

---

When listening and observing, another skill that is very important is *Coping with uncertainty and ambiguity*. Talking to people from other cultures brings along a lot of uncertainty because one is continuously trying to figure out why someone behaves in a certain way or what they mean when they say something. There can be a lot of ambiguity, where one is wondering whether something means one thing or the other. So, how comfortable are you with not knowing exactly what is happening? Box 3.8 has an exercise where you put yourself in new situations so you can see how you react when faced with uncertainty and ambiguity. It can help to expect some uncertainty and ambiguity, since it's usually part of living and working abroad. Having realistic expectations helps adjusting to the host country.[43]

### Analytical and action skills

When we pay attention and reflect on the concrete experiences that we have, we get a lot of information which can be analysed and lead to learning. This is the third stage of the learning cycle, where we think, analyse and build general theories, which can then be experimented with.[45] This process mainly happens in your head, and it is important to create time and space for this reflection. The fourth and final stage of the cycle is where one experiments with the newly learned information, doing things differently than before. For this, one needs action skills such as the ability to take initiative and actively engage in an intercultural situation. The exercise *Get to know the 'other'* (Box 3.6 on p. 88) is a great activity to train your social initiative. How comfortable do you feel with approaching a stranger? To take that first step is to open up a world of opportunities for developing your intercultural competence.

### Adaptive skills

In addition to his famous learning cycle, Kolb and his colleagues have identified another style of learning, namely developmental learning where one learns to adapt to changing situations over time.[46] Flexibility is needed to deal with a changing environment, which is especially relevant for expats who move abroad. The exercise *Let someone else decide* (Box 3.9) challenges especially those who like to be in control and know what to expect. This is inspired by the book *The Luck Factor* by psychologist Richard Wiseman, who studied the differences between lucky and unlucky people. One important lesson is to seek out new experiences in your life – for example by rolling dice to determine what fun new activity you might want to try this weekend – that might bring you the chance opportunities that many consider to be 'luck.'

A second intercultural competence that is very helpful to deal with moving abroad is *stress management*. Some people might get stressed because of the inherent uncertainty and ambiguity in intercultural interactions. It

---

**Box 3.9    Let someone else decide**

The aim of this exercise is to develop your flexibility – one's ability to switch easily from one strategy to another, because the familiar ways of handling things will not necessarily work in a new cultural environment[49] – which might help you take advantage of social opportunities that come on your path. It brings more coincidence in your life, which can make your life more interesting.

- Look for an opportunity where you let someone or something else decide for you (in a very random way). For example, go to the supermarket and buy the same groceries as the first person who walked in just before you (keep it reasonable though!), or walk around for an hour in a new neighbourhood and keep taking left and right alternatively. If you have a free day or evening, you can list six possible destinations or activities and then roll a die to determine where to go or what to do. You can also flip a coin to determine what you will have for dinner, or let your partner or friend order for you.
- Make notes of your experiences and your feelings while doing this exercise. What did you do? Who made what decision for you? What did you experience while doing it? How did it feel to have someone else decide? Did you find it difficult? Was it fun? What were the positive sides of letting someone else decide?

---

is essential for effective communication and intercultural adjustment to manage this (Box 3.8 on p. 90) because it helps one to feel comfortable in the host culture.[47] Remember – some anxiety and uncertainty is actually good because it questions whether you understand what is going on, and motivates you to find out more. It is important to get out of your comfort zone because that's where the learning takes place.

For managing stress, it is worthwhile to know a bit more about stress and coping. The process starts when someone perceives a situation as stressful to them. This is different for everyone; what stresses one person, does not stress another. Coping is about what happens next. There are a lot of different strategies to cope with stress, and which one is best depends on the situation.[48] Two general types of coping are distinguished: problem-focused coping is aimed at solving the problem, for example by making a plan of action; whereas emotion-focused coping is about managing the emotional stress that is caused by the problem, for example by venting to a friend. When one can influence the situation to some extent, problem-focused coping is very helpful because it removes the root of the problem. If that is not possible, then it is often better to use emotion-focused coping strategies to change how one feels about the situation. A third category that is often distinguished is meaning-focused coping, where the person uses their values, beliefs and goals to change the meaning of a stressful situation. This is often used when a person has to deal with adversity, and it can help to seek meaning in this stressful situation. For example, losing a job could also be seen as an opportunity to change directions and find something one would really like to do. Similarly, intercultural situations that might be stressful also can be seen as opportunities to develop oneself.

Since coping is very dependent on the context, it is impossible to say which coping strategies are best. It might also shift over time; what works in the beginning of a stressful situation, might not work later on. For example, when students have a difficult exam, it helps to study a lot for it (problem-focused coping) but when the exam is done, it is better to distract oneself while one waits for the result (emotion-focused coping). In many cases, people use combinations of problem- and emotion-focused coping strategies. Let's take giving a presentation for a large audience as example. Many of us – but not everyone – will feel stressed about this to a lesser or larger extent. A problem-focused coping strategy is to prepare as well as possible for this presentation, both in terms of content as well as presentation techniques. Maybe you have a friend or colleague who is good at this, and who could help you fine tune your presentation. Then, the evening before the presentation, you might want to go for dinner with some friends to distract yourself from what is happening the next day, or you talk to your partner or a friend about how nervous you feel, and they can reassure you. These are emotion-focused coping strategies.

One can also prepare for potentially stressful situations, which is called future-oriented proactive coping. For example, when an expat is sent abroad, they know they will have to work in another cultural context on a daily basis, and that this might be stressful. The expat can make sure they have the resources to deal with these situations, for example, that they get some cross-cultural training. They also might already think about which situations they would find especially stressful and how to cope with such situations when they occur. As mentioned earlier, some stress is actually good for learning – one needs to get out of one's comfort zone to develop. This is inherently stressful, so it is important to accept some level of stress and see it as an opportunity for learning.

As with the other skills, it helps to first become aware of how good you are at stress management. You can do the exercise *Let someone else decide* (Box 3.9) to put yourself in unknown situations, and then see how you react. If you find that stressful, then it is important to find out which coping strategies work best for you in specific situations. One student in my class focused on developing his ability to deal with stress:

> During the semester I tested out my stress limits to see in which kind of situations I tend to feel more anxious and try to step-by-step minimize the level of anxiety and react to those situations more calmly. I focused on not panicking or stressing myself out when things go south, or when I am experiencing stressful situations, I tried to stop over-thinking and exaggerating about stuff that are not so serious or can be handled calmly and simply. I joined the gym and I started practicing mindfulness, something that I found really interesting and helpful for my everyday anxiety.

This chapter helps you develop your intercultural competence specifically with regard to making new friends abroad. To do this, it is important to take this first step and talk to people you do not yet know – such interactions with strangers can actually be more pleasant than you might expect! Once you are in contact with 'others' it is helpful to be openminded about what happens in such an intercultural situation. Try to listen and observe well, learning as much as you can, while at the same time managing the uncertainty and stress that such situations will invariably carry. But remember: it is when you are outside of your comfort zone that you learn the most!

## Notes

1 Bird, A., Mendenhall, M., Stevens, M. J., & Oddou, G. (2010). Defining the content domain of intercultural competence for global leaders. *Journal of Managerial Psychology, 25*(8), 810–828.
2 There are many different terms that all indicate this ability of communicating with people from different cultural backgrounds, see also: van Bakel, M., Gerritsen, M., & Van Oudenhoven, J. P. (2014). Impact of a local host on the intercultural competence of expatriates. *International Journal of Human Resource Management, 25*(14), 2050–2067.
3 Wiseman, R. (2002). Intercultural communication competence. In W. Gudykunst & B. Mody (Eds.), *Handbook of international and intercultural communication* (2nd ed., pp. 207–224). Thousand Oaks, CA: Sage, p. 208.
4 There has been much discussion about conceptualisation and definition of intercultural competence. I can recommend the SAGE *Handbook of intercultural competence* if you want to dive deeper into the topic; one of its chapters is about how to measure it.
5 Richter, N. F., Schlaegel, C., Taras, V., Alon, I., & Bird, A. (2023). Reviewing half a century of measuring cross-cultural competence: Aligning theoretical constructs and empirical measures. *International Business Review*, 102122.

6  Ott, D. L., & Michailova, S. (2018). Cultural intelligence: A review and new research avenues. *International Journal of Management Reviews, 20*(1), 99–119.

7  One reason why companies sometimes don't think intercultural training is necessary is when someone is sent to a relatively nearby country - say, from the Netherlands to the United Kingdom, or from Denmark to Sweden. This can be tricky, however, because differences are underestimated or not recognised, and the expats think it will be easy to adjust to the host country. If the reality is then more difficult than expected, this can make adjustment more difficult (Vromans, P., Van Engen, M., & Mol, S. T. (2013). Presumed cultural similarity paradox: Expatriate adjustment and performance across the border or over the globe. *Journal of Global Mobility, 1*(2), 219 – 238).

8  Bennett, J. M. (2009). Cultivating intercultural competence: A process perspective. In D. K. Deardorff (Ed.), *The SAGE handbook of intercultural competence* (pp. 121–140). Thousand Oaks, CA: Sage.

9  Yamazaki, Y., & Kayes, D. C. (2004). An experiential approach to cross-cultural learning: A review and integration of competencies for successful expatriate adaptation. *Academy of Management Learning & Education, 3*(4), 362–379.

10  Bennett (2009), p. 127.

11  Eichinger, R., & Lombardo, M. (1996). *The career architect development planner*. Minneapolis, MN: Lominger Limited.

12  Kolb, D. A. (1984). *Experiential learning: Experience as the source of learning and development*. Englewood Cliffs, NJ: Prentice-Hall.

13  Yamazaki and Kayes (2004).

14  Lew, D. N. M., & Schmidt, H. G. (2011). Writing to learn: Can reflection journals be used to promote self-reflection and learning? *Higher Education Research & Development, 30*(4), 519–532.

15  Yeager, D. S., & Dweck, C. S. (2020). What can be learned from growth mindset controversies? *American Psychologist, 75*(9), 1269–1284.

16  Definition of curiosity by Opdal (2001) as cited in Bennett (2009), p. 128.

17  Van Oudenhoven, J. P., & Van der Zee, K. I. (2002). Predicting multicultural effectiveness of international students: The Multicultural Personality Questionnaire. *International Journal of Intercultural Relations, 26*, 679–694, 680.

18  Bennett (2009).

19  Schaetti, B., Ramsey, S., & Watanabe, G. (2008). *Personal leadership: Making a world of difference: A methodology of two principles and six practices*. FlyingKite Publications.

20  Schaetti et al. (2008).

21  Yeager and Dweck (2020).

22  www.smithsonianmag.com/innovation/7-epic-fails-brought-to-you-by-the-genius-mind-of-thomas-edison-180947786/ (accessed on 14 August 2023).

23  I've always said that I'm not good at drawing, but then for a project of Young SIETAR, where we produced an intercultural storybook for children, I tried to draw one particular drawing for the book's cover. After many tries, I was actually pleasantly surprised that I managed to draw this particular drawing

quite nicely - and it made it to the back cover. I am still not very good at drawing, but I did realise that if I practice a lot, I can certainly improve my drawing
skills.

24 www.bbc.com/worklife/article/20210624-why-doesnt-the-us-have-mandated-
paid-maternity-leave (accessed on 14 August 2023).

25 https://data.oecd.org/emp/part-time-employment-rate.htm (accessed on 14
August 2023).

26 For a contemporary overview of various conceptualisations of culture, see
Adler, N. J., & Aycan, Z. (2018). Cross-cultural interaction: What we know
and what we need to know. *Annual Review of Organizational Psychology and
Organizational Behavior, 5*, 307–333.

27 Adler and Aycan (2018).

28 Johnson, D. R., Jasper, D. M., Griffin, S., & Huffman, B. L. (2013). Reading
narrative fiction reduces Arab-Muslim prejudice and offers a safe haven from
intergroup anxiety. *Social Cognition, 31*(5), 578–598.

29 President Obama and Marilynne Robinson (2015): A conversation – II.
New York Review of Books. Retrieved from www.nybooks.com/articles/2015/
11/19/president-obama-marilynne-robinson-conversation-2/ (accessed 14
August 2023).

30 Adler and Aycan (2018).

31 Bennett (2009).

32 Osland, J. S., & Bird, A. (2013). Process models of global leadership development. In M. Mendenhall, J. Osland, A. Bird, G. Oddou, M. Maznevski,
M. Stevens, & G. K. Stahl (Eds.), *Global leadership: Research, practice and
development* (pp. 97–112). New York and London: Routledge.

33 Yamazaki and Kayes (2004).

34 Van Oudenhoven and Van der Zee (2002).

35 Pettigrew, T. F., & Tropp, L. R. (2008). How does intergroup contact reduce
prejudice? Meta-analytic tests of three mediators. *European Journal of Social
Psychology, 38*(6), 922–934.

36 In my study of why expatriates find it more difficult in Denmark to make
friends with locals, one of the explanations was the large divide between
work and private life. I have observed similar patterns in the Netherlands (van
Bakel, M., & Vance, C. M. (2023). Breaking out of the expatriate bubble
in Denmark: Insights from the challenge of making connections with local
Danes. *Journal of Global Mobility, 11*(1), 21–42).

37 Schroeder, J., Lyons, D., & Epley, N. (2022). Hello, stranger? Pleasant conversations are preceded by concerns about starting one. *Journal of Experimental
Psychology: General, 151*(5), 1141–1153.

38 www.ted.com/talks/elizabeth_lesser_take_the_other_to_lunch?language=en
(accessed on 14 August 2023).

39 Jarmon, B., Brunson, D. A., & Lampl, L. L. (2007). The power of narratives
in the process of teaching and learning about diversity. In D. A. Brunson,
B. Jarmon, & L. L. Lampl (Eds.), *Letters from the future: Linking students and
teaching with diversity in everyday life* (pp. 26–42).

40 Schaetti et al. (2008).

41 Huerta-Wong, J. E., & Schoech, R. (2010). Experiential learning and learning environments: The case of active listening skills. *Journal of Social Work Education, 46*(1), 85–101.

42 McNaughton, D., Hamlin, D., McCarthy, J., Head-Reeves, D., & Schreiner, M. (2008). Learning to listen: Teaching an active listening strategy to preservice education professionals. *Topics in Early Childhood Special Education, 27*(4), 223–231.

43 Caligiuri, P., Phillips, J., Lazarova, M. B., Tarique, I., & Burgi, P. (2001). The theory of met expectations applied to expatriate adjustment: The role of cross-cultural training. *International Journal of Human Resource Management, 12*(3), 357–372.

44 Schaetti et al. (2008), pp. 97–98.

45 Yamazaki and Kayes (2004).

46 Yamazaki and Kayes (2004).

47 Gudykunst, W. B. (1998). Applying anxiety/uncertainty management (AUM) theory to intercultural adjustment training. *International Journal of Intercultural Relations, 22*(2), 227–250.

48 Folkman, S., & Moskowitz, J. T. (2004). Coping: Pitfalls and promise. *Annual Review of Psychology, 55*, 745–774.

49 Van Oudenhoven and Van der Zee (2002), p. 681.

Part II

# Connecting with locals

# Experience

A German expat in Mexico – "Families which are just here for having a career are not that happy here"

*Kathrin is a 38-year-old German assigned expat working in the automotive industry in Mexico. Her assignment was for 2.5 years but she extended it with a year. She has two kids and a husband at home.*

**What were your expectations when you came to Mexico in terms of making contacts here?**

We were very interested in making contact because it was the first decision not to go to [city] where all the Germans live. We wanted to stay in the more typical Mexico. So, we decided to live here in [city] which is not that overwhelmed by Germans. Normally all my Mexican colleagues live here, and it was a concrete decision to go, also in this *fraccionamiento* [housing subdivision] without any German people for getting in touch very quick. Yeah, so that was the plan. Learning Spanish very quick, getting in touch with some Mexican people. Our family who is renting the house [to us] are Mexicans. And they helped us a lot and we get friends during the time, so. [...] Getting in touch with the real Mexico and not being here just for working and being with Germans like in Germany.

**How did you start making contacts when you arrived here in Mexico?**

We met them [landlord] very often at the beginning and they invited us for their typical family parties. So, like the religious communion. So, I think that's a very special party here in Mexico. Or we met their parents. So, I think that's, that's the first step getting in touch with Mexicans. They invite you for, for eating, for celebrating with their families. So that was the first steps and then we started to invite some of my Mexican colleagues.

DOI: 10.4324/9781003246855-11

And our oldest daughter was starting getting in touch with the Mexican girls in her class. And they were invited to our house as well. And then the parents came here and then you get in touch very quick.

**And in your first months here who did you meet the most?**

My colleagues [laughs]. Most time I'm at work [...], my colleagues. But nearly all of them are Mexicans. [...] It was the natural thing and therefore 13 hours per day and we have one hour in the bus in the morning and one hour in the bus in the evening and then I could ask them all my questions I had and where to, where to go out for eating or where to go buy some stuff. So that was the main contact in my case.

**What else have you done to establish your social network here in Mexico besides work?**

Yeah, I think the kids. Together in combination with the school, because also the kids have a very long day here and our son was in the kindergarten first when we came, and he was the only German kid in his group. And he adopted to Spanish very very fast. And in the case of our daughter, she was in a mixed class of German and Mexican kids but she was contacting all the Mexicans as well. And then it was the next step that the kids brought all these kids here and then the parents as well.

**And how did your social network develop after the first year?**

I think now it's a good mix, we are within the Mexican circles. And the weekends we spend [at] some beaches or hotels or renting some houses of Airbnb, that we mainly do with the Germans but I think that's also a financial point. [The German families] have the financial status to go nearly every weekend somewhere and I think the Mexican families which are having local contracts here even at [Western multinational organisations] do not have that much money. So, in fact we are going to holidays with German families but still meeting and still agreeing on some afternoons with Mexican families.

**What would you recommend to a new expatriate in terms of meeting local people in Mexico?**

My first big recommendation is not to go here because you think you will earn a lot of money but just to come here and having interests and getting known to the culture and the people. Because Mexico is, I don't know but I think there is no fact which is similar to Germany. Mexico is a very very different country to Germany regarding the climate conditions, regarding the people, regarding work situations, regarding having a family. [...] And that's my experience from the two, last two and a half years. Families which like to be here because of country and people and culture are very very happy here. Families which are just here for having a career are not that happy here.

### What was your best strategy to meet local people in Mexico and why?

Mexicans really like to eat and when you are interested in the local food, when you are on the market or when you are making some trips in not very touristic regions, and you are interested going to small restaurants where normally there are no tourists. Then you always get in a very quick contact with the locals because they are interested where you come from. Then they are interested in the kids, for example asking them, then the kids are responding in Spanish. And that's a very quick bridge you can build with local people and then you can sit together, drink something together.

### Would you say it's easy or difficult to meet local people in Mexico?

It's very easy because they are very open but just until a definite point. So, when you meet them on the street for making some small talk they are very open and when you are doing a weekend trip you can get to know 100 Mexicans if you like because everybody wants to talk to you, everybody's interested where you are from but I think that's a very basic small talk.

### Is there any local person you would call a friend?

I think Mexicans are not really interested in kind of making friendships because Mexican families are very very big. A lot of sisters, brothers, parents, nephews. So really big families, we experienced that when we were invited to their families. And I think they are fine with being, with being with their families. So, there were times when we tried to invite them on weekends and there was often the excuse that they have to be with their families every Sunday for example. So, I think that's quite normal here. And that's also what we heard from Mexicans, like the people who rent the house [to us] that, that it's not that easy getting in a close friendship with Mexican people.

# Chapter 4

# The benefits of expat contact with locals

## Introduction

> I have very few close Dutch friends in the Netherlands. Most of the friends I've made here are foreigners. It's difficult to break into any foreign society I think, difficult to get past the point of just being an acquaintance rather than a friend.
>
> English expat in my PhD research[1]

Many expats stay within an 'expat bubble' and mainly meet other expats and not the people of the host country itself. That is a shame, because this contact can be very helpful because locals can offer social support to deal with the stress of moving abroad as well as be a source of information about the host country. A lot of research has been done on the interactions between expats and locals, both in and outside the workplace, and generally, contact with locals has positive effects for expats, with regard to culture learning, adjustment, competence development and performance.[2] In this chapter I would like to share these studies and what we can learn from them.

## The value of getting in touch with locals of the host country

Getting in touch with locals can have many benefits for expats and their partners, both at work and in private life. Moving abroad for a job brings along a lot of stress, and friends and other contacts can help the expat and partner by offering support with this. Although it's much easier in today's age to keep friendships back home alive through digital means, expats and their partners also need to make new connections in the new host country. There are four different groups that could support the expat: compatriots (expats with the same nationality), expats from other countries, locals of the host country and people back home. These groups support the expat in different ways, as is shown in a study that asked

DOI: 10.4324/9781003246855-12

*Figure 4.1*  The benefits of expat contact with locals. Illustration by Heldermaker.

42 single expats working in 21 different countries to keep a diary for a month of their social interactions.[3] Locals of the host country help expats to learn about the new culture and the language, and to feel accepted in the host country and feel like they fit in. As one expat said: "I'm invited to all local events. My presence is valued here. I feel privileged to be accepted within the group." Compatriots offer the opportunity to compare home and host cultures and provide relevant advice, as well as a sense of belonging to a community. They – just like people back home – give emotional support and are a way to maintain ties with the home country. Expats from other countries can empathise with the expat, easily give a lot of good practical advice and tips and offer many opportunities for learning to communicate with people from other cultural backgrounds. Where people back home and compatriots help the continued attachment to the home country, contact with locals of the host country and expats from other countries push the expat out of their comfort zone and into a growth zone where (culture) learning occurs. This is where intercultural competence is developed, as we have also seen in the last chapter: "I have such great teachers! Every day I'm learning new things, things that are very different. Things I cannot see on the surface … It would take so long to discover these on my own."

So, how do these types of support help the expat, and does it matter who supports the expat? One study examined exactly this question among 131 English-speaking expats and repats in New Zealand, who were asked about their work experience abroad.[4] You may remember from Chapter 1 (p. 24) that two main categories of social support are usually distinguished, namely informational/instrumental support such as lending a hand or giving a suggestion for solving a problem, and socioemotional support such as a listening ear. The study showed that both informational/instrumental and socioemotional support were important for the satisfaction with the foreign work experience, but it turned out that it was also important who provided the support. Receiving more support from locals and less support from the home network meant higher satisfaction with the international work experience. For expats to be happy with their stay abroad, they need to be supported by locals – in particular with socioemotional support; having someone to do activities with when they have time off, but also to chat about difficult experiences. Locals particularly can help there, by explaining what happened from a cultural viewpoint. Other expats might not know the culture as well, or are struggling themselves, with the risk of both starting to complain about the host culture. Another interesting finding was that the support from the home network actually worked counterproductive; the expats were less happy with their work experience abroad if they had a lot of support from friends back home. This support might increase feelings of homesickness, but it might also be that expats do not fully engage in the host country if they are still spending a lot of time to talk to their existing friends. That would also leave less time to do new activities in the host country, and make new friends there. Being embedded in the local community is very important for expats to want to stay in the host country.[5]

### Contact with locals in the workplace

Many studies have focused on the contact between expats and locals of the host country in the workplace; expats often work on a daily basis with locals, and this contact can help expat adjustment and performance.[6] When an expat first arrives in the new workplace, they need to learn how things work in the new environment. Locals can act as socialising agents[7] and make sure the newcomer gets the organisational information that they need to become effective employees. Such socialising agents can also provide instrumental and emotional support when the expat is stressed. While there is evidence that contact with locals helps the adjustment of both the expat and the spouse,[8] several studies suggest that locals in the workplace might be more important for expat performance than for expat work adjustment.[9] It seems that local colleagues are better at providing relevant information helping job performance than they are at offering emotional support which might help the adjustment to the host country. Perhaps this is because relationships with locals of the host country are often not so easy to establish, and a contact usually needs to develop before emotional support is offered. Local colleagues can also cause extra stress that can actually make adjustment more difficult. An interesting study was done among 70 mainly Western expats in China,[10] which showed that local colleagues helped expat performance, but negatively impacted expat adjustment. To understand this surprising effect, we have to look at the context in which the study took place. Thirty-five follow-up interviews were held, and these pointed indeed to the Chinese context as possible explanation. Expats already worked long hours, but then were also expected to socialise with Chinese colleagues after work hours, blurring the boundaries between work and personal time in a way which according to some expats "just blows your mind." Many expats were also frustrated by the clearly different cultural background of their Chinese colleagues, especially their indirect communication style. This suggests that it is very important whether the relationship with a local from the host country is voluntary or not; basically, whether a local is a colleague or a friend. It makes sense that frustrating relationships with local colleagues one has to work with on a daily basis, as is the case in this study, would have a very different effect than when one has a good relationship with them and gets all kind of help. The study did show a positive relationship between local contact at work and expat performance. Good relationships with the Chinese are crucial for doing well in your job. One expat urged others to "be prepared to have fun with your relationship building, because if you don't build those relationships with people in China, you won't succeed." This shows how important it is to know the context of a study. Generally, local colleagues offer a lot of good information about the workplace that can help expat performance, but such contacts are extra important in contexts where personal relationships when doing business are emphasised.

Good contact with the local workforce can also help assigned expats to transfer practices from headquarters to the local subsidiary, which is often done to ensure the efficient running of the local subsidiary. One study on the transfer of HR practices of Taiwanese multinational corporations to their British subsidiaries[11] found that the transfer of HR practices such as training, selection and recruitment, and performance management from Taiwan to the United Kingdom was quite difficult. The Taiwanese expats were mainly on technical assignments and were unfamiliar with the HR practices, which made it hard to explain to the locals why they were being transferred. They also ran into a language barrier because many expats did not speak English very well. They also had difficulty creating a good relationship with the British locals because headquarters kept them so busy there was little time to socialise during work hours. Different cultural values and lifestyles made it difficult to socialise outside of work. One expat said:

> We are not familiar with these HRM practices transferred from the head office. We do not know whether these practices or measurement can fit into our local practices and markets. Maybe we can use local firms' practices because we are working in the North England not Asia Pacific.

Locals from the host country can play an important liaison role as Change Agent in situations like these, and this will be further discussed in Chapter 5.

### Role of contact with locals in knowledge management

Sharing relevant information about the organisation is an important way in which locals can contribute to the success of both the (assigned) expat and the organisation itself. Several studies have focused on knowledge management, which is nowadays seen as a key competitive advantage for multinational corporations, and show that locals of the host country play a very important role in effective knowledge management.[12] Expats who are sent on an assignment to a local subsidiary are able to act as a link to the host country, and thereby feed important local information and opportunities back to the rest of the organisation.[13] The expat gets much of their information from their local colleagues, who know the country much better. The important roles that locals of the host country can play in this process – as a liaison between the expat and the local workforce – are highlighted in Chapter 5. One study focused on how these intercultural knowledge sharing relationships between Australian expats and locals are built in NGOs in Vietnam.[14] At the beginning, the relationship has to be built, where it is important that the expats tune into the host environment and listen to the needs of the locals from the host country. The locals, for their part, helped the expats feel at home in their new environment and make them feel part of the organisation. This laid the foundation for the second stage of the knowledge sharing relationship, where expats invite the locals to put forward ideas and try to make them feel safe in challenging the expat's ideas without losing face. Locals from the host country helped clarify cultural differences and promote the expat's ideas in the local context. This could then further develop into a collaborative intercultural knowledge sharing relationship where new ideas are co-created by the expat and the locals drawing from the cultural perspectives of both. As one expat formulated it: "There was sort of the clash of the cultures, where we ... we talked and we discussed it, discussed it from our cultural standpoints and then came to, what we thought was the best conclusion and then moved forward."

In this knowledge sharing process, having a common language is, of course, an important factor. As we saw in Chapter 2 (p. 113), expats who speak the host language are more easily able to make local friends, and a similar effect can be seen in the workplace: expats who speak the host language are able to create larger social networks and receive more support from local colleagues.[15] As one expat in that study explained: "The big thing different from elsewhere is that Chinese partners here do not speak English. [...] It is very difficult to build up social relations. You cannot make a telephone call. [...] You do not build up the connections." Another consequence of a lack of host language proficiency is that having to translate constantly for the expat puts an extra burden on the local from the host country.

Another important reason why expats are hired is to develop the local subsidiary or organisation. In such cases, the desired outcome of the contact between expats and locals from the host country is learning by the local colleagues. Another study on NGOs in Vietnam,[16] where expats were specifically hired to develop the organisation, showed that locals from the host country mainly learn 'soft' capabilities such as management skills from the expats, rather than technical knowledge. The locals develop

English language skills and other communication abilities such as negotiating and listening, and they develop their intercultural awareness and competence. They also develop at a personal level which contributes to their work quality, for example by increased motivation and greater self-confidence. One local expressed it as follows: "I learn so much skills and knowledge from [expats'] general activities like communication skill, planning skill or negotiation skill, many skills that are not items of the project activity but I can learn from them."

## What influences the contact between expats and locals?

It is clear that the connection between expats and locals from the host country can have many benefits for both parties as well as the organisation. Of course, these potential positive outcomes do not always happen, as was clear in the aforementioned study on expats in China, who became frustrated with their local colleagues. One study focused on the 'dark side' of these interactions,[17] and found that both expats and locals do not always act positively towards each other. While locals from the host country, who often are subordinates, sometimes withhold their support and can be resentful and even xenophobic towards the expats, expats might discriminate against locals in their selection or promotion decisions and expect very high performance without allowing a flexible approach to the work tasks. Many factors determine how the contact between expats and locals from the host country works out. They fall into three categories, namely individual level factors related to either the expat or the local, interpersonal factors that are about the relationship between the expat and the local and contextual factors.

### Individual factors of the expat and the local of the host country

#### Personality and attitudes

One of the things that easily comes to mind when thinking about what might influence the contact between expats and locals are personality aspects such as openness and extraversion. Openness to people really helped because it made the expat interested to learn from the contact with people from different cultural background.[18] This willingness to learn helps adjustment to the new host country. Extraversion – the extent to which one prefers social activities – is also generally found to help connect with locals of the host country and get familiar with their way of interacting.[19] Aspects such as self-esteem and self-efficacy (the extent to which one believes one can accomplish a certain level of performance) also help to connect more with locals because of approaching these interactions in a positive way.[20]

A related aspect is the attitude one has towards interacting with people from other cultures. In the context of expat-local interactions, the research has focused on local attitudes towards the expat. Ethnocentrism is one factor that can hinder good quality contact between expats and locals because the person believes their own culture is the centre of everything, and that other cultures are inferior. Both expats and locals can be ethnocentric, which makes people more wary of learning from and interacting with someone from another cultural background.[21] It can also cause intercultural conflicts by feeding negative stereotypes of the other group, for example expat being pocket-fillers or "exploiters of the local, under-developed economy."[22]

At the heart of these issues is something called outgroup categorisation. Social categorisation theory[23] suggests that people tend to categorise people who have the same attributes or characteristics into social groups, and that if someone is categorised as not belonging to one's own social group, negative consequences may occur. This process also happens when expats and locals meet and locals categorise expats as an outgroup because they have a different nationality or they speak a different language. This negatively impacts on expat adjustment and performance because locals are less likely to offer support to the expat, and the expat feels isolated, which makes them want to return home early.[24]

Much research has focused on the local's willingness to help the expat,[25] and shows how it varies depending on how trusting, good-natured and cooperative the local is, and how much they like the expat and have in common with them. The organisational and job context also influences the willingness of the local colleague to support the expat. Many organisations do not treat expats and locals equally, for example in terms of salary, even if they are in similar positions or have similar qualifications. This can create resentment among locals, decreasing their willingness to help the expat.[26] The work environment itself can also stimulate locals to help the expat, if they share work-related goals and are committed to them so the local feels they can trust the expat.[27] Locals from the host country are also more willing to help expats if they feel they are supported by the organisation.

It is important, however, not to jump to conclusions too fast, and think that ethnocentrism and prejudices must be behind certain behaviours of locals of the host country. An interesting case study was done in an Australian organisation operating in Asia,[28] where one expat discovered a knowledge gap between him and his local colleagues, which might explain their unwillingness to change their behaviour.

Staff need to know where they sit in the big picture. Why do they make the products they make? Right now, all they know is that they are making a product for an anonymous customer. But, if they knew it was for an important customer or that it was a new product specially designed in response to customer feedback, I think it would lift their performance.

### Skills and competences

Intercultural interaction between expats and locals of the host country is also facilitated by certain skills and competences of an individual. An important competence for both expats and locals is intercultural competence, which helps with communicating effectively and appropriately with people from other cultural backgrounds (see Chapter 3). It's not enough to know a lot about other cultures, one also needs to want to interact with people from other cultural backgrounds and have the skills to do so successfully.

Another skill is host language proficiency, which obviously helps the interaction with locals, both at work and in private life, especially if there is no common other language such as English.[29] If one cannot really communicate with someone because of a lack of shared language, it is difficult to build a relationship and get support. And it is not only about the actual language proficiency, but also about whether the expat is willing to learn the language and makes an effort. An interesting study in China shows how willingness to learn the language or even only throwing in a few words here and there can already make a difference. One expat said:

> I want to integrate even better into the Chinese society and the work community here. I want to understand China and Chinese and Chinese people. I think it doesn't hurt to have some basic understanding of the language. [...] I definitely want to learn Chinese. That's not the main drive, but it shows my commitment to China and our business in China and to my colleagues that I am taking it seriously. I am not here to visit, but I want to integrate.

And this helps build positive relationships with locals from the host country. If an expat doesn't express any interest or makes any effort in learning the language, the locals may become suspicious and guarded:

> He [expat] has never studied it [Chinese], although there are free classes provided by the company [...] He seems to understand many things though. However, he cannot learn the positive side of Chinese. Instead, he picked up the bad habits of Chinese.

### Interpersonal factors connecting the expat and locals from the host country

#### Similarity

The relationship between an expat and a local from the host country is also influenced by interpersonal factors, which are factors that are related to both parties and not just the individual. An example is the similarity between the expat and the local. We saw in Chapter 1 (p. 30) that it is important to find some similarity one can build a relationship on, and this also goes for intercultural relationships where culture is a major factor. People more easily associate with people from a similar cultural background; this contributes to the creation of these expat bubbles where expats only see other expats. These cultural differences also influence the support that expats get from locals from the host country. When locals perceive expats as having the same values, they are more likely to categorise them as an in-group member and are likely to offer more support to them than if values are much more different.[30] In a study of nurses of Indian origin in the United Kingdom,[31] the importance of the support of locals was, once again, confirmed for the adjustment to the new host country. The support that was provided by locals was dependent on the perceived value similarity: if the locals believed they had similar work and social values as the expat, they were providing more role information such as information on behaviours and attitudes that were valued and expected in the workplace, as well as social support. This support of locals is especially important for this specific group of expats; nurses are part of the group of self-initiated expats who are not sent by an organisation, and, hence, get no or very little support with their move abroad.

#### Trust

Differences between expats and locals from the host country can also make it more difficult to build trust, which is a crucial factor for good communication and information sharing between expats and locals. Another study on Australian expats in Vietnamese NGOs[32] showed that trust plays a central role in working relationships between expats and locals from the host country, especially those focused on developing the capabilities of locals, which is core to much NGO work. How does one build this trust? Small talk is one way to go about; an ethnographic study[33] of Japanese and Indonesian staff in a subsidiary of a Japanese company in Indonesia showed that people talked all the time, and this helped build trust as well as the exchange of information. Another study[34] focused on how assigned expats in Western multinational corporations in Shanghai, China, build trust with the locals they temporarily work with. Both the expats and the locals said they decided to start trusting the other after witnessing some form of work competence. It starts with 'cognition-based trust' – based on talking content, setting goals and efficiency and effectiveness at work – but when the parties have gotten to know each other, 'affection-based trust' takes over. One important way to gain the trust of locals was for expats to protect their local subordinates professionally – 'take the bullet' – and thereby show that they have the locals' best interests at heart.

### Type of relationship with the local

The aforementioned studies are about expats and locals in the workplace, as colleagues. As we have seen before, this can influence the relationship; remember the study done among Western expats in China that showed a negative impact of contact with local colleagues on expat adjustment. Expats had to socialise outside of work hours, and they were frustrated by the clearly different cultural background of their Chinese colleagues. Contact with Chinese friends that one has sought out themselves may have very different effects. It is, therefore, very important to distinguish the type of relationship the expat has with the locals from the host country: are they colleagues, friends or even married with a local? And are local colleagues co-workers or is there a hierarchical relationship? It may be that the earlier mentioned outgroup categorisation is less important for adjustment when expats and locals are co-workers, and not supervisor-subordinate. However, a shortcoming of some of the research on expat-local relationships is that they do not distinguish whether a local is a co-worker, a subordinate or a manager. We still need to find out more about how the relationships between expats and locals are different dependent on the type of relationship they have.

### The importance of context

The context in which expats and locals from the host country find themselves makes a difference for if and how the relationship develops. In Chapter 2 (p. 56) we saw that the organisational context, culture and language influence who an expat makes friends with and how the relationship develops. In the current chapter you have already read about how expats were expected to socialise with Chinese colleagues after work hours, which some found rather frustrating. Both the organisational and the wider cultural context influence how relationships between expats and locals develop, and how beneficial these relationships then can be.

*Culture and language*

There are quite a few studies that show how expats find it difficult to connect with the locals from the host country due to some cultural characteristics. In Chapter 2, I looked at the Danish situation where characteristics such as homogeneity and equality make it more difficult for foreigners to join in with the locals (see Box 2.2 on p. 57). We have also seen how the divide between work and private life is larger in some countries than in others. A Portuguese expat said the following about making friends in the Netherlands:[35]

> In the first years, colleagues never invited me to something. Only recently there was a group of people that invited me to dinners and parties. That's when I got to know Dutch people and get to know the culture. I think they really don't realise how hard it is for foreigners to make such contacts.

Another study in Malaysia suggested aspects such as power distance and collectivism as explanations why expats have difficulty connecting with locals.[36] A higher power distance culture has more of a (invisible) barrier between expats and locals because differences in status are respected. In-group collectivism – the degree to which individuals express pride, loyalty and interdependence in their families – means that people are often more wary of 'outsiders,' and people are more likely to stay in strong cohesive groups since birth. This makes it more difficult for expats and locals to become friendly. Interestingly enough, the Scandinavian countries score high on institutional collectivism, which is another aspect of collectivism, yet low on in-group collectivism.[37] Institutional collectivism is about whether group loyalty is emphasised at the expense of individual goals, but also whether being accepted by other group members is important. This might explain why it is difficult for expats to connect with locals in the Scandinavian countries.

In addition to culture, language can also play a role. Chinese managers working in Europe and Australia felt isolated because they had very few local friends due to cultural and language barriers.[38] Even in countries where English was the native language, they found it difficult to discuss topics such as news, entertainment or religion, because they didn't feel they understood the local culture well enough. Countries also differ in terms of how important it is to speak the host language, which is called linguistic nationalism. One study in local subsidiaries of multinational corporations in China showed how expats noticed that the locals used Chinese in many situations, even if the corporate language was English.[39]

Expats were frequently excluded from conversations, which frustrated and discouraged them to learn the language, and hence better connect with locals. Many other countries value their own language – France would be another example, with the *Académie française* taking an active role in protecting the language from anglicisms such as computer and e-mail. Danes also place a strong emphasis on being able to speak Danish because it is seen as a core of 'Danishness.'[40] On the other hand of the scale, perhaps, is the Netherlands, where some expats got frustrated enough by locals switching to English to develop a badge with the text '*Spreek Nederlands met mij*' [speak Dutch with me] to help expats to develop their Dutch language skills.[41]

### Country context

Relationships between expats and locals from the host country can also be hindered by specific aspects of the country. As we've seen in Box 2.1 (p. 51), many expats live in compounds where cultural norms are less enforced, and safety can be better guaranteed, and are, therefore, surrounded by other expats. Another example is provided by an interesting study done in the 1990s in Arab Gulf countries,[42] where expats often felt socially isolated and homesick. To understand this, we need to look at the historical context. When the demand for oil sharply increased in the 1970s, the Gulf countries earned a lot of money that they wanted to invest in development and modernisation projects. Because a lack of labour threatened to stall these projects, they sourced labour from abroad. This was so successful that a staggering 61% of the labour force in 1985 was foreign. While this number has fluctuated over time, with the Gulf governments trying to decrease their dependence of foreign labour, this large share of expats in these countries also led to hostile attitudes on the part of the locals, who fear the influence on their culture and identity.

A similar situation is presented in a study in Luxembourg, where 45.9% of the city of Luxembourg consists of foreign nationals who live very much separated from local life. Because of the high number of expats in Luxembourg, they felt much less of a need to connect with locals. They get their support from other expats, and they don't need to learn one of the host languages because the corporate language is English. The study also looked at the Luxembourgers themselves and found that they felt defensive and reserved towards foreigners. All in all, it seems like there are two worlds in Luxembourg that are functioning fully separately – that of the expats, and that of the locals. The study is interesting because it shows that expats don't necessarily need locals to adjust and enjoy their life abroad if they are in a sufficiently international environment, but the question is whether such segregation is the best solution for all involved, also the locals and the host country itself.

Finally, a history of immigration can sometimes help expats connect with locals. A study of international students in Hawaii[43] suggests that the cultural mix that is present in the host population – particularly people from Chinese and Japanese descent – helps international students make friends with locals. A significant portion of the population of Hawaii is from Chinese and Japanese descent, and these locals might be more open to friendships with especially Asian students. On the other hand, a multicultural society based on immigration, like the United States and Canada, does not automatically make it easier for expats to connect with locals. Korean expats in the United States[44] and international students in Canada[45] both found that locals were very friendly but that deeper friendships were still difficult to establish. This goes back to the personality layers of a culture mentioned in Chapter 1 (p. 34), where the United States and Canada are examples of cultures where more layers (e.g. the home) are public and the local's friendliness, for example through an invitation to come for a barbecue, is wrongly interpreted as a first step towards a friendship.

### Organisational context

While the culture and language of the host country can make it more difficult for expats to connect with locals, the organisational context can also play a role, and maybe sometimes compensate to some extent a difficult external context. A supportive organisation can positively influence the outcomes of the contact between expats and locals, for example in terms of knowledge exchange. The earlier mentioned study of assignments of Australian expats in Vietnam[46] showed how important a supportive organisational context is for capacity development of locals of the host country. The leaders of the host organisations could make a difference by emphasising the role and contributions of the expat. They can also guide them to create good working relationships with their local colleagues, for example by creating opportunities to clarify responsibilities and boundaries of the working relationship:

(The manager) encouraged me on my arrival to sit with each of (the staff) for an hour or two as the best way of understanding their job. I sat next to them ... just learning about what they did and it did teach me a lot.

In Chapter 9 and the Recommendations for expats, organisations and societies, I will go in more detail into what organisations can do to facilitate the contact between expats and locals both inside and outside the workplace, so that both expats and locals get the opportunity to benefit from this contact.

Getting in touch with locals of the host country can have many benefits for expats as well as the locals themselves. In the past few chapters, we have seen how expats can make new friends in the host country not only with other expats but also with locals. The next chapter shifts the focus to connections with locals in the workplace and shows several liaison roles that the local colleague can take that are valuable for the success of the expat and the organisation. Such a connection between expats and local colleagues can be seen as an intercultural mentoring relationship, which is the focus of Chapter 6.

## Notes

1 van Bakel, M. (2012). In *Touch with the Dutch. A longitudinal study of the impact of a local host on the success of the expatriate assignment*. PhD thesis, Radboud University, Nijmegen, The Netherlands.
2 For more details, see van Bakel, M. (2019). It takes two to tango: A review of the empirical research on expatriate–local interactions. *International Journal of Human Resource Management, 30*(21), 2993–3025.
3 Bayraktar, S. (2019). A diary study of expatriate adjustment: Collaborative mechanisms of social support. *International Journal of Cross Cultural Management, 19*(1), 47–70.
4 Podsiadlowski, A., Vauclair, C.-M., Spiess, E., & Stroppa, C. (2013). Social support on international assignments: The relevance of socioemotional support from locals. *International Journal of Psychology, 48*(4), 563–573.
5 Yunlu, D. G., Ren, H., Fodchuk, K. M., & Shaffer, M. (2018). Home away from home: community embeddedness and expatriate retention cognitions. *Journal of Global Mobility: The Home of Expatriate Management Research, 6*(2), 194–208.
6 van Bakel (2019).
7 Toh, S. M., & DeNisi, A. (2007). Host country nationals as socializing agents: A social identity approach. *Journal of Organizational Behavior, 28*(3), 281–301.
8 van Bakel (2019).
9 E.g., Liu, X., & Shaffer, M. (2005). An investigation of expatriate adjustment and performance: A social capital perspective. *International Journal of Cross-Cultural Management, 5*(3), 235–254.

10 Bruning, N., Sonpar, K., & Wang, X. (2012). Host-country national networks and expatriate effectiveness: A mixed-methods study. *Journal of International Business Studies, 43*(4), 444–450.

11 Chang, Y. Y., & Smale, A. (2014). The transfer of Taiwanese management practices to British subsidiaries: A diachronic perspective. *Asia Pacific Journal of Human Resources, 52*(2), 234–254.

12 Heizmann, H., Fee, A., & Gray, S. J. (2018). Intercultural knowledge sharing between expatriates and host-country nationals in Vietnam: A practice-based study of communicative relations and power dynamics. *Journal of International Management, 24*(1), 16–32.

13 Au, K., & Fukuda, J. (2002). Boundary spanning behaviors of expatriates. *Journal of World Business, 37*, 285–297.

14 Heizmann et al. (2018).

15 Zhang, L. E., & Peltokorpi, V. (2016). Multifaceted effects of host country language proficiency in expatriate cross-cultural adjustments: A qualitative study in China. *International Journal of Human Resource Management, 27*(13), 1448–1469.

16 Fee, A., & Gray, S. J. (2020). Expatriates as catalysts: What and how Vietnamese locals learn from self-initiated expatriates. *Cross Cultural & Strategic Management, 27*(3), 389–416.

17 Ljubica, J., Shaffer, M., Tin, S., & McKouen, K. (2019). A model of the dark side of expatriate–host country national relationships. *Journal of Global Mobility: The Home of Expatriate Management Research, 7*(2), 137–156.

18 Caligiuri, P. (2000). The Big Five personality characteristics as predictors of expatriate's desire to terminate the assignment and supervisor-rated performance. *Personnel Psychology, 53*, 67–87.

19 van Bakel (2019).

20 Johnson, E., Kristof-Brown, A., Van Vianen, A., De Pater, I., & Klein, M. (2003). Expatriate social ties: Personality antecedents and consequences for adjustment. *International Journal of Selection and Assessment, 11*(4), 277–288..

21 van Bakel (2019).

22 Jassawalla, A., Truglia, C., & Garvey, J. (2004). Cross-cultural conflict and expatriate manager adjustment. *Management Decision, 42*(7), 837–849.

23 Turner, J. C., Hogg, M. A., Oakes, P. J., Reicher, S. D., & Wetherell, M. S. (1987). *Rediscovering the social group: A self-categorization theory.* New York: Basil Blackwell.

24 Shen, J., Wajeeh-ul-Husnain, S., Kang, H., & Jin, Q. (2021). Effect of out-group social categorization by host-country nationals on expatriate premature return intention and buffering effect of mentoring. *Journal of International Management, 27*(2), 100855.

25 van Bakel (2019).

26 Bonache, J., Sanchez, J. I., & Zárraga-Oberty, C. (2009). The interaction of expatriate pay differential and expatriate inputs on host country nationals' pay unfairness. *International Journal of Human Resource Management, 20*(10), 2135–2149.

27  Toh, S. M., & Srinivas, E. (2012). Perceptions of task cohesiveness and organ-
    izational support increase trust and information sharing between host country
    nationals and expatriate coworkers in Oman. *Journal of World Business*,
    47(4), 696–705.
28  Massingham, P. (2010). Managing knowledge transfer between parent country
    nationals (Australia) and host country nationals (Asia). *International Journal
    of Human Resource Management*, 21(9), 1414–1435.
29  Zhang and Peltokorpi (2016).
30  van Bakel (2019).
31  Varma, A., Mathew, J., Wang, C. H., Budhwar, P., & Katou, A. (2020).
    Indian nurses in the United Kingdom: A two-phase study of the expatriate–
    host country national relationship. *European Management Review*, 18(3),
    329–341.
32  Fee, A., Heizmann, H., & Gray, S. J. (2015). Towards a theory of effective
    cross-cultural capacity development: The experiences of Australian inter-
    national NGO expatriates in Vietnam. *International Journal of Human
    Resource Management*, 28(14), 2036–2061.
33  Shimoda, Y. (2013). Talk, trust and information flow: Work relationships
    between Japanese expatriate and host national employees in Indonesia.
    *International Journal of Human Resource Management*, 24(20), 3853.
34  Ang, F., & Tan, H. H. (2016). Trust building with Chinese host country nation-
    als. *Journal of Global Mobility*, 4(1), 44–67.
35  Van Bochove, M., & Engbersen, G. (2015). Beyond cosmopolitanism and
    expat bubbles: Challenging dominant representations of knowledge workers
    and trailing spouses. *Population, Space and Place*, 21(4), 295–309.
36  Malek, M. A., Reiche, B. S., & Budhwar, P. (2015). Sources of support and
    expatriation: A multiple stakeholder perspective of expatriate adjustment
    and performance in Malaysia. *International Journal of Human Resource
    Management*, 26(2), 258–276.
37  House, R. J., Hanges, P. J., Javidan, M., Dorfman, P. W., & Gupta, V. (Eds.).
    (2004). *Culture, leadership, and organisations. The GLOBE study of 62 soci-
    eties*. Thousand Oaks, CA: Sage.
38  Wang, D., Fan, D., Freeman, S., & Zhu, C. J. (2017). Exploring cross-
    cultural skills for expatriate managers from Chinese multination-
    als: Congruence and contextualization. *Asia Pacific Journal of Management*,
    34(1), 123–146.
39  Zhang, L. E., & Harzing, A.-W. (2016). From dilemmatic struggle to legiti-
    mized indifference: Expatriates' host country language learning and its
    impact on the expatriate–HCE relationship. *Journal of World Business*, 51,
    774–786.
40  van Bakel, M., & Vance, C. M. (2023). Breaking out of the expatriate bubble
    in Denmark: Insights from the challenge of making connections with local
    Danes. *Journal of Global Mobility: The Home of Expatriate Management
    Research*, 11(1), 21–42.
41  https://directdutch.com/2017/07/spreek-nederlands-met-mij-a-week-of-
    eschewing-english/ (accessed 15 August 2023).

42  Atiyyah, H. S. (1996). Expatriate acculturation in Arab Gulf countries. *Journal of Management Development, 15*(5), 37–47.

43  Hendrickson, B., Rosen, D., & Aune, R. K. (2011). An analysis of friendship networks, social connectedness, homesickness, and satisfaction levels of international students. *International Journal of Intercultural Relations, 35*(3), 281–295.

44  Toh, S. M., & DeNisi, A. (2005). A local perspective to expatriate success. *The Academy of Management Executive, 19*(1), 132–146.

45  Robinson, O., Somerville, K., & Walsworth, S. (2020). Understanding friendship formation between international and host-national students in a Canadian university. *Journal of International and Intercultural Communication, 13*(1), 49–70.

46  Fee et al. (2015).

# Experience

A Danish expat in Malaysia – "You need local management to run the business"

*Anders is a Danish sales director for a Danish multinational corporation in Malaysia, where he has been living for 4.5 years. He covers the Asia-Pacific region and has about 10 country teams of each approximately 5 people. These are headed by a country manager, who report to him. Anders is married, with two small children.*

### How many locals do you work with on a daily basis?

So we have local [country] managers and it's extremely important for us actually. It's actually smaller businesses that we do business with locally, so if we don't speak their language or know the culture, it can be very hard for us to penetrate the market. So that's why we have local managers. [...] If you don't master the local language, then you have a problem. Then I think you really have a problem. You can be a manager in a place, building up something [...], that's okay for some time, but sooner or later you need local management to run the business.

### Did you have any cultural informants?

Nah but they are also good at telling me things about their own culture, right? Not how I should behave but 'this is how we do it here' or something like that. So if you get closer to them yes – some of them will tell you. And they will find it fun, just to talk about differences between where you come from and where they live. Sometimes I also tell them that I find it very strange that people are reacting so and so, "how come that things are … ," and they explain to me how things are working out. And sometimes I have to ask the country managers a little bit, especially when it comes

DOI: 10.4324/9781003246855-13

to how should I dress and so on [when I visit their country]. And in the beginning especially, I didn't really know.

### Do you also meet locals in your private life?

Ah we meet basically only expats. It's very, very little we do with the locals. Very little.

### Why is that?

This is a... I think it actually goes back to the fact that our cultures are also very, very different. What brings us together in the beginning is actually the children. They go to school, they meet other Danish or other foreign children there, parents meet and then suddenly [clicks tongue] – you are linked. And then you start building up your network – that's how it works. It's not at work/I cannot start socialising with all my staff right? Look at the position I'm in now. You never know what I have to do in half a year's time [e.g. lead a firing round]. You need a balance there, right? Not that I don't want to – but anybody else local outside the office would be much better.

### How have locals helped you in your work? For example, do the local country managers assist with the communication?

If, let's say, if I communicate to the whole organisation something, then I will first take in the country managers and do the communication for them. I'd say: "okay this is what I intend to communicate to the whole organisation – do you have concerns about that or any comments? Anything I should change? Anything that worries you about this?" If not, then I will just go ahead. The thing about Asia is also you have to be... you have to know that they are not so open in the communication as we are in Europe. Very often they will not say anything [...]. But talking to people individually will give you a very good impression, especially if you go further down in the organisation, talk to some of the staff and "how is it?" and yeah. Some of them will open up.

### How about change projects that have to be implemented locally?

We have introduced a new finance programme that we're rolling out now. The country managers here will be involved because I've been asking them to provide feedback, how they see this going forward and what kind of load they see coming towards them now with this new way of handling the finances. So, the discussion is, I said: "I need that information," actually to discuss with headquarters. Because they [the country managers] know the details. And yeah, we meet some resistance sometimes. But as long as we can argue and discuss it and so forth, and sometimes we can also change a little bit here and there.

**And is there anybody internally here who would talk to you about: "well two years ago we tried that but that didn't work"?**

Oh yeah yeah yeah. Locally, I would talk to the... actually there's several people I can talk to. In each country you have a unit who ensures that finances and logistics and all this is taken care of. And many of these people have been in the organisation for ages, they know a lot. And they also know the issues in the different divisions, and they even know it down to individual levels, who could be causing problems or who is... you know, all these things. We had a lot of issues in one of the countries [...] and it was related down to specific individuals who were acting funny, who did strange things. And these people know that.

# Chapter 5

# Connecting with locals in the workplace

## Introduction

Contact with locals of the host country can have many benefits, as the previous chapter showed. Many expats work with locals on a daily basis, and they can offer a lot of useful information that can help expats do their jobs well. A useful way of looking at the various ways in which locals can help is the host country liaison (HCL) model.[1] This chapter will look more closely at the five HCL roles that locals can take. It is based on a total of 45 interviews done with Scandinavian and Germanic expats in Malaysia, Mexico and the United States.[2]

## The host country liaison model

The HCL model was developed to highlight the often-neglected role that locals of the host country can play in the success of multinational corporations. Much research has focused on assigned expats who are sent to a local subsidiary, and how they should be selected, trained and supported, so that they are successful on their assignment. While assigned expats are often in strategic positions to influence the running of the local subsidiary, locals of the host country are the largest part of the workforce in a multinational corporation. They can play an important role in terms of knowledge management, which is increasingly seen as a source of competitive advantage. If all employees in an organisation – and not just senior executives and assigned expats – are able to transfer and use new knowledge, the organisation will be much better able to innovate.

Knowledge transfer is one of the major reasons for expats to be sent on an international assignment. The expat acts as a link between headquarters and the local subsidiary, and transfers knowledge – how things are done – from headquarters to the local subsidiary and back. It is very helpful to gain new knowledge in the local subsidiary, and feed that information back to headquarters, and maybe also elsewhere as needed in the

DOI: 10.4324/9781003246855-14

*Figure 5.1* Connecting with locals in the workplace. Illustration by Heldermaker.

multinational corporation. This is where the locals of the host country come in since they know about the local subsidiary and the context in which it operates. The HCL model suggests that locals of the host country can play an important liaison role between the expat and the local environment and workforce. This can be a formal role, for example when an administrative assistant is asked to liaise between the expat and the local workforce because of language issues. But the role can also be informal, such as with a local manager at the same level as the expat who might discuss some concerns in the workforce while meeting for coffee. The roles can also be spread over several local colleagues of the host country; it is not necessarily just one local who takes up the HCL roles. It is also important to realise that the HCL role as a liaison role is meant to go both ways – both towards the expat and towards other local employees.

The model distinguishes five HCL roles, namely cultural interpreter, communication manager, information resource broker, talent manager and change agent. These five roles will be discussed next, using examples from the interviews conducted with expats in Malaysia, Mexico and the United States. The HCL model has been created with the traditional assigned expat in mind, but some roles can also be relevant for the self-initiated expat.

## Cultural interpreter

The first HCL role is about helping the expat navigate the new culture. Cultural differences can present an important barrier for the effective management of knowledge. When expats arrive in the new host country, they often lack a lot of knowledge of how things work there. Locals of the host country can help clarify and explain what is happening. A German quality manager in Mexico had a lot of help from a Mexican colleague in HR, who was familiar with both cultures because that colleague had a German boyfriend. "…when there was a situation during the week and we had the chance next week to talk, I asked her from time to time: 'Okay, there was this, there was that, what does he mean?'" The guidance can also work in the other direction, towards the local employees. For example, a local colleague in the host country can help explain certain policies or decisions that headquarters has made to the other local employees.

The local colleagues can also go a step further, and actively guide the expat in what they should or shouldn't do. A German expat working in the chemical industry in Mexico mentioned that the local colleagues "helped me to understand the way of thinking in the business, because the way of working is completely different compared to Europe, also to the United States and they are neighbours. It's completely different." Especially if the local colleagues have lived abroad themselves, they can be very good cultural informants. A Danish vice-president of Asia-Pacific in Malaysia had a local colleague who had been to Denmark but had also lived in the United States. He sought him out to discuss the local context:

> He speaks openly about all the corruption, all the inefficiency in the Malaysian system, and the lack of talent, the brain drain, and all that – so he has that western angle too. He can put it into a more holistic context. So, people like that are the most valuable you can find.

Informal chats with local colleagues can also be very enlightening. A German marketing director in the United States (see also Experience on p. 137) learned a lot by just chatting about things with colleagues, and comparing notes about how things are done in the United States and in Germany. She also found it a lot of fun. This cultural guidance can also be very helpful in private life, to understand what is happening but also to get tips, for example on whether it is safe to go to a specific location during the weekend, as several expats in Mexico mentioned.

Expats and locals might misunderstand each other because they lack a shared cultural frame of reference, which can lead to frustration and conflict. A local colleague can mediate in such situations, trying to resolve it by explaining about cultural differences and managing the conflict. They can also minimise the chances of conflict by tackling stereotypes that each party might have towards the other and addressing rumours. A German HR manager in the United States realised that she created some conflict at the beginning of her stay because she used her very German direct approach where she pointed out things that needed to be worked on "maybe a little bit more pushy than the Americans would do it normally. So that created some conflict in the beginning, but we also find a way to talk through it and find out why that's a conflict."

## Communication manager

Local colleagues can also help with several communication challenges the expat is faced with. When the expat doesn't speak the language of the host country, local colleagues can translate – both in the workplace and in private life, such as when an expat receives an official letter or a bill. Many expats also learn from them about the local language. A German logistics transport planner in Mexico learned a lot from local colleagues pointing out when something was Spanish, not Mexican Spanish. Two German expats in the United States commented on how U.S. American English is different from the British English that they learned at school. One of them learned to use new expressions that were unique to the

United States, such as 'hitting it out of the ballpark' and 'throwing a curveball.'

A local colleague can also be necessary to talk to the local employees who don't speak English. An Austrian head of manufacturing in Mexico said:

> At the beginning, my Spanish was really really poor. And sometimes you are on the shop floor, standing next to the line, want to interact a little bit with the guys working, asking them for "How was it going? What can we improve?"

A local colleague can help by acting as a communication mediator, passing messages from the work floor to the expat. In the opposite direction, local colleagues can also help deliver messages from headquarters down to the work floor. For example, a Danish sales director in Malaysia (see also the Experience on p. 123) used his country managers to deliver news to their teams in their respective countries.

Local colleagues can also help the communication flow between the expat and the local colleagues in other ways. A local colleague can help adjust the communication to fit the local context. A German chief executive officer (CEO) in the United States always sends his written communications to one of his local colleagues to make it sound more American. Local colleagues can also help create a climate of trust so that local employees will reach out to the expat, and vice versa. Several expats talked about the importance of establishing trust with local employees. A Danish head of business finance in Malaysia said:

> In the beginning people told me: "You can't do that," so I didn't do it in the very beginning actually. Some of the locals said: "Don't go out and ask that question, you need to gain the trust from the team first."

### Information resource broker

Local colleagues can also be a great source of information, for example about the local market. Several expats commented on how the information of locals is crucial for doing business because they know the local situation. Even if processes are largely standardised around the world, as was the case for a large car manufacturer in Mexico, there are still some local influences. The German logistics transport planner working for this company said:

> So, with the knowledge of some plants you are normally also able to work here in Mexico in a good way. But you have to understand, let's

say, the last 10%, how it works here in Mexico, and also for these topics they can help you.

The local context can also influence the running of the business, which
the expat might not be aware of. A German sales and project manager in
Mexico mentioned how her colleagues told her about issues with local gas
pipes which meant there was no gas for the factory, and a tsunami which
disrupted their shipping.

Local colleagues also know a lot about the organisation and what
happened in the past that could be relevant for the expat to know. The
German marketing director in the United States learned a lot about their
facility during informal chats with her colleagues in the team, how it used
to be back then, what it looked like, and what changed recently. Locals
are also the go-to person to learn more about how the organisation works.
A German engineering technician in Mexico said:

> The locals in that matter are always very important, not only when it
> comes to hard facts but also when it comes to rumours [laughs] and
> gossip and talks of course. I mean if you don't listen to them, you will
> lose a lot of information but always you have to be, of course, careful
> how to use this kind of information.

The Danish vice-president of Asia-Pacific in Malaysia used both local
colleagues and other Danish expats for such information. He would ask
a local colleague what was going on when he picked up some vibes and
strange behaviour, to get a more complete picture of the situation. At the
same time, he also appreciated talking to some of the Danish expats who
had been there for a longer time, because he got the Danish perspective
on how the office works. This saved him a lot of time figuring it out
himself.

Not all local employees would give the best information. An Austrian
general manager in Malaysia experienced that he should go around his
middle managers, directly to the work floor, to get them to open up about
what could be improved. He said:

> ... once a month I'm selecting people from different departments, rank
> and file staff, entry level staff, and I just sit with them and not have
> their manager present. And that's very important. That doesn't mean
> I don't trust my managers, but I know when the manager is present,
> they don't open up. So, you find out things that you would normally
> not find out.

## Talent manager

Local colleagues in the host country can also spot local talent and help develop them and their careers. The HCL role of talent manager focuses on helping the organisation to acquire, develop and retain the necessary talent to be successful.

The first aspect is to identify local talent, both within and outside of the organisation. Local colleagues usually know the external labour market better than the expat and can help recruit people from outside of the organisation. Internally, the spotting of talent often is done in a structured way through a performance management system, where managers rate their employees. Several expats mentioned how they look at talent together with the local managers and make decisions together on who will be developed further. A Danish head of sales in Malaysia describes the process like this:

> So in the management team together with all middle managers we consult the full organisation, so we calibrate every single person and say who wants to work here, who wants to go abroad, who wants to have a career in marketing, who wants to have a career here.

Once the right talent is identified, it is important to develop and retain them. One way to develop local talent is by sending them on an assignment to headquarters so they get experience there. This increased understanding helps the local colleague to fulfil their liaison role between the expat and the local culture, as the Danish vice-president of Asia-Pacific in Malaysia had experienced with his country manager in Japan:

> [he] also lived in Denmark so we try to, these talents, we try to bring them out of their cultural context in order to promote exactly this. So that they become translators both ways. Because you are a part of a Danish company, so you need to understand that aspect also.

Local colleagues of the host country can help develop knowledge, skills and other abilities, and help further the careers of other local colleagues as well as the expats themselves. Whenever someone starts a new job, they will need to be introduced to how things are done, and for expats, it is often a local colleague who introduces them. A Danish senior manager in Malaysia had one person who "was in charge of getting me used to the processes, used to the plant, to the country, to the people, introducing, taking me basically at the hand and bringing me into the company's way to work." Local colleagues have valuable knowledge about what works best in that particular environment and can also act as a type of mentor to help expats in their career. A German vice-president of operations in the United States had a mentor in his U.S. American manager, the CEO of the company, who stimulated him to do an MBA and gave time off to enable him to do it.

## Change agent

Change is part and parcel of everyday life in most companies. Many expats have to implement changes that come from headquarters and it can help greatly if local colleagues of the host country work with the expat to effectively manage this process of change. First, it can be very helpful to have local input on the change itself, and how it can work best in the local context. Many expats commented on how they changed small aspects of a project or guideline that came from headquarters to make sure it would work in the local context, and often local colleagues helped with their input. A German HR director in Mexico said:

> daily [we] have to implement new processes where we need the experience of the Mexicans to adapt this. That it is not a copy and paste process from let us say Germany, but it's really a Mexican process which fits to this company.

The German marketing director in the United States explains how she asks for input of the local colleagues:

> for example, in Brazil, and Mexico, does it work for you? Like, this is my idea, I think this is a good thing to do, like, what do you think? And I'm really getting that open feedback, and I'm having them tell me, for these three reasons, it's not going to work. And then I'm trying to understand, okay, can we overcome these obstacles, or do we really need to change the approach?

The local colleagues in the host country are also often crucial to getting the change implemented, and getting their input is a first step to get them engaged and supportive of the change. Local colleagues can also act as ambassadors. The German logistic transport planner in Mexico commented:

> but it helps a lot when you have Mexican colleagues that they, you can convince them for the change and then it's important, you have a like it multiplicator in an organisation when you convince some guys in a

certain level, and they will also, they have the understanding of the new process, they will help you and support you a lot, also to teaching the guys also for the change.

The HCL model shows different ways in which locals of the host country can contribute to the success of the expat and the local organisation. As a Russian supply chain manager in the United States said: "You need locals, it is the only way you can succeed."

## Notes

1   This model was originally called the Host Country National Liaison model but has since developed to Host Country Liaison because it became clear during the interviews that it can also be other expats who take up some of these roles. (Vance, C., Vaiman, V., Andersen, T., & Gale, J. (2014). A taxonomy of potential contributions of the host country national local liaison role in global knowledge management. *Thunderbird International Business Review, 56*(2), 173–191.)
2   While 11 of the interviews in Malaysia were done by Torben Andersen and me, the rest of the interviews were done by my students Anna-Lena Schwarz and Zuzana Satková (Malaysia and Mexico), and Lisa Schlichting (U.S.), for their respective master theses.

# Experience

A German expat in the United States – "You don't have to reinvent the wheel"

*Lisa is a 34-year-old German marketing director working since early 2019 in the United States, where she also spent a year as a student. She has regional responsibility for both North and South America and her teams sit in the United States, Mexico and Brazil. The interview took place in March 2021 toward the end of the COVID-19 pandemic.*

### How much contact do you have with U.S. American colleagues during your daily work?

My team and my direct reports are spread across the Americas. So, I'm basically on the phone all day. And since COVID, [this] increased even more. I'm on the phone all day, I have to lead and guide my team remotely, entirely remotely, since a year now.

### When you arrived in the United States, did you get help from your colleagues in understanding the local culture?

Yes, for sure. [...] there were a couple of things that were really stunning and surprising to me. And then I asked them, like is that a thing here? Like, I don't know for example, Fourth of July or Thanksgiving, like all those traditions and the way people handle things. The way they work, the way they live their everyday life. I learned a lot just chatting about things with colleagues and talking and I'm like, 'I observed this and that and I thought that was really interesting.' And they're like, 'Oh, yeah, how do you do that in Germany?' So, we are talking about, and we still do, about the differences we see in the cultures. It's really fun.

DOI: 10.4324/9781003246855-15

**And in what way have your U.S. American colleagues contributed to your performance at work?**

Oh, that's an interesting question. I would say I underestimated the cultural impact. So, if you think about American culture, how to deal with the way they work, what they expect from a manager… Yeah, and what they deliver, the worker results, and the way they communicate, it is very different. I think they taught me a lot. They taught me a lot in the sense of, what do I need to do in order to achieve the best results as a manager, because the working style really differs a lot from the German way of working. The German way of working […] is very detailed, […] you have your plan laid out, where Americans are more like, yeah, okay, I want to do this, you can trust me that I can do it. […] As a German manager experiencing this I was like, yeah, you can, but I have questions, because I don't see the detailed plan behind it. And they were a little bit confused why I wanted to know all this, and why I did not trust them.

**And to what extent have colleagues been a source of important information for you, for example, about the local environment?**

Yeah, absolutely a lot. So, for example, [when a tornado hits] that you have to go in a certain area and wait till the storm is over. […] So, they made us aware of how serious it is, and then other things I think you learn here pretty quickly and that is also enforced by trainings that you get through HR. I mean, you know, that anti-discrimination, and sexual harassment and things like this are super important in the U.S., right? What you learn right away is what you can say and what you can't say. And especially if you have employees, you have to have a certain training.

**How did you get informal knowledge about the subsidiary, about the history, for example?**

I talked to colleagues and then of course, also, HR has some processes. They showed us the history of the plant here and the different other plants that we have across the U.S. I think actually really the colleagues here in the team, so the ones who work here, in the same facility, they told me a lot about it and how it used to be back then, what it looked like, what changed recently. Yeah, there were a lot of informal chats about these things.

## And have they helped you carry out change projects?

Yeah, absolutely. I think it's, also like a matter of how you approach people, I mean, if you, if you tell them, okay, this is how we do it, and you don't provide further information on why you want to do it that way, it's always difficult for people to understand and support it. [...] I'm trying to explain to them why we want to do it and ask them also for their experience [...], for example, in Brazil, and Mexico, does it work for you? Like, this is my idea, I think this is a good thing to do, what do you think? And I'm really getting that open feedback, and I'm having them tell me, for these three reasons, it's not going to work. And then I'm trying to understand, okay, can we overcome these obstacles, or do we really need to change the approach?

## And what would you recommend to an expat who is new to the United States?

I would recommend being openminded, to try to introduce yourself in a friendly way and in a way that is common in the culture. That's what I would recommend and then trying to connect to somebody who has been through the process, I think that's really what helped most, to find someone who relocated recently as well and who knows how things go. You don't have to reinvent the wheel and you don't have to go through all the pain by doing it all by yourself. So just ask for help.

Chapter 6

# Intercultural mentoring

## Introduction

In the previous chapter we saw how connections with local colleagues can really help expats in their work. Such a relationship between an expat and a local can also be seen as a form of mentoring.[1] Mentoring in the workplace[2] has many advantages for both mentors and mentees and the organisations they work for. For mentees, it is a great opportunity to learn and develop one's career. Expats who receive mentoring get a better introduction to their new workplace, and this form of support positively influences their intention to finish their assignment as well as their understanding of global business issues.[3] Mentors also benefit from a mentoring relationship through more motivation, job satisfaction and career success.[4] For the organisation, peer mentoring is a key HR practice to stimulate knowledge creation and increase knowledge transfer.[5] Mentoring also has the potential to develop a learning organisation,[6] and helps retain valuable employees.[7]

The academic interest in mentoring started in the 1980s, mostly with a domestic focus. Nowadays, however, many of these mentoring relationships take place in an international context or between people from different cultural backgrounds. In this chapter, we take a closer look at mentoring in an international context,[8] such as the mentoring of expats and locals of the host country, which is very relevant particularly for multinational corporations that value all their global talent. Intercultural mentoring is a powerful tool to develop global leaders by enhancing both emotional and cultural intelligence,[9] and can contribute to organisational knowledge development and sharing that are crucial for global success.[10]

So, what is intercultural mentoring and how should organisations go about when they want to set up mentoring programmes that might cross cultural boundaries? How can one tailor mentoring to the needs of various groups of global talent? And how can an organisation facilitate mentoring to achieve the best results? I will discuss these topics in this chapter.

DOI: 10.4324/9781003246855-16

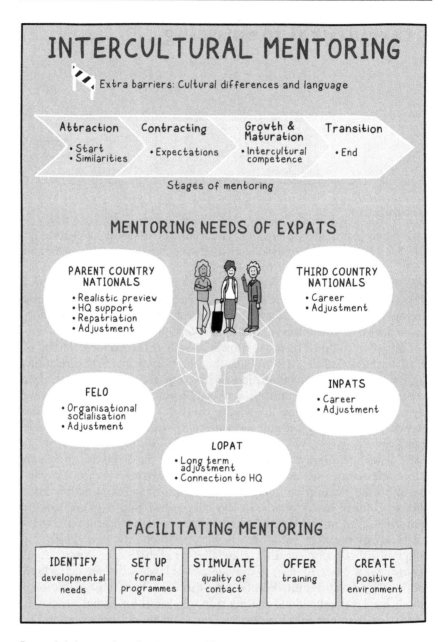

*Figure 6.1* Intercultural mentoring. Illustration by Heldermaker.

## Mentoring: what is it?

Mentoring has traditionally been defined as "a relationship between an older, more experienced mentor and a younger, less experienced protégé for the purpose of helping and developing the protégé's career."[11] An example of this traditional view of mentoring is a senior manager who mentors a high-potential young employee. A core feature of a mentoring relationship is that it is developmental in nature, with the main focus on career development and professional growth. Typically, mentoring relationships provide two major functions to their mentees: those behaviours that help protégés advance in their career (career functions) and those behaviours that enhance the protégé's professional and personal growth, identity and perceived self-worth and self-efficacy, which is one's judgement of one's capability to accomplish a certain level of performance (psychosocial functions).[12] For example, a mentor can discuss various career possibilities with the mentee, both within and outside of the organisation, or even give them opportunities they otherwise would not have, such as an interesting and challenging project. The mentor can also coach the mentee with challenges in their daily work, for example, by providing political or cultural knowledge that will help the mentee deal with these challenges, as well as give feedback on their performance. These mentoring behaviours are examples of career functions.[13] But a mentor can do more than just boost their mentee's career; they can also help the mentee develop further both professionally and personally, which are called the psychosocial functions of mentoring. For example, as a role model, the mentor can show which behaviours, attitudes and skills would help the mentee be successful at their job. This helps the mentee feel more confident that their behaviour and attitudes mirror what is appropriate in that particular workplace. The mentor can also provide personal counselling to the mentee. Through listening and demonstrating warmth, encouragement and trust, the mentor can help the mentee cope with situations they find difficult. For example, a mentor could share some of the challenges they encountered in their career, and how they managed them.[14]

Nowadays, there are many variations to the traditional mentoring relationship. A first important distinction is whether a relationship is formal or informal, depending on whether it is set up by the organisation, or the individual asked a certain person to be their mentor. Many more organisations have now set up their own mentoring programmes to capitalise on the many potential benefits of mentoring. They don't want to leave mentoring to chance. Such programmes are expected to deliver unique benefits for the organisation by helping new employees integrate into the organisation and develop leadership potential, but also as a way to help women and minorities gain needed support to enhance diversity within management ranks. Formal mentoring relationships typically are developed with organisational assistance and with a limited time frame. There is some evidence, however, that suggests that formal mentoring programmes are less effective than informal ones because less career and psychosocial support are being offered to the mentee.[15]

Another variation on the traditional hierarchical mentoring relationship is peer mentoring, which occurs at the same hierarchical level.[16] The peer mentor is usually a more experienced colleague, at the same or similar level, teaching new knowledge and skills and providing encouragement to a less experienced colleague. Despite the mentor not being at a higher hierarchical level, they still can provide both the career and psychosocial functions that 'normal' mentoring provides. Peer mentoring is a valuable alternative to traditional mentoring, particularly in today's flatter organisations where not as many senior managers are available for mentoring. Mentoring also does not have be done by only one person but can be provided by a 'developmental network,' where the key idea is that a person can have multiple mentors who support career as well as personal development. In addition, a mentoring relationship does not have to be restricted to one and the same organisation; employees can also have mentors from outside the organisation. More junior employees can also function as a mentor to a more senior employee, for example to help the latter understand new technologies, the changing marketplace or other topics where the younger mentor may have greater skill and familiarity. This arrangement is called reverse mentoring.[17]

And, of course, in today's highly connected world, more and more mentors and mentees find each other online; geography is no longer a barrier for mentoring. E-mentoring relationships mostly take place via e-mail and other electronic means, and they cut across internal and external organisational boundaries as well as geographic boundaries and time zones.[18] The mentoring can also be a mix of online and face-to-face contact, depending on the situation and wishes of those involved (e.g. when the mentor and mentee are not located in the same office).

### Intercultural mentoring

The more and more diverse workplace nowadays also means that mentoring is often intercultural. Intercultural mentoring, where the mentor and mentee come from different cultures,[19] has not received the much-needed attention it deserves to address the additional barriers to overcome, such as cultural differences and language barriers. These cultural differences can also lead to more benefits. Both the mentor and mentee get the opportunity to develop their intercultural competence, and the mentor becomes more emphatic through seeing the challenges the mentee faces.[20] As we have seen in Chapters 2 and 3, intercultural competence is very important to develop intercultural friendships, and this is also applicable to intercultural mentoring relationships.

Cultural differences influence mentoring in various ways. Both mentor and mentee bring their own cultural frame of reference to the relationship and might have different expectations of what a mentor is. Already in the very first phase of mentoring – when one meets someone who might become a mentor – cultural differences influence how interested one is in having that person as a mentor (or mentee). In Chapter 2 (p. 55), I discussed the similarity-attraction hypothesis which shows the importance of similarities in building a new relationship. This also goes for mentoring relationships: people will be more interested in mentoring or being mentored by someone who is similar to themselves, and they will also like the other more. Cultural differences also influence whether mentoring actually occurs. In Hispanic cultures people often place a high emphasis on the family unit for support, and this tendency might make individuals from those cultures reluctant to reach out to a mentor outside of this family circle.[21] The culture of the host country also influences how much informal mentoring an expat receives. A study of 179 expats in 19 countries showed that expats were more likely to receive informal mentoring in countries with a lower power distance and uncertainty avoidance.[22] In cultures with a high power distance there is more of a gap between supervisors and subordinates. Supervisors are seen as inaccessible, which does not make it easy for their subordinates to reach out for mentoring. A low score on uncertainty avoidance means that people in authority positions feel the responsibility to help others, and that conflict and doing things differently is more accepted. This attitude helps informal mentoring relationships to develop.

The second stage of mentoring is about setting up the relationship where cultural differences influence the expectations that both individuals have about their roles. What is a good mentor? The United States and Europe have a different emphasis in mentoring, where in the United States there seems to be more emphasis on the mentor being a senior employee who will help the career of the mentee by giving them opportunities or helping them be more visible. The German vice-president of operations in the United States mentioned in the previous chapter (p. 134) has such a mentor in his boss:

> I'm studying MBA, and he approved that and pushed me to do that and gives me… I mean, that's pretty time intense and he does give me the time off to do that. […] He always supports me, and he has a good network in the U.S. if I need somebody or something he helps me with that, it's for sure one major reason why I'm still here. He is pretty good in that.

In Europe, many mentoring relationships are more focused on personal development and growth, with career development only coming second.[23]

Even though these differences in emphasis are important to be aware of, mentoring in general has developed over the years towards two-way learning, and towards dialogue and asking good questions instead of the mentor having all the answers.

The third stage of mentoring is where the relationship is built. Cultural differences might make communication more difficult, so it is important to be aware of this challenge and have the intercultural competence to deal with these differences. Individualism versus collectivism – whether a society emphasises the individual or the community – is one dimension where cultures differ, which can have an influence on the mentoring relationship.[24] For example, a mentee from a more collectivistic culture might be more relationship-oriented rather than getting a job done. A mentor from an individualist culture might then draw the wrong conclusions if the mentee is late for a meeting and interpret a cultural difference as evidence of a weak character or a lack of professionalism. Also, in collectivist cultures it is important to build relationships first, to spend time with each other to establish trust and not to jump right in to immediately focus on the task. This trust is key for mentoring relationships to work. In more collectivist cultures it is important for mentors to be sensitive when giving feedback to avoid the mentee losing face. Another cultural dimension that is important in this growth phase is power distance, since mentees in a high power distance culture might not want to disagree with their mentor. A low power distance mentor might become disappointed in a high power distance mentee who does not engage in lively discussions where different opinions are being debated. The high power distance mentee might remain silent to avoid being seen as confrontational, and the low power distance mentor might in turn conclude mistakenly that the relationship is simply not working out.[25]

A mentoring relationship can continue to develop and become more stable, reaching the maturation phase. The cultural differences as described previously still play a role in this phase, but to a decreasing extent because the mentor and mentee have learned how to best deal with these differences. Then, at some point, the mentoring relationship will end, or transition into another type of relationship such as a more meaningful and long-term friendship that also exists outside of the workplace. A mentoring relationship might end prematurely if expectations are not met, trust is lost or priorities shift.[26] Cultural differences also influence this final phase of the mentoring relationship. Collectivist cultures value loyalty and relationships of infinite duration, so collectivist mentees might feel offended if an individualist mentor feels their job is done and would like to end the mentoring relationship.[27]

## Mentoring needs of expats

Mentoring can really help expats in their workplace. An important starting point is to look at the needs of the mentee, when determining what kind of 'developmental network' should be set up. A person might have different mentors, not only over time, throughout their career, but also at one particular moment in time. It is very difficult for one mentor to meet all the mentee's needs, especially with careers changing much more quickly than they used to in the past. Two Professors at University of Miami, John M. Mezias and Teresa Scandura, have made an overview of the different needs an expat has before, during and after their assignment, and what kind of mentor could address those needs.[28] They mainly focus on expats who are sent from headquarters to the local subsidiary in a host country (the so-called parent country nationals or PCNs), but in this chapter I will also look at the mentoring needs of other types of expats, such as third country nationals (expats from a different nationality than headquarters and the host country), inpatriates (expats who are sent from a local subsidiary to headquarters) and self-initiated expats. It is important to take into account all types of global talent in an organisation, and not just take care of the PCNs. Especially host country nationals – those who work in the local subsidiary – are an important group to also take into consideration. They are the largest group of employees in a multinational corporation and play an important role in knowledge management. Sending host country nationals on expat assignments can be a great way to develop this source of global talent.

### From headquarters to a host country: parent country nationals

The most traditional type of expat is the so-called parent country national (PCN), where an expat from headquarters is sent abroad to a local subsidiary. When expats are offered an international assignment, they could benefit from discussing this opportunity with a home country mentor. A mentor at headquarters who is higher in the hierarchy than the expat would be able to give a realistic preview of what the assignment would be like, and whether it is a good idea or not in terms of their career. Such a 'sponsoring mentor' could also provide ongoing support throughout the assignment, in linking the expat with headquarters so that they are not 'out of sight out of mind.' A mentor at headquarters can also be very valuable for when the expat returns home. They can make sure that the repatriation is considered from the beginning, when the decision to send an expat abroad is taken. They can also help the expat settle back into the home office. A sponsoring mentor can also support the expat in their further career, assessing how best to use the knowledge and skills gained from the international assignment, and thereby retain the expat – turnover after repatriation is one of the biggest problems when managing expats.[29] A sponsoring mentor often has the same nationality as the expat, but even though there are no cultural differences, there is a geographical barrier, once the expat is abroad, that can provide challenges and has to be managed.

The expat will also need to adjust to a new culture both in the workplace and in private life. A peer mentor is the best choice here – someone who is on a similar hierarchical level as the expat, because peer mentoring relationships offer more informational and social support than a hierarchical mentoring relationship. To make sure this mentoring takes place, organisations can appoint a local colleague as buddy or local host (see Chapters 7–9), or they can stimulate the creation of informal relationships through organising events where colleagues come together (see the Recommendations for expats, organisations and societies). Organisations can also encourage expats to join local expat clubs that support newcomers – there are even local clubs that encourage networking among expats. One example is the Professional Women's Network[30] that has a global community with presence in many different countries. For better adjustment to the new challenging work role – for example, expats often have more responsibility abroad than they had in their previous position – it can be very helpful to also have a hierarchical mentor. The expat's supervisor in the host country can be very helpful because they are likely to have a good grasp of the role of the local subsidiary in the multinational corporation and can also discuss longer-term career goals with the expat.

Multinational corporations often have many expats, and their expertise can be used in many ways. Returning expats or 'repats' can serve as a peer mentor for expats who are going on an international assignment; they can help with preparing the expat for working abroad in the often very short period of time between the decision and departure. Similarly, they can mentor newly returned repats and help them readjust to the workplace. An additional benefit is that this is an excellent way to use the knowledge and skills a repat has gained during their international assignment. One of the most important reasons for turnover upon repatriation is a lack of interest and value placed by the organisation on the international experience that is gained.[31] By using their knowledge and skills in this way, the organisation can show that the international experience is indeed valued.

### From one host country to the next: third country nationals

Multinational corporations can also choose an expat of a different nationality than headquarters, and these expats are called third country nationals (TCNs). These can be host country nationals who are given the opportunity to work in another country, which is a great way to develop their global leadership capacities. TCNs are often used because they are familiar with a specific region and maybe also the language, and are often cheaper to send than a PCN from headquarters. TCNs could benefit from peer mentoring by local colleagues from the host country to help adjust to the new culture, as well as by local PCN expats who have a greater knowledge and understanding of career opportunities and more network connections within the organisation. Mentoring should take into account that TCNs might lack background knowledge about the organisation because they do not come from headquarters. Another potential barrier is that the locals of the host country might not be very supportive of TCNs who come from neighbouring countries; there might be historical, political and social sources of tension and conflict, which organisations should be aware of when sending a TCN to a host country. Also, even if TCNs might be more familiar with the country and language, there still might be cultural differences that they have to adjust to. This is the cultural similarity paradox which happens when expats move to a country where they presume more cultural similarity and easier adjustment than is actually the case.[32] Having more difficulty than expected hinders their adjustment and performance.

### From a host country to headquarters: inpats

Locals from the host country can also be sent on an expat assignment to headquarters and become so-called inpatriates or inpats. Inpatriate assignments are a very good way to develop locals of the host country, who are often a neglected source of global talent. Such assignments often have the goal to develop the leadership capacities of the inpat before they return to their home country and continue their careers in the local subsidiary of the organisation. In the previous chapter (p. 130), the Danish vice-president of Asia-Pacific in Malaysia had a country manager whom they had brought to Denmark on an inpat assignment, so that he could learn about Danish culture and the company and become a 'translator' both ways. The inpat will need to adjust to the new workplace culture, which is where a hierarchical manager, for example the manager of the inpat at headquarters, can offer support. Such a mentor can also discuss career opportunities in terms of returning to the host country. The inpat also will need to adjust to a new culture outside of the workplace, and, as with the other types of expats, a peer mentor from the host country is most suitable for this support.

### Self-initiated expats

An additional category of expats are self-initiated expats who are not sent by an organisation but go abroad on their own initiative. Organisations who are interested in using mentoring to support their global talent should consider two specific types of self-initiated expats with regard to their mentoring needs. The first group consists of assigned expats who decide to stay in the host country when their assignment ends, when they transition to a local contract. They are called localised expats or LOPATs.[33] They are in for the long run and could use peer support with settling into the host country on a more permanent basis. Locals from the host country – colleagues and/or friends – could help the expat with this support, and an organisation could stimulate this by connecting the expat with a local host (Chapters 7–9). In the workplace, LOPATs face specific challenges because of their distance to headquarters now that they decided to not go back. They might feel more rooted in the host country and 'go native,' and this new identification might be negatively seen by headquarters. The best mentors for these challenges are probably other LOPATs who know the feeling and have found ways to manage it.

The second group of self-initiated expats whose mentoring needs should be considered are foreign executives in local organisations, or FELOs.[34] These are people who are hired by a local organisation because they possess the skills to lead the organisation. This can be a good solution when the organisation is growing very fast, and there is no time to develop talent from within the organisation. When such a foreign executive is hired, the organisation would do well to appoint a formal mentor who can help introduce them to the organisation and ways of working. In addition, the foreign executive could benefit from peer mentoring by locals of the host country – both within the workplace as well as in private life – to facilitate settling into the host country on a more permanent basis, especially if the foreign executive is new to the host country.

### Facilitating mentoring

So, how should one set up a mentoring programme that best enables the mentee to learn? For this task, we can use a process model for personal learning introduced by Melenie J. Lankau and Teresa Scandura,[35] which provides a guiding framework with several choices an organisation needs to make for each developmental relationship. They argue that one should first determine the learning context; what development need does the mentee have? We have seen in the previous section that expats have different needs depending on what type of expat they are and their particular stage of the assignment. Clearly defining mentee needs will help in the selection of multiple mentors who can then support the expat throughout the assignment; for example, a host country mentor to help with the adjustment to both the new workplace and the host country culture, and a home country mentor to help maintain a link to the home country. To make sure that these mentoring needs are met, organisations may want to set up formal mentoring systems, and not rely only on informal mentoring relationships being created by the expats themselves. This way, organisations can be sure that the mentoring actually happens. One example is setting up a buddy programme where expats are connected with a local from the host country, as is discussed in the next chapter.

Several other aspects of the mentoring relationship influence the outcomes in terms of personal learning and growth, such as how the mentor facilitates learning by providing challenging assignments and offering social support to the mentee. This learning can go both ways, if the mentor is willing to change roles from expert to learner. The learning in a developmental relationship is also influenced by characteristics of both the learner and the developer, such as whether one is openminded and willing to learn from the other and believes they can improve their competence (I have also discussed this growth mindset in Chapter 3 on p. 79). Carefully considering all these aspects of a mentoring relationship will increase its success.

Implicit in the process model of personal learning is the quality of the relationship, which has been shown to be important when setting up mentoring relationships.[36] But how can organisations influence this? I also delve deeper into this particular aspect in Chapter 8 when discussing how the quality of the contact was important for expats who were put in touch with a local host – one way of increasing the likelihood of informal peer mentoring taking place.

The literature on mentoring has some tips as well. To increase the chances of successful intercultural mentoring relationships, it is important that both mentor and mentee are interculturally competent (see also Chapter 3 which contains exercises for developing intercultural competence). Cross-cultural training can help raise intercultural awareness and develop the skills needed for effective and appropriate intercultural interactions. Such training is often offered to expats when they are sent on an international assignment, but can also be very helpful if one takes part in an intercultural mentoring relationship. Both mentors and mentees should learn as much as possible about each other's cultural values, assumptions and expectations before engaging in a mentoring relationship to get off to a good start and realise the full potential of the relationship. Organisations can also offer specific mentoring training,[37] with an emphasis not only on how cultural differences may influence the mentoring relationship but also on what mentors and mentees can do to increase the chances for successful interactions. One example is to set ground rules to enable open communication, and to discuss the expectations of both mentor and mentee early on in the relationship.[38]

Apart from setting up formal mentoring programmes and offering training, organisations should provide an environment that values and rewards mentoring relationships, for example through reward systems.[39] The organisation could emphasise the importance of developing others through mentoring and evaluate and reward employees on their effectiveness as mentors. The HR department could also explore various strategies to enhance cultural awareness between mentoring partners, which can benefit the entire workforce of the organisation. More will be covered on this topic in Chapters 7–9 and in the Recommendations for expats, organisations and societies, where I discuss how organisations can encourage contact between expats and the locals of the host country. One way of facilitating this interaction is through connecting the expat with a local host or buddy. In the next chapter, I will discuss these buddy systems and my research on this topic.

Intercultural mentoring is on the rise, and it is important to take cultural differences into account to increase the success of such developmental relationships. There are many different types of expats, and this chapter has shown that all these types of expats have their own specific developmental needs that are important to take into account when setting up mentoring relationships. In particular, it is important to pay attention to the role of locals of the host country in mentoring: they can act as mentors for expats and help them adjust to the new host country (see also Chapter 5 for the various roles that locals of the host country can play), and they also can be mentees themselves. Locals from the host country are the largest group of employees in multinational corporations, and, therefore, an important source of global talent that should not be neglected.

## Notes

1  In this chapter I focus on mentoring, which is more long term than coaching and has a primary focus on professional and career development instead of immediate, current work performance (van Bakel, M., Vaiman, V., Vance, C. M., & Haslberger, A. (2022). Broadening international mentoring: Contexts and dynamics of expatriate and HCN intercultural mentoring. *Journal of Global Mobility: The Home of Expatriate Management Research, 10*(1), 14–35).

2  Ragins, B. R., & Kram, K. E. (2007a). *The handbook of mentoring at work: Theory, research, and practice.* Thousand Oaks, CA: Sage.

3  Feldman, D., & Bolino, M. (1999). The impact of on-site mentoring on expatriate socialization: A structural equation modelling approach. *International Journal of Human Resource Management, 10*(1), 54–71.

4  Gentry, W. A., Weber, T. J., & Sadri, G. (2008). Examining career-related mentoring and managerial performance across cultures: A multilevel analysis. *Journal of Vocational Behavior, 72*(2), 241–253.

5  Bryant, S. E. (2005). The impact of peer mentoring on organizational knowledge creation and sharing an empirical study in a software firm. *Group and Organization Management, 30*(3), 319–338.

6  Klinge, C. M. (2015). A conceptual framework for mentoring in a learning organization. *Adult Learning, 26*(4), 160–166.

7  Payne, S. C., & Huffman, A. H. (2005). A longitudinal examination of the influence of mentoring on organizational commitment and turnover. *Academy of Management Journal, 48*(1), 158–168.

8  Not all mentoring in an international context is intercultural, for example when an expat has a home-country mentor and share the same culture. Although there may be minimal cultural differences between the two, the mentor and mentee have to deal with geographical separation and being immersed in different cultural environments.

9  Alon, I., & Higgins, J. M. (2005). Global leadership success through emotional and cultural intelligences. *Business Horizons, 48*(6), 501–512.

10  Crocitto, M. M., Sullivan, S. E., & Carraher, S. M. (2005). Global mentoring as a means of career development and knowledge creation: A learning-based framework and agenda for future research. *Career Development International, 10*(6/7), 522–535.

11  Ragins, B. R., & Kram, K. E. (2007b). The roots and meaning of mentoring. In B. R. Ragins & K. E. Kram (Eds.), *The handbook of mentoring at work: Theory, research, and practice* (pp. 3–15). Thousand Oaks, CA: Sage.

12  Ragins and Kram (2007b).

13  Hall, D. T., & Chandler, D. E. (2007). Career cycles and mentoring. In B. R. Ragins & K. E. Kram (Eds.), *The handbook of mentoring at work: Theory, research, and practice* (pp. 471–497). Thousand Oaks, CA: Sage.

14  Hall and Chandler (2007).

15  Baugh, S. G., & Fagenson-Eland, E. A. (2007). Formal mentoring programs. In B. R. Ragins & K. E. Kram (Eds.), *The handbook of mentoring at work: Theory, research and practice* (pp. 249–271). Thousand Oaks, CA: Sage

16  McManus, S. E., & Russell, J. E. (2007). Peer mentoring relationships. In B. R. Ragins & K. E. Kram (Eds.), *The handbook of mentoring at work: Theory, research, and practice* (pp. 273–298). Thousand Oaks, CA: Sage.

17  Harvey, M., McIntyre, N., Thompson Heames, J., & Moeller, M. (2009). Mentoring global female managers in the global marketplace: Traditional, reverse, and reciprocal mentoring. *International Journal of Human Resource Management, 20*(6), 1344–1361.

18 Ensher, E. A., & Murphy, S. E. (2007). E-mentoring. In B. R. Ragins & K. E. Kram (Eds.), *The handbook of mentoring at work: Theory, research, and practice* (pp. 299–322). Thousand Oaks, CA: Sage.

19 Osula, B. and S. M. Irvin (2009). Cultural awareness in intercultural mentoring: A model for enhancing mentoring relationships. *International Journal of Leadership Studies, 5*(1): 37–50.

20 Young, C. A., Haffejee, B., & Corsun, D. L. (2018). Developing cultural intelligence and empathy through diversified mentoring relationships. *Journal of Management Education, 42*(3), 319–346.

21 Murphy, S. E., & Ensher, E. A. (1997). The effects of culture on mentoring relationships: A developmental model. In C. S. Granrose & S. Oskamp (Eds.), *Cross-cultural work groups* (pp. 212–233). Thousand Oaks, CA: Sage.

22 Feldman, D., & Bolino, M. (1999). The impact of on-site mentoring on expatriate socialization: A structural equation modelling approach. *International Journal of Human Resource Management, 10*(1), 54–71.

23 Clutterbuck, D. (2007). An international perspective on mentoring. In B. R. Ragins & K. E. Kram (Eds.), *The handbook of mentoring at work: Theory, research, and practice* (pp. 633–656). Thousand Oaks, CA: Sage.

24 Osula and Irwin (2009).

25 Osula and Irwin (2009).

26 Murphy and Ensher (1997).

27 Osula and Irwin (2009).

28 Mezias, J. M., & Scandura, T. A. (2005). A needs-driven approach to expatriate adjustment and career development: A multiple mentoring perspective. *Journal of International Business Studies, 36*(5), 519–538.

29 Kraimer, M., Bolino, M., & Mead, B. (2016). Themes in expatriate and repatriate research over four decades: What do we know and what do we still need to learn. *Annual Review of Organizational Psychology and Organizational Behavior, 3*(1), 83–109.

30 https://pwnglobal.net/ (accessed on 18 August 2023).

31 Szkudlarek, B. (2010). Reentry – A review of the literature. *International Journal of Intercultural Relations, 34*, 1–21.

32 Vromans, P., Van Engen, M., & Mol, S. T. (2013). Presumed cultural similarity paradox: Expatriate adjustment and performance across the border or over the globe. *Journal of Global Mobility, 1*(2), 219–238.

33 Tait, E., De Cieri, H., & McNulty, Y. (2014). The opportunity cost of saving money: An exploratory study of permanent transfers and localization of expatriates in Singapore. *International Studies of Management & Organization, 44*(3), 80–95.

34 Arp, F., Hutchings, K., & A. Smith, W. (2013). Foreign executives in local organisations: An exploration of differences to other types of expatriates. *Journal of Global Mobility, 1*(3), 312–335.

35 Lankau, M. J., & Scandura, T. A. (2007). Mentoring as a forum for personal learning in organizations. In B. R. Ragins & K. E. Kram (Eds.), *The handbook of mentoring at work: Theory, research, and practice*. Thousand Oaks, CA: Sage.

36  Eby, L. T. d. T., Allen, T. D., Hoffman, B. J., Baranik, L. E., Sauer, J. B., Baldwin, S., . . . Evans, S. C. (2013). An interdisciplinary meta-analysis of the potential antecedents, correlates, and consequences of protégé perceptions of mentoring. *Psychological Bulletin, 139*(2), 441.
37  Osula and Irwin (2009).
38  Clutterbuck (2007).
39  Murphy and Ensher (1997).

# Part III

# How to bridge the gap

# Experience

A Belgian expat and his partner in the Netherlands – "We have created a friendship"

*Antoine and Marie are a cosmopolitan couple, originally from Belgium, in their forties and with three kids, two of which who are grown up and moved out. They have lived for 2-3 years each time in many countries around the world for Antoine's job at a French multinational corporation, and arrived in the Netherlands for a stay of three years. In 2008, they enthusiastically signed up for my PhD project, in which I put them in touch with Johan and Annelies, a Dutch host family that was 20 years older than them, also with two grown up kids, and having lived abroad in two different countries for a total of 5 years. When I contacted them again in 2023, they had continued the friendship, and had met several times in Belgium and also in Uganda and Singapore when Antoine and Marie were posted there.*

## What have you done together?[1]

Johan: For our first meeting, they came for tea at our house, and we went for a walk. Then they invited us for dinner at their place, which was very *gezellig*.[2] We also visited a few places and museums together, for example, we went for a walk in Gouda and Katwijk, and we visited the *Keukenhof* – also together with Marie's parents – and a Japanese garden.

## Why did you sign up for this project?

Marie: When we returned from our previous posting in Africa, I felt a bit alone here. I also thought it was interesting to meet people of the country itself, and learn about their culture.

Antoine: I was curious about it, but I would say it's more Marie who pushed it because she is a bit more by herself during the day. I meet colleagues all the time. But I am very happy we

DOI: 10.4324/9781003246855-18

participated because Johan and Annelies were basically the only Dutch family we met outside of work.

## How did you enjoy the contact?

*Antoine*:    It was good from the start. They are really very kind, both of them. It was really great.

*Marie*:    It worked out very well, the host family is super, they are very pleasant. They also speak French very well. We don't have to make an effort to talk, not in English nor in French. They really wear their hearts on their sleeve, and we have done a lot of things together.

*Johan*:    It was very relaxed. We shared a common interest in art, we had enjoyable dinners together, and *gezellige* conversations about anything and everything (children, parents, living abroad).

*Annelies*:    The expats were really nice and enthusiastic.

## What did you enjoy the most?

*Marie*:    Just the *fact that you can meet up with people, other families outside of the workplace.*

*Antoine*:    *The m*ost important part for us was the discovery of the place we are in, and to do this with nice people, with whom it is a pleasure to be.

## Did the contact help you in any way?

*Antoine*:    At least now we know a little bit of the Dutch, have a better understanding of the country we are in. This is always a bit frustrating, if you go somewhere and you leave without having met any locals, then somewhere you tell yourself you're missing something. I don't want to lock myself into the world of expatriates.

*Marie*:    Yes, I have a very different opinion of the Netherlands than at the start, when I didn't feel like going out to discover another country. It's not always easy to make new friends. We are changing countries every three years, so… My husband goes to work where he meets colleagues, so it's much easier for him. I am at home, and then it's up to me to go meet people, because if I have to wait until people come to me, then you will wait forever. The project has facilitated a lot in terms of having this contact with a local family. And we have created a friendship. That is important for me and I think that we'll keep in touch and keep being friends.

## Was the contact always with the four of you?

*Antoine*:  Yes, and sometimes my parents and parents-in-law joined us, for example when we went to the *Keukenhof*. What is very nice with the host family, is that we visited a new place every time. So we learned a lot about the Netherlands, and then we always had a nice dinner.

## Could anything be improved in the contact?

*Johan*:  The only issue sometimes was that Antoine and Marie were very busy with visits to family and friends – now that they are located close to their home in Belgium as opposed to somewhere in Africa, they are catching up. Marie also has started up all kinds of social activities, and our calendars are also quite busy.

*Antoine*:  No, honestly, I don't see any downside. Seriously. If there would have been downsides, we would have stopped somewhere seeing each other. I think it worked well because they also have been abroad. They have this first opening of the mind and know what it is, to change to a new country. [...] I believe that if you meet nice people, you will find things in common.

## Notes

1  All the information comes from e-mails, open-ended questions in surveys of all four participants, and individual interviews with Antoine and Marie.
2  *Gezellig* is a unique Dutch word that means something like 'conviviality,' 'coziness,' 'fun'. It is somewhat similar to the Danish word *hygge*.

# Chapter 7

# The value of buddy systems

## Introduction

Buddy systems have been long in use in many different variations to indicate that someone pairs up with another person. The term goes back to 1895, and originally the goal of this pairing is to look after each other's safety or welfare,[1] for example when diving. Nowadays, there are buddies for many different reasons and in many different settings, such as the army, churches and schools. Also in the health sector, buddies have been found to be useful to stimulate the right behaviours that support health, for example for people who have diabetes or who want to stop smoking. A buddy system is a way to support a person and can be seen as a form of peer mentoring (see also Chapter 6).

## Buddy systems for international students

Quite a few studies have been done on how a buddy can help international students when they arrive. Many international students would like to have more contact with local students during their studies, but it is hard for them to form such friendships.[2] To support international students, many universities and student associations now offer a peer mentor or buddy,[3] which has a lot of benefits. A buddy helps international students integrate better into the host society and interact with locals. In one Canadian study,[4] international students were put in touch with a host student for 3 months. They were encouraged to meet weekly, explore campus and the local community together, and practice conversational English. The results show that the international students were better adjusted socially, felt more comfortable living in the host country and were less stressed about this whole process than those who did not have a buddy. A buddy helps the international student to adjust to social life in the host country, which can also help the international student in their academic life. One study done in Canada and Australia[5] showed that international students

DOI: 10.4324/9781003246855-19

*Figure 7.1* The value of buddy systems. Illustration by Heldermaker.

who were put in touch with a host student for a period of 8 months had higher academic averages and were less likely to have dropped out than a comparable group of international students without buddy.

Connecting international students with host students also has effects on the buddy, especially with regard to intercultural learning and the development of intercultural competence. One host student said about their experience of being a buddy to an international student in New Zealand: "This project has enhanced my awareness of cultures around me. It helped me to learn the value of communication and the importance of sharing cultures with different people."[6] The host students also became more aware of their own culture, and when they were ethnocentric or using stereotypes. Many host students also felt personal satisfaction to help an international student settle in:

It was very rewarding and satisfying to know that I had done a small part for one person in helping them to incorporate and integrate themselves into our society and making a lifelong friend in the process made it even more gratifying.[7]

Being connected with a buddy from a different cultural background can also help the development of intercultural friendships. As compared to several initiatives to increase intercultural contact such as housing international students together with host students and putting them together in the classroom, it was the connection with a buddy that led to more friendships with local students in Argentina.[8] A study at an urban U.S. college[9] showed that having a buddy led to intercultural friendships through increasing knowledge and developing a positive attitude about the other's culture, especially if the student did not know much about that culture beforehand. For an intercultural communication course, students had to complete an assignment where they would focus on a different 'culture' through connecting with another student who could be different not only in terms of nationality but also religion or lifestyle. Six months after being connected with a culturally dissimilar buddy, 23% of the students had become friends or close friends with them.

Buddy systems have been applied to international students for many years in many different countries, and have resulted in a better social adjustment to the host country, more intercultural learning and even in better academic results. What if you were to do the same but then for expats who go abroad for their jobs, and might also need some support?

## In touch with the Dutch

For my PhD project,[10] I put 33 expats in touch with a buddy or local host, as I called them, in the Netherlands for 9 months, and compared them with 32 expats without a host. Through surveys and interviews I wanted to see whether this local host would help with adjustment, performance, intercultural competence and social support. The expats were matched to a Dutch local host, where I mainly ensured that they would live close to each other so that it would be easy to meet up, and that they had a similar age and family situation with regard to having a partner and children. You can read more about the matching process and what I learned about it in Chapter 9. The expats and host family were put in touch via e-mail with a short introduction of both parties, and then they could organise the first meet up. The expats did a great variety of activities with their hosts, from just having drinks or dinner together to touristic outings such as a visit to a city, a brewery or the floral park *Keukenhof*. I have to admit I got slightly jealous when I heard that one expat took their host flying in a little plane over the Netherlands, so they could see it from the sky.

### The effect of contact with a local host

While there certainly were some effects of the contact with a local host in terms of adjustment, social support and intercultural competence, I didn't find any effect on expat job performance. This was also not very surprising since the contact with the host took place outside of the workplace, and job performance is influenced by a whole host of other factors such as one's knowledge and skills which are probably more important than whether someone has a local host where they learn more about the culture and get social support.

### Adjustment

The first finding was that the contact with a local host helps with adjusting to the interactions with people from the country in general,[11] which makes a lot of sense. A U.S. American expat said:

> I think that, you know, when I go back and tell people stories about the Dutch and I certainly do tell things about the office, but a lot of things I've learned about the Dutch I learned more from watching how the host family interacts with their kids, how they interact with their neighbours, how they serve their meals and have coffee, and snap the cookie jar shut.

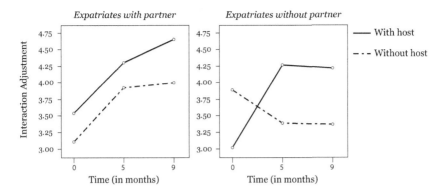

*Figure 7.2* Effect of a local host on the interaction adjustment of expats (with partner and without partner).

It is common in the Netherlands to present only one cookie with a cup of tea or coffee. This caused some stress for another expat in my study when she was getting a visit from her Dutch host. She was a bit torn by the number of cookies she should present on a platter, being aware of this 'rule' but also wanting to appear hospitable. A local host was especially important for single expats because having a partner also helps this interaction adjustment; it seems that partners are an additional source of information about interacting with the host population (Figure 7.2).

## Social support

The results also show that a local host is a good support system for the expat.[12] Expats who had a local host received more social support from locals than those without a host (Figure 7.3). A Canadian expat said: "Meeting with the host meant caring stimulating encounters and it made me feel welcome and cared for. There was someone to listen to me. It is a very meaningful connection." This effect took some time to show, which makes sense because the contact with the local host is newly created. The relationship has to be built up first before an expat would feel comfortable talking about what they struggle with and the local host could offer emotional support, as in the quote above. Expats and hosts also became friends, already within the time span of the project. A U.S. American expat said:

I think for us it worked because we became friends very quickly; we have a lot in common; we enjoy each other's company a lot and did

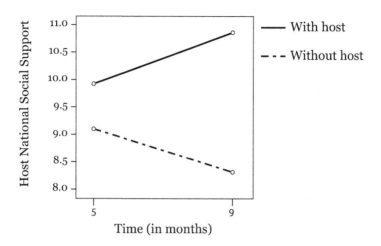

*Figure 7.3* The effect of a local host on social support received from locals of the host country.

quite a few things together very early on. In the first few weeks, we met up about twice a week.

Some of the connections also stood the test of time. About 2 years after the data collection had finished, I contacted all the participants of the study, and found that 31% of the expats were still in touch with their host. Almost half of these relationships even spanned more than 3 years, and expats had become long-term friends with their host. A British expat (see also Experience on p. 179) said 2 years and 4 months after the project finished: "We have become friends and share our social circles." The expat couple in Experience on p. 159 were even still in touch with their local host 15 years later. This suggests that the contact with a local host has potential in the long run, when a friendship is developed between the expat and the local host.

### Intercultural competence

A third area of results was with regard to intercultural competence, which is very important when building new relationships across cultures (see also Chapter 3). I looked at aspects of all three components – knowledge, attitude and skills – to see whether a local host influenced the intercultural competence of expats.[13] Starting with intercultural knowledge, the majority of the expats learned about Dutch culture during the contact with their local host. A German expat said: "Just getting a reliable 'Dutch'

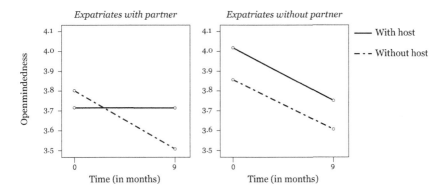

*Figure 7.4* The effect of a local host on the openmindedness of expats (with partner and without partner).

opinion about aspects of other Dutch people's behaviour helps to break down mental barriers – prejudices, misunderstandings due to stress and everyday hassles."

The second component of intercultural competence is the motivation or attitude one has with regard to communicating with people from other cultural backgrounds. I looked at openmindedness, and found an unexpected effect. Instead of increasing in openmindedness, I found that a local host buffered a decrease for expats who had a partner (Figure 7.4). The general decrease on openmindedness that I found might be explained by the expats coming to the Netherlands with an open mind, ready to establish life there and make contact with the Dutch, and then found the reality more difficult than expected. Their expectations might have been too optimistic, resulting in a decrease in openmindedness. One U.S. American expat partner told me that they started out very enthusiastic with the aim of making the Netherlands their home, but that they realised over time that she did not like many small things of daily life in the Netherlands:

And I've noticed more and more [these little things] and I think "is it me?" am I doing something that is pissing them off? Or is it just how people are here? Because I don't understand them. I don't know if they do it to me, or if they do it to themselves as well. Because if I would understand Dutch, I could see "oh, they do it between themselves as well, it's fine." But I don't know.

Ultimately, they decided they did not want to stay in the Netherlands and would leave as soon as the contract expired. They did not want to live in a society that they felt did not accept them, no matter what they tried.

Having contact with a Dutch local host might counteract this decrease in openmindedness. Another U.S. American expat said:

> But if you have that family contact, a normal family, whether it's a guy with his girlfriend or just a guy that takes you to meet his parents one day for a weekend, you go bowling or whatever, where you see normal Dutch people interacting, I think you get a different perspective of their cultures, not to see the negatives that you see here by yourself.

Interestingly enough, the buffering effect of a local host only happened for expats who had a partner. There are two possible explanations for this. First, I tried to match for family situation, which means that expats who had a partner were, where possible, also put in touch with a local host that was a couple. This means that there were two Dutch persons willing to meet the expat, and the interaction also got richer because there were more people involved. This might prevent this decrease in openmindedness. Another explanation is that single expats can't share their experiences with a significant other. If an expat has been in touch with the host and the partner is also part of that experience, they are likely to talk about it, reinforcing the positive effect of the event. This is called capitalisation.[14] By retelling and reliving a positive experience, it might become more salient and easily remembered, and it might counterbalance more successfully any disappointing experiences the expat might have had with the Dutch. This would explain the buffering expat of contact with the local host for partners. Single expats might not benefit from this capitalisation because they don't have a significant other to share the experiences with.

The third component of intercultural competence are skills. There are a great many skills that have been linked with intercultural competence,[15]

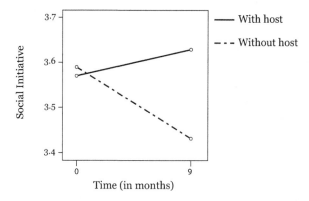

*Figure 7.5* The effect of a local host on the expat's social initiative.

but here I focus particularly on social initiative and cultural empathy. For social initiative, which is about actively approaching social situations and taking initiative, I found a similar result as for openmindedness: expats decreased on social initiative unless they were put in touch with a local host (Figure 7.5). Also here, a local host had a buffering effect. Expats might have too optimistic expectations with regard to trying to make contact with the Dutch after arriving in the Netherlands. If they can't get in touch with the Dutch as easily as they expected, they might take fewer initiatives to meet Dutch people, and decrease in social initiative altogether.

A second skill for which I, surprisingly, did not find an effect was cultural empathy, or the ability to empathise with the feelings, thoughts and behaviours of members from different cultural groups. While my study showed that the expats learned about Dutch culture, this knowledge might not so easily translate into behaviour. One U.S. American expat partner had an interesting experience with the Dutch waiting in the queue to pay for tickets for the floral park *Keukenhof*. In her opinion, the Dutch behind her were standing too close, and when she had paid for her ticket, the man behind her told her she should be more careful when entering her pin code, because he could see it. She said:

> At first this man made me very mad. I kept thinking about how in the US people allow much more distance between each other when they wait in line. It is an unspoken rule that you do not touch people when waiting in line and therefore I would not have to hide entering my pin because there would be enough distance between me and the person behind me to protect this information. After a few deep breaths and some logical thinking, I remembered that I am a guest in another country and that in this country lines are very different and that the man behind me was giving me good advice based on the unspoken rules of this country.

### Partners

In my PhD I focused both on expats – those who came to the Netherlands for their work – and their partners, who might not be working (yet). It might be that a local host has similar benefits for partners as for expats themselves;[16] the data did show some indication of similar effects with regard to interaction adjustment, the establishment of friendships and learning about Dutch culture. It is also possible that the contact with a local host should be adjusted so that non-working partners would benefit more from this contact, since they could meet up more easily during the week than the expat who would be at work. One of the criteria for matching an expat was the family situation, so I tried to connect an expat couple with a local host couple. This often meant that much of the contact took place with all four there, even though meeting up with one of the hosts separately was certainly also possible. A French expat partner said:

[one of the hosts] normally works a bit less, so only the two of us should have met up, but she was very busy with the house and her son, so in fact we didn't see each other that much. I think we've seen each other four or five times. And each time it was with the four of us.

It could be interesting to see what benefits a partner would experience if the local host was particularly matched to the partner, and not to the couple, so that they could meet up more regularly than the expat might have time for due to their job.

## Connecting with a Danish colleague

In 2018, I had another opportunity to connect expats with locals through funding I received from a Danish ministry that wanted to find ways in which better to integrate expats into Danish society. This time I connected expat academics at my own university to a local colleague, to study whether this would have more work-related effects. The contact was expected to last 6 months, and the buddy was a colleague at the university – but preferably not a direct colleague. The participants also filled out a survey before and after those 6 months, and with the help of some students I interviewed 17 expat academics and 10 hosts.

Over a period of 2 years, I put 42 expat academics in touch with a local colleague. In six cases, this colleague was 'local' in a different sense, namely that they had lived in Denmark for a very long time but were not Danish. In Chapter 9, we'll also have a look at the choices an organisation can make in the setup of a buddy system, one of them is whether the local host is from the host country or not but has lived in the host country for a long time. The contact was facilitated through vouchers. Every pair received a voucher for the canteen, so they could have a free lunch together. During the 6 months of the contact, I also offered each pair at least twice another voucher with a discount for a café or restaurant in Odense, where most of the pairs were located.

### Making local friends

I was, of course, curious about whether having a local host in the workplace had additional effects, for example in terms of expat performance but also their attachment to the organisation. For the quantitative analyses, I compared this group of expat academics with a comparable group of 45 expat academics who did not get a local colleague as host. While the groups were similar in terms of gender, age and having partner and/or children, the group who signed up for the project had less contact with Danes and fewer Danish friends and were more motivated to stay in Denmark. This might explain why they signed up for the project in the first place, and shows that there is a need among expats to participate in activities that help them socialise with locals.

Unfortunately, it still seems like the sample size is too small to be able to find many statistically significant differences, but there are some patterns in the data that suggest that having a local colleague as host does have a positive influence. One effect that is significant is that expat academics with a local colleague as host increased the number of Danish friends that they have, whereas this number decreased for the control group. Similarly, expat academics who were put in touch with a local colleague were more satisfied with the number and quality of local friendships they had than those without a local colleague as host. No effect was found on job performance, apart from perhaps one aspect, namely team performance. This difference was, however, not statistically significant, so this can easily be due to chance and should be examined in future research (with larger samples) to find out whether a colleague as local host might help expats work together in teams.

I also examined whether a local colleague as host could help retain expat academics, and there is some indication in the data that a local colleague as host might make the expat academic more committed to stay with the university, but this, again, would need to be tested with a larger sample because the effect was not significant. Being put in touch with a local colleague does not make a difference in the intentions to leave the country – here, it was rather surprising to find that all expat academics increasingly wanted to leave the country, regardless of whether they had a host or not. After 6 months, the expat academics all wanted to leave Denmark more than when they filled out the first survey. Whether this has something to do with the university or with Denmark as a country is the question, but it does suggest that quite a few of the expat academics are seriously considering leaving the country. It also fits in the larger discussion about Denmark's ability to retain the much-needed international talent; it looks like there are challenges there, at least with regard to retaining academic expats.

### Social support and culture learning

To find out more about what precisely happened in the contact, I interviewed 17 expat academics and 10 local colleague hosts. These interviews show many similar benefits as found in my PhD research. The two ways in which contact with host nationals can contribute to expat success are very clear in the data, namely social support and culture learning. In terms of social support, we have seen on page 24 that it consists of two main types of support, namely informational/instrumental support and socioemotional support. Expat academics received both types from their host, although it was clear that informational support was what was provided most. That also makes sense, because informational support is about giving information that can help solve a problem for an expat, and is quite easily provided. For example, one expat academic talked about how to buy a house in Denmark with their host, another got a list of websites with activities that mums can do with their babies. A Norwegian expat academic said:

> she would give me information about anything that I would ask it, if I had any kind of question, I would just run to her and ask her a bunch of questions and she would provide me with any information. No matter if it was job related or it was something about, anything, so she, now we are friends so it's more like [...] she provides me any information that I want.

Another expat academic, from Germany, also really appreciated having a designated person for questions, simply knowing there is someone to ask.

Sometimes the information was related to the workplace: expat academics learned from their host about events at the university, how to get an extension of their contract and the Danish system with regard to unions and how they negotiate salaries for their members. A German expat academic found the contact with her host useful because she could learn about

> how does the university function, what is the university's strategy and so on. So, he is the senior academic in a different department and he has a very good insight into how, you know, a lot of these political processes. And that is often very valuable, because that is the kind of knowledge that you don't find written down anywhere, it is kind of implicit knowledge.

Some hosts also offered instrumental support, for example, help in moving house, translating Danish e-mails and one host even set up a meeting with the spouse of the expat academic to help her find a job in Denmark.

Socioemotional support is about spending time with someone in one's spare time as well as having someone with whom one can discuss problems. Even though emotional support happened much less frequently because a relationship usually needs to have developed a bit before one would find comfortable enough to vent frustrations, there were quite a few examples (see also the Experience of a Chinese expat academic on p. 195). A German expat academic said: "Sometimes we both complained [about something] at some point. Then we would listen to the other," showing how this support also goes both ways, and not just from the host to the expat. Another Chinese expat academic felt supported by her host when he explained that it is normal to feel that it is difficult to make friends with Danes. "So, he was telling me, you know, don't feel like you are kind of alienated. That's the culture here." A participant from India simply appreciated having the opportunity to meet someone and to do activities together.

There was also a lot of learning during the contact with the local colleague, about Danish culture but also the language. Many talked about Danish culture and traditions with regard to birthdays for example, but also about working culture. The local colleague could give a Danish perspective on activities and events. An Italian expat academic said:

> She helped me in understanding better Danish cultural traits. As she works in the same place, but we don't really have occasion to work together, our relation is not biased by the stress of appearing smart. That is why it is a good occasion to investigate about habits and cultural expectation with more freedom, even asking stupid questions. It is also an occasion to explain my life without to risk to be perceived as a complaining kind of person.

This quote also hints at what made this connection a success – something I will delve deeper into in the next two chapters.

A few expat academics also learned some more Danish, although this was often only a few words since they didn't really speak any Danish to start with, so the contact was mainly in English. One German expat academic did develop their Danish language skills in the contact with the host:

> [...] actually we started to talk Danish during the last meetings we saw each other, and that's super helpful for me, because I, my Danish is not too bad right now, but I don't see many opportunities to talk, or talk about a variety of topics, so that we made that switch. So, it's not definite, right, so even afterwards we had meetings where we would talk in English and then we switched to Danish for a while and then we switched back, so it's still, you know, depending a little bit on my energy level, if I talk Danish or [not]. And on the topic, of course, if I talk Danish or English with him. But that has perhaps become a quite nice aspect, that we do that.

Being put in touch with a local colleague is a first step towards making new contacts, which can sometimes be difficult for expat academics, especially if they are on the shy side. One expat academic from China said:

> I think this is a very good way to get to know people, so it is very good to get to know the culture in Denmark and get to know people. You may become friends in the future. So, you have someone to talk to apart from work. I think that part is the best.

Some participants did indeed become friends with their local colleague. Having a local colleague as host also helps feeling integrated in the local community. One of the participants said: "I think that before I had the contact, I was really, I was really feeling lonely, because I did not feel included in a way, not in a work sense, but in a Danish environment sense."

### Benefits for the hosts

The hosts also often got something out of the contact. Learning about another culture is what was most often mentioned because they would not only talk about Danish culture but also the culture of the expat academic. As one host said: "So, in terms of having cultural exchange I think it has been profitable both for him and for me." This host certainly got an inside view into the culture of the expat academic because he was invited to their wedding in their home country. Some of the hosts also developed their English language skills through talking with the expat academic. Other hosts appreciated that they got a new contact that otherwise would probably not have been established. One host, who was supporting staff, enjoyed having a researcher as his contact because over the years he had found it difficult to get into deeper contact with the researchers he was supporting. This way, the host could also learn more about a different part of the university. And sometimes the expat academic also gave some social support to the host because the host was also sharing some of their frustrations that they wouldn't necessarily share with a direct colleague. One host said:

> Yeah, yeah just talking five minutes that means a lot [...] It contributes immensely to one's work life and everyday life [...] [The expat] often comes in and says "Good morning" and "Hi" and ... almost everyday when she is here, we have a small chat with each other.

Many hosts got something out of the contact with the expat academic and participated because they felt it was rewarding to do. One host said:

[...] it is also making my work more diverse, learning something about other people and their background. And so it is rewarding for me. If I didn't think it was rewarding, I wouldn't do it. But I'm just helping and listening. So, I got a lot out of it.

Other hosts could see that it is not so easy for expats to get in contact with Danes, so they wanted to contribute to the workplace by supporting an expat academic. One Danish host commented:

I think your initiatives are really important in the sense that I do know that the Danes are really, really bad at taking care of foreign colleagues. They, and I don't think it's bad will on the part of the Danes but it's more that the Danes have this tradition of, you know when you invite people to the home or to your home, it really has to be a formal dinner. [...] And it takes a bit of preparation to do that. I mean if they would just relax and say, you know, coming over for dinner, you know, eat with our kids etc. etc., most, you know formless, is what they would be happy with that, that's actually what they're looking for. They're not necessary looking for these formal things. Or just inviting if you are going on a trip somewhere and, you know, go sightseeing over there or you just ask them along. But Danes think this has to be something special when we do. And then in the end we never get to do it.

Connecting expats with a local buddy can help the expat settle into the host country. Even if the buddy was a local colleague, the focus of much of the contact was more on life outside of work and most of the benefits were of a more personal nature with regard to receiving social support and learning about the host culture. If an organisation would like to improve an expat's performance in the workplace, it is recommended to look into a mentoring programme (Chapter 6). A buddy system is especially a valuable option with regard to the social aspect of settling into a new host country. In Chapter 9, I will discuss different choices an organisation can make with regard to supporting their expats through a buddy system.

## Notes

1 *Oxford English Dictionary*, www.oed.com.
2 For example, Thomson, C., & Esses, V. M. (2016). Helping the transition: Mentorship to support international students in Canada. *Journal of International Students*, 6(4), 873–886.
3 For example, the BuddySystem created and supported by the Erasmus Student Network France. The system is expected to spread to about 30 European

countries and around 300,000 students., Read more at https://buddysystem.
eu/en/.

4  Thomson and Esses (2016).

5  Westwood, M. J., & Barker, M. (1990). Academic achievement and social adaptation among international students: A comparison groups study of the peer-pairing program. *International Journal of Intercultural Relations, 14*(2), 251–263.

6  Campbell, N. (2012). Promoting intercultural contact on campus: A project to connect and engage international and host students. *Journal of Studies in International Education, 16*(3), 205–227, p. 211.

7  Campbell (2012), p. 216.

8  Hendrickson, B. (2018). Intercultural connectors: Explaining the influence of extra-curricular activities and tutor programs on international student friendship network development. *International Journal of Intercultural Relations, 63*, 1–16.

9  Gareis, E., Goldman, J., & Merkin, R. (2019). Promoting intercultural friendship among college students. *Journal of International and Intercultural Communication, 12*(1), 1–22.

10  van Bakel, M. (2012). *In Touch with the Dutch. A longitudinal study of the impact of a local host on the success of the expatriate assignment.* PhD thesis, Radboud University, Nijmegen, The Netherlands. You can find the PDF on www.intersango.dk, where I have also posted blog posts about all the articles published about this research.

11  van Bakel, M., Gerritsen, M., & Van Oudenhoven, J. P. (2011). Impact of a local host on the success of an international assignment. *Thunderbird International Business Review, 53*(3), 391–402.

12  van Bakel, M., Van Oudenhoven, J. P., & Gerritsen, M. (2017). Expatriate contact with a local host: An intervention to increase social support. *Human Resource Development International, 20*(3), 215–235.

13  van Bakel, M., Gerritsen, M., & Van Oudenhoven, J. P. (2014). Impact of a local host on the intercultural competence of expatriates. *International Journal of Human Resource Management, 25*(14), 2050–2067.

14  Gable, S. L., Reis, H. T., Impett, E. A., & Asher, E. R. (2004). What do you do when things go right? The intrapersonal and interpersonal benefits of sharing positive events. *Journal of Personality and Social Psychology, 87*(2), 228–245.

15  See for example the overview in Bird, A., Mendenhall, M., Stevens, M. J., & Oddou, G. (2010). Defining the content domain of intercultural competence for global leaders. *Journal of Managerial Psychology, 25*(8), 810–828.

16  Unfortunately, it was difficult to find out how a local host affects the partners because not every expat had a partner, so only 23 partners participated in the study (of which 10 had a local host). This limited sample size made it difficult to do statistical analyses.

# Experience

A British expat in the Netherlands – "Together we had some great fun and will continue to be friends"

*James is a 40-year-old British expat who participated in my PhD project, working for a big cable operator in the Netherlands with a lot of international work and travel experience. Other than working in the United States for a little less than a year, he has worked extensively across Western and Central Europe. He plans to stay in the Netherlands for about 5 years. His local host is Bram, a 31-year-old Dutchman who has lived in Canada for 3 years and has travelled widely and has a passion for culture and intercultural communication. They became very good friends.*

## What have you done together?

Almost immediately after we met, we arranged a few different activities and went out and had beers, got to know each other a little bit. And then started doing various activities, we went flying, we also went to concerts, those types of things. [...] We're friends now, still in contact, I was around there for dinner last week and so we got on very well, and did various things, but mainly kind of socialising I would say, dinner, socialising, drinks that kind of stuff.

## How did you enjoy the contact?

He's an approachable and friendly person with similar interests and perspectives. Together we had some great fun and will continue to be friends.

DOI: 10.4324/9781003246855-20

### What did you enjoy the most?

I think having the regular contact. Because it was at a time when [...] I was in a bit of a quiet spell and for me it was quite good, it was another avenue, another channel to go out and make friends so, I enjoyed the socialising bit of it and, yeah all the stuff we did, I enjoyed that as well.

### Did the contact help you in any way?

Yes, it gave me more insight into Dutch culture and ways of thinking. Bram became a trusted friend also. [...] Having another friend and doing the stuff we do, yeah, helped to, kind of contributed to my overall well-being which has meant I felt settled and secure and happy here so yeah.

### Has it also helped in other ways? For example practical things?

For sure, yes, I've asked him for advice on various things in terms of dealing with the Dutch systems and that kind of stuff. Asking for, if he knows a plumber, that kind of things, recommendations for all sorts of things. Otherwise, I might have struggled, or find it a bit more difficult having to search through the yellow pages. And also on a business level we both shared and confided in each other and talked about our situations at work and that kind of stuff. There was also a situation where one of his suppliers was causing him some pain and I remember we had a long discussion over dinner where I gave him some advice about how to deal with this guy, and some options and strategies. So, it worked both ways.

### What did you think was the most important in the contact?

I would say for me it was more about having personal contact, and having a person, it wouldn't have mattered what nationality, yes it helped the fact that he's Dutch so he understands local systems and all the rest of it and gave insight there, but it was more about having a good friend to confide in and discuss and all that kind of stuff, so the value of that, really. It helps that he was Dutch but it wouldn't have mattered if he was South African.

### Why did you think it worked well?

I think for us it worked, because we became friends very quickly. We have a lot in common, we enjoy each other's company a lot, did quite a few things together very early on, in the first few weeks, we met probably twice a week and do stuff. He is pretty broad-minded, he's got that breadth to him, that he has lived in other countries, so he has that perspective and because of that he is very interested in other cultures and he has got that natural inquisitive thing so I think that's not always the case with them. And I can speak for that, because when I first came to Holland, I had a Dutch girlfriend and I was very much immersed in the Dutch live, in fact I had no expat friends so the other people I knew were Dutch, that didn't work out. Perhaps unfortunately I was kind of left to my own devices, in which case I had to start again and it was interesting that none of the Dutch people that were her friends and associated with me, stayed friends with me. None of them made an intent to, and this was after about nearly two years... Bram is very international in his thinking anyway... whilst he is Dutch, he's not I would say, a real patriot, no, I think he himself has got a quite international background, I thinks he's almost an expat himself living in Holland.

# Chapter 8

# The importance of the quality of the contact

## Introduction

Connecting an expat with a local from the host country – as a colleague or in private life – can have many benefits, as the previous chapter showed. Those benefits also depend on the relationship between the expat and local. Do they meet very often? Are they close? And what do they talk about when they meet? These three questions reflect the three aspects of social ties that are usually distinguished: frequency, depth and breadth of the contact. In this chapter I will look more closely at these aspects, and how organisations can stimulate this.

## The importance of the quality of the contact

It makes a lot of sense to look at the quality of the contact between expats and locals of the host country because one would be more likely to support a friend than just an acquaintance.[1] So, what is the quality of the contact? Many studies use the frequency of meeting as a way to measure what is going on in the relationship, the idea being that the more often expats meet locals, the more opportunities they have to receive support or to learn about the new culture. As one British expat in my PhD research said: "…because the more people we meet, who we can have a real conversation with, the more likely we are to understand the Dutch culture." The frequency of the contact is something else than the quality of the contact, although the two are often related.[2] Those who meet more often are able to build a closer relationship, as was also the case in my PhD research. It does not necessarily mean, though, that someone we meet frequently is also a close connection, or that we are always able to meet our closest friends on a frequent basis. Especially for expats, their closest friends often live back in their home country. So, it is important to distinguish both aspects when looking deeper into the contact between expats and locals from the host country.

DOI: 10.4324/9781003246855-21

*Figure 8.1* The importance of the quality of the contact between expats and locals. Illustration by Heldermaker.

The quality of the contact is important because those with good contact get more benefits out of it. The mentoring literature shows that how the mentee feels about the mentor and their relationship is important for satisfaction with the workplace and career, and that the most development happens when the quality of the relationship is high.[3] In the expat literature, research has shown that locals from the host country who like the expat are more willing to give them important information for doing their jobs well, and to make their work-life easier for them.[4] A study on foreign physicians in Sweden also highlighted the crucial role of the quality of the contact – friendships – for social integration.[5]

In my PhD research, I also looked at the role of the quality of the contact, which was related to the frequency of the contact, and it was clear that expats who had high-quality contact with their local host benefited the most.[6] It was not just being linked to a local host, but it was the quality of the relationship that allowed the expats to make the most of the experience. There is also some indication that expats who had low-quality contact with their host still benefited a little bit from the contact, although it was impossible to be sure about this due to the fact that there were not so many expats who had low-quality contact with their host (only about a third). This is encouraging because the mentoring literature has shown that mentoring actually can have negative effects. If the mentoring relationship is of low quality, the mentee might be more stressed and lose self-esteem. Happily, this does not seem to be the case with expats being matched to a local host.

While it is clear that relationship frequency and quality are key, it might also be that the type of support offered is what is important to look at – this is sometimes also called the breadth of the contact. We have seen in Chapter 1 that there are two main types of social support: informational/instrumental support and socioemotional support. While informational/instrumental support such as tips about the best restaurant in town are easily talked about at the start of a new contact, an expat usually needs to get a bit closer to the local host before sharing the more difficult aspects of living and working abroad. In my PhD research it was clear that a local host can offer both types of support, but we don't know much yet about which of those is more important at what stage of the stay.

## What makes a relationship work?

Since we know that the quality of the contact plays a crucial role, it is very useful to delve deeper into how high-quality contact is created. In my PhD research, I analysed 33 expats and 10 of their partners who were put in touch with a local host.[7] About two-thirds of them developed a high-quality relationship with their local host, and the data showed quite a few factors that influenced the development of the contact.

These factors are divided in three categories of factors that, according to social penetration theory,[8] influence the development of the relationship. The first category of factors are personal characteristics such as personality and the extent to which people need new friends that might influence the development of the contact (see also Chapter 2, p. 45). For expats and their hosts, this was about the similarities between them, their motivation to connect with each other and the expectations they had about the contact. The second category is about what comes out of the contact. Social penetration theory states that people are continually looking at the cost and rewards of interactions,[9] where costs can be things such as physical or mental effort or anxiety one might feel. Rewards can be that the contact is fun or helpful in one way or another, for example in terms of social support. The third category is about aspects of the situation that may influence the development of the contact, for example how much time the participants have for meeting up, and the fact that the expat and the local host are from different countries. One of the key factors here is proximity because the closer people live to each other, the more they interact. For this reason, I took this already into account when matching the expat and the local host, to make sure they would be able to meet up easily.

### Does it click?

The expat and the local host need some common ground to build the relationship on. To increase the chances for the contact to work out, I tried to match the expat and local host with regard to age and whether they had a partner and children. A difference in age can but does not have to hinder the contact; one expat who had a 16-year age difference with their host said that "age is only a problem if we make it a problem." It could also be that life stage is the more important factor. For one expat, who only differed 3 years with their host, this was an issue since the host was still studying whereas she had started to work already. Similarly, having children usually leads to a very different lifestyle, and matching for this criterion – especially when they have similar ages – will really increase the chances of the contact developing. Being matched to a local host who also has a partner also can be more helpful because then both the expat and their partner would have a counterpart in the local host couple. For one couple who was matched to a single host, this was the main reason why the partner of the expat didn't really participate in the contact.

While matching for similarity in age and having a partner and children is a good basis to start from, similarity in other respects can be more important to make the relationship develop. Many expats mentioned how they 'clicked' with their local host because of having something in common. One British expat said:

> I think you need to have enough communality for people to at least [...] find some common ground to have a relationship, and then some differences too, make the other person go outside of their normal comfort zone. So they try something new or extend a little bit.

A lack of common interests can hinder the development of the relationship. In one case, the host invited the expat to several activities but often got 'no' as answer, which dampened the enthusiasm.

In this study I didn't match for similar interests simply because I only had a limited number of hosts to choose from. One factor that probably helped the development of many of the contacts was that most of the hosts had also lived abroad or had travelled extensively. And sometimes it was unpredictable what would spark a connection between the expat and the host. One good example of this is when a local host asked me in the interview whether the fact that they both had a link with Israel was the reason they were matched together. While I did know from the registration form that the expat had lived in Israel, I did not know that the father of the host grew up there. The conclusion is that there has to be something in common to build the relationship on, and what that is, might be surprising.

## Motivation

Another personal characteristic was the motivation of both parties to meet up. Simply wanting to meet the other and make it work was an important reason for the relationship to develop. A French expat commented on how the host really wanted to help them understand their country and their life, and a French expat partner appreciated the time their host took out of their busy daily lives to meet with 'foreigners.' One of the Dutch hosts thought it was great how the expat and their partner were very enthusiastic and curious about what the Netherlands had to offer. Expats and hosts might also influence each other's motivation by showing enthusiasm about an activity they did together, or even send a 'thank you' e-mail afterwards. Since both the expat and the host signed up for the project on a voluntary basis, you would expect both parties to be motivated to make it work, but that was not always the case. In one case, a French expat couple had managed to find some friends by themselves by the time they were put in contact with their host, so they were less interested in making the contact work. In addition, this expat was not as interested in the contact with the local host, which made the partner push a little less for it.

### Different expectations

Expats and local hosts might also have different expectations of the contact, which does not help the development of the contact. Sometimes they had different expectations of the goals of the contact, for example when one host thought it would be about 'helping someone' and did not realise that an important way of helping an expat is to simply go for a drink or a walk with them. Expats and hosts were sometimes also confused about the type of activities they were supposed to do. I left that very much open, only suggesting a long list of potential activities on the project website, from having a drink to more touristic activities. Some hosts thought they had to explore the Netherlands together with their expat, and two hosts had issues finding activities that the expat had not yet done. Of course, it would have been very fine to simply go for drinks or dinner – the important thing is that the expat and the local host meet up. Having different expectations with regard to the activities does not have to be a problem. One host said how she laughed together with the expat about how it was becoming more of a friendship between women. The expat had expected to be matched to a family and occasionally go to a museum, so she was joking how she was thinking about which typical Dutch family they could join to eat something very Dutch. One thing that can help here is to talk about the expectations in the very first meeting. One U.S. American expat said:

> The host took initiative at the first meeting to say: how can we help? Do you want to keep in touch about this or that, do you want to get together? I was like, once a month, touching base, having conversations, talking about experiences, asking questions, that would be great. I really don't want to impose on your life, but I would love to keep the relationship going. We both agreed that was good [...].

A third area where different expectations caused issues was who should take the initiative to meet. One could argue that it is the local host who should take the initiative, since they are 'hosting' the expat, but also that it is the expat who has just arrived and would like to get 'in touch with the Dutch.' In 6 of the 33 contacts, the host said that the initiative was mainly on their side, which they found a shame and does not help to meet up again. It could help to be clear about this from the outset as well, with the ideal situation of both the host and the expat taking the initiative for meeting up.

### Benefits of the contact

Social penetration theory states that if one receives a lot of benefits from a specific relationship, one is more likely to want to continue and develop it. The interviews showed that expats were particularly aware of benefits in terms of adjustment, social support and that the contact was enriching.

The contact with the local host helped the expat adjust to the Netherlands. Having a local host who sends messages and asks questions can help the expat feel included and at home. Many expats also learned about Dutch culture and practiced their Dutch language skills with their host. The expats and partners talked to their host about the culture but also learned from observing their behaviour. One U.S. American expat said:

> If you're not familiar with the culture the first thing you need to do, is have some insights to the culture. You're just left on your own, with no context to put the Dutch culture into, it's really easy to become depressed and very anti Dutch. Because if all you do is go to work and when you come home and have your own little world, you never really understand why all this stuff is happening around you. Why everyone acts this way and why this happens.

In one case, a French expat partner really enjoyed that sometimes she was able to contradict fellow French expats who were criticising the Dutch or generalising too much. Based on her contact with the Dutch local host, she could tell them something they said was not true.

The local host was also a way to meet Dutch people, which was difficult for quite a few expats, and they could offer a lot of social support. You may remember that there are two main categories of social support: informational/instrumental support and socioemotional support. Many expats got a lot of information and advice from their host, for example about restaurants and shops but also about finding a plumber, buying a house and giving birth in the Netherlands. In general, a local host could be very helpful in helping the expat deal with the Dutch system, even assisting in a very practical way by, for example, meeting up to buy a bike. The local host was also company for the expat, and, in many cases, became someone to talk to about issues or problems (socioemotional support). They provided a listening ear, which made one expat 'feel welcome and cared for.'

The contact with the local host was also very enriching for many expats and partners. It made them discover places they didn't know before.

A French expat went to *Museumnacht*[10] and a Spanish workshop with her host, which she would never have done otherwise. This is a good example of how connecting with someone from a different cultural background can lead to some new experiences that might stretch your comfort zone and offer lots of opportunities for learning (see also the intercultural competence development exercises *Get to know the 'other'* (Box 3.6 on p. 88) and the *Road less travelled* (Box 3.5 on p. 86). A U.S. American expat discovered a different perspective on historic events when they went to a museum together and looked at displays about the wars between the Dutch and the English.

### Costs of the contact

While contact with a local host can have many benefits, there are also some costs involved. In general, interacting with people from different cultural backgrounds and in a different language might cause anxiety. In the specific case of this project in which I put expats in touch with a local host, there can also be extra anxiety about how the contact with the host will work out, whether one will make a good first impression and whether one has sufficient language skills to make it work well.

The expats and hosts signed up for the project and then were put in touch by me. Some expats commented on how it was slightly peculiar because they had never met the other before – in a way, it was a blind date, as one host mentioned. A French expat partner thought it was a bit artificial and was afraid that they wouldn't have anything to say to each other. Her partner said he wouldn't even have signed up for the project had it not been for her, but also acknowledges that "in hindsight it's stupid, but I know that I would not have taken that step." In two cases, this feeling of artificialness remained during the whole 9 months of the project. In contrast, in a case of very high quality contact, a French expat mentioned how natural the relationship was, and how they talked about everything.

Some participants were also worried about whether they would get along with the other. All participants introduced themselves to each other in a short text that was included in the e-mail with which I put them in touch with each other. In two cases, these introductions made the impression that the other was of much higher status than they were, leading to anxiety. A French expat partner constructed an image of a "very classy Dutch couple" but found that they were not like that at all, but were very approachable, nice and even "like us." One host got worried when they heard what kind of job the British expat had, and wondered whether they would have anything to talk about. But when they met, they really didn't notice it and talked about all sorts of things.

A final point about which some participants were anxious was about what to do together, especially for the first meeting. A British expat also was nervous because she knew there were cultural differences between her own country and the Netherlands in terms of what hospitality means. She loves cooking but also realised that her efforts when entertaining could be perceived as extravagant and trying to impress people.

I think in Dutch culture I get the sense that maybe the concept of prudence, not overdoing things, being frugal in some ways, keeping things simple and not indulging too much in things, comes across a little bit. And I wonder whether it, therefore, makes me a bit more nervous when I entertain Dutch friends.

### Available time

Both expats and local hosts often had very busy lives, and this was the most often mentioned barrier to the contact. Also those couples with high-quality contact only met up about seven times on average during the 9 months of the project, even though all participants were encouraged to meet up once a month. In one case busy schedules led to a breakdown of the contact because the participants could only meet on Monday evenings. The expats and partners were also often busy visiting family back home over Christmas or the summer holidays or receiving visitors from abroad. But this can be overcome by being motivated to meet up, as one host said, "we all try and it works out."

### Timing of the contact

To make sure expats and partners would benefit as much as possible from the contact, I made sure that they had not been in the Netherlands for longer than a year. Only two participants commented that they thought the expat had been in the Netherlands for too long to benefit from the contact, and these contacts did not really develop. This also depends on the expectations one has – if a host feels they should help the expat with a lot of practical issues, then the contact would have to be established as soon after arrival as possible. Timing in a different sense, namely the date on which the expat and partner were put in touch with their host, can also make it more difficult for the contact to develop. In one case I put the expat in touch with their host in June, but then the expat as well as the host went on holiday, and it took them until September to meet up. They still developed a high-quality relationship, but it could have easily derailed it as well.

## Communication difficulties

In some cases, the contact was prevented from developing further for technical or personal reasons. In two cases, e-mails did not arrive, even if the participants were both eager to meet up again. In one case, the expat asked me to chase their host, and it turned out that their e-mail had arrived in the spam folder. There were sometimes also personal reasons why the relationship was interrupted; one host moved to another part of the Netherlands, and two participants had a baby which interrupted the relationship.

Cultural differences played a role in one of these cases because of different cultural conventions that one might not be aware of. In the Netherlands it is common to send out a *geboortekaartje* (birth announcement) to family and friends within a few days of the birth. This card informs when the mother and baby can be contacted and visited, so the host was waiting for this announcement before reaching out. She was a bit disgruntled that she only heard the baby was born a month later, though she commented: "Maybe they do it differently in England, no idea." The expat, on the other hand, was disappointed because she had hoped and expected the host to reach out because she might want to visit her and come see the baby. The relationship didn't survive this incident; they did not meet up again in the four remaining months of the project.

Cultural differences might also put a break on the contact if they are not recognised as such. The British expat who commented earlier on being anxious when entertaining Dutch people because she was aware that how she liked to cook for parties might be seen as over the top, had another experience that drove her and her host further apart. She organised a children's birthday party which was full of people and children which made it hard to talk to anyone, but, in her opinion, that is how birthdays are. She did note that birthdays in the Netherlands seemed to be much smaller and only for very close friends and a few family members, whereas in the United Kingdom also children from day care and their parents would be invited. The host did not recognise this cultural difference, and felt it was done to impress others. This will not have helped their relationship to develop further.

A final example of cultural differences that could hinder the development of the contact comes from a French expat who mentions how they usually aren't available before 20.00 or 20.30, while Dutch people are already on the second part of their evening by then. This might make it more difficult to find a common time to meet up.

Connecting expats with a local host is a great way for organisations to support their expats when they are abroad – even if the expat only meets their host one or two times and does not develop a high-quality contact relationship, they still seem to benefit to some extent. In many cases, the contact between the expat and local host will develop into high quality, and if not, it is highly unlikely that it is going to make things worse for the expat, so it is a safe intervention. We have also seen that quite a lot of factors influence the development of the contact between the expat, partner and local host. Some are more important than others. Having some common interest is one of the most important factors, which is tied in with having the motivation to make the contact work. Dissimilarity between the expat and their host, a lack of motivation together with few benefits meant that a relationship would often not get beyond the first meeting. These similarities and the motivation to make it work are crucial when barriers are present such as difference in age of life phase or living in different cities, making it less easy to meet up. In a few cases, the expat and their host overcame these barriers simply because they wanted to make it work. In the next chapter I will discuss in more detail how organisations can best set up a buddy system for their expats.

## Notes

1  Dunbar, R. I. M. (2018). The anatomy of friendship. *Trends in Cognitive Sciences, 22*(1), 32–51.
2  Hall, J. A. (2018). How many hours does it take to make a friend? *Journal of Social and Personal Relationships, 36*(4), 1278–1296.
3  Eby, L. T. d. T., Allen, T. D., Hoffman, B. J., Baranik, L. E., Sauer, J. B., Baldwin, S., Morrison, M.A., Kinkade, K.M., Maher, C.P., Curtis, S., & Evans, S. C. (2013). An interdisciplinary meta-analysis of the potential antecedents, correlates, and consequences of protégé perceptions of mentoring. *Psychological Bulletin, 139*(2), 441.
4  Sonesh, S. C., & DeNisi, A. S. (2016). The categorization of expatriates and the support offered by host country nationals. *Journal of Global Mobility, 4*(1), 18–43.
5  Povrzanović Frykman, M., & Mozetič, K. (2020). The importance of friends: Social life challenges for foreign physicians in Southern Sweden. *Community, Work & Family, 23*(4), 385–400.
6  van Bakel, M., Gerritsen, M., & Van Oudenhoven, J. P. (2016). The importance of relationship quality: Maximizing the impact of expatriate contact with a local host. *Thunderbird International Business Review, 58*(1), 41–54.
7  van Bakel, M., van Oudenhoven, J. P., & Gerritsen, M. (2015). Developing a high quality intercultural relationship: Expatriates and their local host. *Journal of Global Mobility, 3*(1), 25–45.

8  Altman, I., & Taylor, D. A. (1973). *Social penetration. The development of interpersonal relationships.* New York: Holt, Rinehart and Winston, Inc.
9  For a discussion of how rational people are when it comes to making friends, please check out my academic work on expatriate social network formation at www.intersango.dk.
10  During the *Museumnacht* event, many museums across the Netherlands open their doors at night, in Amsterdam usually from 7 pm until 2 am the next day. Museums collaborate, so people can buy one ticket and visit several museums.

# Experience

A Chinese expat in Denmark – "You feel like you are mentally supported"

*Ling Wang is a 31-year-old Chinese researcher who moved to Denmark with her partner about 1.5 years before participating in the Connecting with a Danish colleague project. She lived in Finland for 8 years. Her Danish host is a colleague who is close to retirement, and who lives about 1.5 hour away from university.*

### Can you tell me about the contact you had with your buddy?

I think we usually meet in the campus, once per month on average. Because it also depends on whether she was busy, or I was busy. But we usually talk about working life, and also personal life.

### And in the beginning what was your actual motivation to participate in the buddy programme?

I think it is because I lived in Finland and then I realised it's quite important to know the working culture, also the social culture in one country if you just move there. It would be nice and also respectful to the people or your colleagues, it is always good to know more.

### How did your participation in the buddy programme influence how you adjusted to living in Denmark?

Oh, I think, of course it has a positive impact because it can help you know more about the local people. For example, there is actually a culture shock for me. When I moved to here, even though I stayed for 8 years in Finland, which is also a Nordic country. [...] Because in Finland, students are usually quite quiet. And they don't talk that much in the class, they don't

DOI: 10.4324/9781003246855-22

complain about your teaching or these kinds of things. But when I moved to Denmark I realised, okay it's a bit different here and students are usually more demanding and they complain about things in the teaching, in the exam. And this is a kind of like culture thing, because they have more opinions, so to speak. It is not a good or bad thing, but back then I had a hard time to deal with it because [...] I took it personal. But [...] when I talked with my [host], and she said like this is the kind of culture thing, it is not like a target on you. Even though she is Danish, she still needs to deal with such kind of comments [...]. So, this somehow made me feel a little bit relieved [...], I mean I'm not used to that. [So,] it is not about really saving your time or make your work easier. But you feel like you are mentally supported. Yeah, that's what would be my expression.

**What would you say, what else kind of information have you received by your buddy?**

[...] Oh the rest is more or less about our life. Because we share some kind of common interests. Both of us like [...] this art. And we talk about like the architecture in Denmark and also some designs in Denmark. Which is very enjoyable conversation, because if it's about life, you feel like you have some social attachment with someone else. And yeah, actually it can help you [...] integrate into the society.

**Did you ever encounter any other kind of negative feelings, experiences or problems in Denmark and how did your buddy help you in handling these difficulties then?**

[...] I think the only a little bit negative [thing], but you probably can't call it negative. I think that's an institutional difference, it is, there are some, because it is a big university. I was working in a relatively small business school [in Finland]. So, the work is a bit different, so to speak. Here, it is sometimes hard to find information [laugh]. You don't know on which site to look at, even though you search on the webpage, you may not find the information you want. So [...] yeah, then, we just talked about that. But the thing is we are not working in the same department. So, there is limited information we can share. But we just, it's more or less about sharing the feeling or share the opinion. Even by doing that, which helps me like relieve some negative, sometimes negative emotions or like temporary feelings, things like that.

## Did you encounter any language barriers?

Well [...] of course, there were some language barriers at the beginning. Because, for example if we want to talk some topics, which is a little bit complicated, for example, like politics or [...] I don't know, social conflicts, such kind of things. And you need to really understand what the other party means. Because otherwise you can create some miscommunication. So, in this sense, like [...] but we, I think we deal with that. Because we use a lot of time to explain what we really mean about, of the topic, so, and sometimes we also [laugh] show each other like, for example, the picture on the phone, which helps quite a lot.

## Do you have any suggestions for organisations who would like to set up a buddy system?

I think it would be more beneficial if you can find the host from the same department. Because in that sense you can share more about your work, and it has more synergy. But, of course, I'm pretty happy about the buddy I got. Definitely, I think there, there is some matching process, seeing as she is quite interested in Finland, she is quite familiar with, like the Finnish design, those are kind of things we share, so kind of common hobbies. Obviously, someone has already selected and matched us based on our common interest, I guess. So, yeah, that's definitely an enjoyable experience. As I said, you can't ask for more [laugh].

# Chapter 9

# How to set up a buddy system

## Introduction

In the previous two chapters, we have seen how connecting an expat and their partner with a local host or buddy can have many benefits, and how those with high-quality contact benefit the most. Connecting expats with a local host is a great way for organisations to support their expats when they are abroad, especially for those expats who will have to work closely with locals and in countries where it is not so easy to make local friends. A buddy system can be a great addition to cross-cultural training because it takes place after arrival, when the expat actually encounters the new host culture. A good connection with a local host provides a safe environment to learn about the host culture – both by talking about it but also by observing how the local host acts. Buddy systems have also increasingly been used for refugees, and Box 9.1 on p. 210 dives deeper into how they are different from buddy systems in organisations, and what one should keep in mind when setting up a buddy system for refugees.

So, how can an organisation best set up a buddy system? In this chapter I integrate all that I learned from my research on connecting expats with a local host in the Netherlands and Denmark. I discuss the choices an organisation has when setting up a buddy system, what the process looks like and what they should pay attention to when matching an expat to a local host. Once the contact is established, the organisation can stimulate the development of a high-quality relationship between the expat and their local host.

## Setting up a buddy system

A foremost aspect to consider when an organisation wants to set up a buddy system is what they expect it to be about. My research has shown that the majority of the benefits expats get from participating in such a programme are within the private sphere: it helps them settle into the host

DOI: 10.4324/9781003246855-23

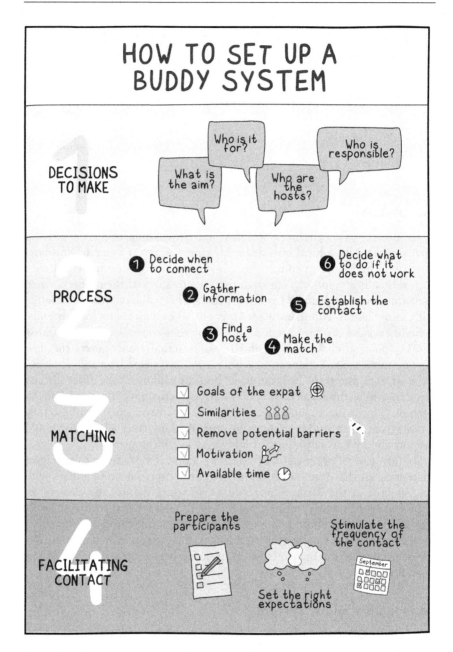

Figure 9.1 How to set up a buddy system. Illustration by Heldermaker.

country and learn a lot about the local culture. When an expat gets a local colleague as buddy, there are also some work-related benefits, such as extending one's network in the workplace and getting specific information that is helpful for doing one's job. Organisations should not expect a direct effect on the expat's performance; if that is what is needed, then I would recommend looking into setting up a mentoring programme (see Chapter 6).

A choice to make is whether the local host should assist the expat with all the practical matters from day one. If there is no dedicated unit within the organisation to help with these practical aspects– like many multinational corporations have – a buddy can be allocated right from the start to help. Organisations could also choose to appoint a direct colleague in the team or an administrative assistant of the department to help with the practical aspects, and add a buddy for the social aspect of settling in the host country in the longer term. It is important to be clear about the choices that are made, so the local host knows what is expected of them (see also the section "Facilitating the contact," about setting the right expectations). If a buddy system is launched, it should also be decided whether all existing expats can sign up for it, or only those who have recently arrived. To offer as much support as possible, it makes sense to include any expat who feels they might benefit from a local host.

A very good, practical, way to set up a buddy system in organisations with benefits for all participants is to include repatriates and potential future expats as hosts. Expats who have returned from their assignment – repatriates – would have the international experience themselves as well as being a local, making them very suitable to being a local host for a new expat. It could also give them some recognition that many crave of that their international experience is actually valued by the organisation. Many repats leave the organisation because they feel their international experience isn't appreciated and does not bring them anything.[1] Being asked for a buddy system could be a way to acknowledge and highlight this valuable experience. Potential future expats – local talent who have expressed a wish of potentially working abroad – could also be great to have as local hosts in a buddy system because they are interested in working and living abroad and it would offer an opportunity for them to learn more about this and develop their intercultural competence.

The organisation should also decide who could participate in the buddy system, whether it is only for expats, for expats and their partners or only for partners. Partners of expats are often struggling, especially if they do not have the possibility to work in the host country due to visa regulations, and this heavily influences the adjustment of the expat. Many organisations underestimate the importance of the expat's family, and do not adequately support them.² Including the partner in a buddy system – or even exclusively set up a buddy system for expat partners – would be a good way for the organisation to support the family of the expat. The expat's children can also be included and supported if the host family also has children of a similar age.

The organisation should also decide who the hosts are. My research has focused on connecting expats with locals of the host country because that is often not easy to do as an expat. A buddy system is a way to circumvent this barrier and create a connection between expats and locals. The buddy does not have to be a local, though, it can also be another expat. Some expats are more or less local themselves after having lived in the country for 20 years and/or having married a local from the host country. They could also be great hosts because they have been through the experience of moving abroad themselves yet have extensive knowledge of the host culture. The buddy can also be another expat who has only been there a bit longer than the new expat. Obviously, such a buddy would not (yet) have the advantage of being deeply rooted in the host environment, and I think one should be careful with making such matches. While other expats can be a great support since they have recently gone through the same transition, this type of support is quite easy to get for expats in the many expat communities and there are disadvantages to staying in this 'expat bubble' (see also Chapter 4). It diminishes the expat's satisfaction with the stay in the long run, and there is also a risk that the expat host does not have correct knowledge about the host culture or is simply not very happy there. I would like to echo the advice of a German expat in Mexico (see also her Experience on p. 101) received from their intercultural trainer:

> Be careful that you don't end up in the choir of people that are just complaining about the place [...] because people tend to just complain, complain, complain, instead of just settling in and living under the conditions that are given them. You need to adapt to the environment that you are installed in and you need to learn to live here.

A final decision point is about who in the organisation would be responsible for setting up and coordinating the buddy system. The HR department would be a good place to anchor the buddy system – especially if there already is a dedicated unit that supports expats and their partners. It helps to cooperate with key persons in the rest of the organisation. In the buddy project I ran at the University of Southern Denmark, I established connections with the person at each department who knew about the new international hires (these were all self-initiated expats academics). They would provide me with the information I needed to contact the expats, and they also helped me find local colleagues who might want to act as a buddy, for example through including information in the department's newsletter. Having someone responsible for the running of the buddy system – and facilitating this by allocating work hours for this task – will also greatly increase the effectiveness of the buddy system. In the section 'Facilitating the contact,' I will discuss the various things a coordinator could do in more detail.

## Process

The process of connecting an expat with a local host kicks off when a new expat joins the organisation. The best time for connecting the expat with a buddy depends on the choices made by the organisation and the preference of the expat themselves. The expat will need a lot of support during those first few months, so if the contact with the buddy is about socialising, then the best time to make the connection is after the first few months, when the initial bustle of settling in has died down and the expat will have time and space to think about meeting up. If the buddy is supposed to also help with all kinds of practical matters during those first few months, then the earlier the match is made the better. It also depends on the wishes of the expat, whether they feel they have time and space for the buddy right after arrival. Most of the expats in my research told me they preferred the contact to happen after the first few busy months. It is also important to not put expats in touch with their local host just before the summer or Christmas holidays. These are busy periods where the expat might also travel, which will make it more difficult to meet up for the first time.

When expats sign up for the buddy system, it is important to get some information that will help match them with a local host such as which countries the expat has lived in and what they would like to get out of their participation (see the next section on matching). It is also relevant to know how long they have been in the host country in case they do not sign up right after arrival. In cases where the expat has been in the host country for a longer time, the host should know about this and what the expat might still want out of the contact. Such contact is probably even less about 'helping' the expat with anything, and more about socialising together.

After the expat signs up, a local buddy needs to be found. I recommend gathering a pool of potential local hosts to choose from – for multinational corporations, these could be local talent that might be sent abroad at some point as well as those who have come back from an expat assignment. Regular communication about the buddy project through newsletters, social media and the organisation's website will help reach local hosts. Stories of existing participants can be used for this – in my research I found that many local hosts signed up because they heard somebody talk very positively about their own experience. Current participants can also be asked to spread the word to their colleagues.

To increase the likelihood of finding enough local hosts – this was a bit of an issue in both of my local host projects – it is also possible to align it more closely with what is expected of employees in the organisation. If the organisation would like to develop the intercultural competence of their employees, a buddy system can become a central aspect of this. Participation in such a system as well as reflections on the experiences could be seen as a way to train intercultural competence and can be encouraged as such by the HR department as well as line managers. It could also be a way to express corporate values such as cooperation and mutual support – 'supporting our colleagues is what we do in this company.' To anchor it in daily life in the organisation, it could become part of a performance management system, and be discussed between employees and their managers on a regular basis.

The matching should be done as soon as possible. In my two local host projects, I only had a few locals to choose from, and often the location was the main deciding factor, together with age and whether the expat had a partner and/or children. I will discuss the considerations to take into account when matching in the next section. The matching can be done via a simple spreadsheet, but it also could be automated (or maybe even done by artificial intelligence!). Buddy systems as a way to support international students are quite popular among universities, and an online platform has been developed centrally to facilitate the matching process.[3] Organisations could develop their own system, or work together and create a central one. Such a system might also offer the possibility for the expat to choose their own host, or express their preference. Another way of doing the matching which includes the preferences of the expat is to organise it as a speed dating event, as one expat in my research suggested. At such an event, expats meet a lot of potential hosts and then indicate their three preferred hosts. It could be interesting to see whether this results in higher quality contact.

Once the match is made, the contact needs to be established. The organisation can choose how much time and effort they would like to put in this. In my two projects, I had each participant write a short introduction, and once I had received both, I introduced the participants to each other via e-mail. These introductions were included as a conversation starter, and it was then up to the participants to connect and have a first meeting. This is a relatively easy and not time-consuming way of managing this process. Alternatively, a preliminary meeting could be set up between the expat and the host to see if they indeed want to be connected.

An organisation should also decide what to do when connections do not work out. The coordinator of the buddy project can monitor and help where needed (see also the section "Facilitating the contact") but sometimes it simply does not work out. The participants might not have enough in common, or the local host may leave the organisation. The expat could then be connected with a new buddy, if they are still interested in participating.

## Matching an expat and local host

It is very difficult to predict beforehand what makes a match successful. The mentoring and coaching literature struggles with this too, although it is clear that mentoring needs should be taken into account.[4] Matching with a mentor who can fulfil these needs leads to more satisfactory relationships (see also Chapter 6 on p. 147 where I discuss the mentoring needs of different types of expats). For this reason, it is worthwhile to enquire about what the expat would like to get out of the contact when they register – would they like someone to support them with practical matters? Would they like to meet up outside of the workplace as well? And if so, would they like to explore the host country with that person or would they simply like to have lunch or an occasional dinner?

Many other aspects influence the quality of the contact (see also Chapter 8). A good starting point when matching expats to a local host is to create similarities between them. While there is clear evidence for the importance of similarities for the quality of the contact (see also p. 186), it is not so clear what exactly those similarities should be. As in mentoring, 'chemistry' is important,[5] though it is difficult to pinpoint the factors that contribute to it. Ori and Rom Brafman dedicated a whole book to the search for the factors which stimulate the 'magic of instant connections,' of which similarities are one.[6] In my research, I have mainly matched for proximity so that it is easy to meet up, and similarities in terms of age and having a partner and/or children. The underlying similarity that the local hosts had often travelled a lot and sometimes also worked abroad probably also helped in creating common ground to build the relationship on. It is also advisable to remove as many potential barriers for the contact, for example, being in a different life phase, and living far from each other which makes it more difficult to meet outside of work. It would be great if the match could go beyond that, and also take aspects such as similar interests into account, but this might simply not be practical due to the limited number of local hosts that might be available. An alternative approach is to invest in encouraging participants to find out what they have in common with the other.[7] Unpredictable similarities might be the key to a high-quality relationship, as was the case for the host mentioned in the previous chapter whose father had grown up in Israel, where the expat had also lived.

Matching an expat to a local in the workplace begs the question who this colleague should be. My research showed that many of the contacts with local colleagues were more focused on socialising and private life. It worked better when the local colleague was not a direct working relationship, because this made some of the participants feel there was more openness to discuss all kinds of things. One host commented:

> We had an open, trustworthy relationship so he could tell me things that he couldn't tell colleagues because I am like a third person. I have no stake in his work. I'm just a colleague but not a boss and not a colleague in the department. Just a third person who is interested in hearing about him and his background.

Another expat felt she got the "freedom to ask stupid questions" because her local colleague was not a direct working relationship. The choice of who should be the local colleague buddy also depends on what the organisation and the expat would like the contact to be about. Some expats also expressed that the focus on socialising (outside the workplace) is what they wanted in the first place, because they already had someone in the department who helped them with the practical aspects. If the organisation would like more of an effect in the work domain, I recommend moving closer to a mentoring relationship (see Chapter 6), for example matching with a local colleague within the same department or even team. This can be complicated, though, for example when the expat and the local colleague are in the same team and at the same level, and might both want to get a promotion. Careful assessment of the individual mentoring needs and situation is needed to make the right choice with regard to a mentor or buddy.

The motivation to make something of the contact is very important as well because it helps overcome the barriers that may be present for the development of the contact. This is something to take into account when an organisation decides on whether participation is completely voluntary, or whether there is some push for people to sign up, for example, if it's part of a performance management system. It is best if participants are intrinsically motivated for the buddy system – that they really want to be put in touch with the other. It would be interesting to see in what way intrinsic motivation can be encouraged, possibly through the sharing of stories of previous connections on how interesting they found it and how much fun it was.

It is also important to check whether the participants have the time and (mental) space to meet up, and whether they are on the same page with regard to meeting outside of the workplace. If that is indeed a possibility, the organisation should make sure the expat lives close to their host and not that both commute for an hour in different directions. It is good to realise that when an organisation matches their expats to a local colleague, they already have the company in common, and maybe even the department or the type of job (see also the Experience on p. 195). This creates a basic level of similarity as well as proximity – the expat can easily meet up for lunch in the canteen with their local colleague – which should help the contact develop.

### Facilitating the contact

First, it helps to prepare the participants for the contact. In Chapter 6, I already discussed that training is recommended for participants in inter-cultural mentoring relationships; this training should not only focus on cross-cultural aspects and increase intercultural competence but also can how to establish ground rules for an open communication and talk about mutual expectations. A short training could be helpful for participants in a buddy system as well, especially if the organisation sees the buddy system as a way to develop intercultural competence throughout the organisation. Alternatively, a short handbook or instruction for both expats and local hosts could be helpful and reduce the anxiety that some participants might have about the contact. Expats who get a buddy could also support each other, and the same goes for the hosts, if given the opportunity to connect.

Such a handbook could also help setting the right expectations, which is a second important aspect that facilitates the development of the contact. The organisation should be very clear about what the buddy system is about. Is the host supposed to help with practical affairs? Is it about social-ising and potentially building up a contact outside of the workplace? And who should take the initiative to meet up? The organisation should also encourage participants to talk about their expectations at the first meeting. Some participants might like to explore the country together, others would prefer to simply go for a drink. When an expat has been in the country for a bit of time already, it is important that the host knows about this and has the right expectations of what the contact could be about. Two hosts in my PhD research who were matched with expats who were in the Netherlands for 7 and 8 months got a bit disappointed. They were expect-ing to really help the expat with all kinds of things, but that was no longer really needed. It is possible that the contact could still have developed if they had had the right expectations, that contact could also mean simply going for a drink or a walk. The participants could also discuss where and how often they would like to meet, what they would like to do and if they want to include their families in the contact as well. Topics like these could be listed in the handbook that could be sent to the expat and the local host. This handbook could also include a list of questions that could be used as a guideline for the first meeting to increase the chances of finding out about what the participants have in common.

Third, a coordinator could greatly increase the effectiveness of the buddy system through monitoring the contact and stimulating the frequency of the contact. The mentoring literature shows that ongoing guidance and supervision of mentors increases the effectiveness of the programme because this support and encouragement helps increase the mentor's self-efficacy or belief that they can be a good mentor.[8] The coordinator could also regularly enquire how the contact is going, which might serve as a reminder for the participants to reach out to each other and meet up. The coordinator could also be an intermediary to prevent breakdown of the contact, in the rare cases where e-mails end up in spam folders or unrecognised cultural differences cause issues, which happened a few times in my PhD project (see Chapter 8 on p. 192). The monitoring of the contact also can be perceived negatively by the participants, though. One of the local hosts in my PhD research commented how they were doing the best they could but were not able to meet more often because of travelling a lot for work and family, and that my mails gave her the feeling that she had to account for herself. A coordinator should find a balance between expressing interest in the contact, gently encouraging it, yet not appearing too controlling or demanding.

A coordinator could also stimulate the frequency of the contact between the expat and their local host. The quality of the contact was clearly related to the frequency of the contact in my PhD research. Even though it was impossible to know cause and effect from that study, it is likely that increasing the frequency of the contact would lead to an increase of the quality of the contact. In any case, meetings between the expat and the local host offer the opportunity for the contact to develop and for support to occur, which is why I asked the participants in my research to meet at least once a month, preferably more. It is important to be clear about the time investment needed and facilitate the contact where possible. One possibility is allowing participants to take an extended lunch break once a month, so they have proper time to talk. This, of course, also depends on the extent to which the participant is able to plan their own work hours, but the organisation would do well to communicate that it is okay to use some work time for this buddy task.

The coordinator of the buddy system could also create more opportunities for expats to meet their host, for example through organising events where the host could take their expat. An additional benefit of such dedicated events is that hosts might find out who else of their colleagues are hosting an expat, and they might team up together and support each other. This happened one time in my PhD research, when a family member of a local host also got enthusiastic and signed up for the project, and they appreciated sharing their experiences with the host and with each other, and also even met up as a group of four. This could also be a way to create more connections within the organisation, across departments and levels, which can increase knowledge exchange throughout the organisation.

Another way to stimulate the frequency of the contact is through vouchers. I experimented with this in the research project at my university in Denmark, where participants received a voucher for a free lunch in the canteen. This worked very well – most participants used the voucher, and met up for their first meeting in the canteen. I also organised other vouchers at local restaurants, for example 10% off the bill, which inspired some participants to meet up outside of the workplace. It can also be a way for the organisation to encourage the participants to discover new places and activities, and such new, enriching experiences can also stimulate the development of the contact.

All in all, organisations have several choices to make that determine how costly a buddy system would be. It can range from a simple programme with minimal work beyond simply putting an expat in touch with a local colleague, to a more elaborate programme with several elements to increase its effectiveness. Matching expats with a local colleague in the workplace has several advantages because it makes it easy to meet up and already creates a common bond and an initial basis of trust. It also creates a common context, where the participants know the people they might be talking about.

Setting up a buddy system within the workplace can be a very valuable way to support expats. Buddy systems mainly have an effect on the social aspects of the expat experience, which are crucial for retaining them in the long term. A buddy system also is a way for an organisation to stimulate intercultural interactions in the workplace and develop their intercultural competence (see Chapter 3), because just having expats and locals in the same workplace does not mean they will develop positive attitudes towards each other. Organisations should encourage expats and their local colleagues to interact, and one relatively simple way of doing this is by connecting them through a buddy system. The next chapter will look at what else organisations can do to stimulate the contact between expats and locals. I will also discuss recommendations for expats themselves and the societies they live in.

## Box 9.1   Buddy systems for refugees

Since the increase in refugees coming to Europe in 2015, buddy systems have become popular as a way for volunteers to provide personalised support to one or several newly arrived refugees. Studies have now been done in Germany[9] and Belgium,[10] and I also connected with Hanne Lee, who set up and coordinated the refugee buddy system for the Red Cross[11] in Slagelse, Denmark.

How are buddy systems for refugees different from buddy systems in organisations? They are different in two important ways. First, while all buddy systems are based on unequal footing with a buddy helping the other, this inequality is much more pronounced in the case of refugees than with expats. Depending on the country's laws and regulations, a key difference between the buddy and the refugee is the latter's lack of citizenship, which both volunteers and refugees are very aware of in the German study. Volunteers felt privileged because they had access to all kinds of services where the refugees did not; and refugees felt they needed to justify the legitimacy of their claims for staying in Germany, and that they were aware they should be grateful for the help received. Another inequality is expressed in how each was able to support the other. Often, volunteers felt it was their role to teach cultural values such as ways of behaving and being in Germany. The refugees felt obliged to act in a certain way in order to be a 'good' buddy partner and were frustrated they could not support their buddy in a more meaningful way than by helping with moving house or fixing a lamp. Also, volunteers and refugees are often much more dissimilar than when matching an expat to a local colleague. The German study showed that the volunteers were mainly middle class, female and between 50 and 65 years old, where the refugees were male, around 20–30 years old, coming from Mali, Guinea, the Ivory Coast, the Balkans, Syria and Ghana. They usually had an insecure or temporary residence status. This inequality between the volunteers and the refugees often was expressed in a positive way, however, by seeing the other as family. In this sense, the buddy relationship was often very similar to informal caring relationships between family members or friends.

A second difference is that the contact often focuses on solving urgent bureaucratic, administrative, legal issues that the refugee faces in the beginning, whereas many expats have much fewer issues to deal with and often get support from their organisation. Volunteers help with translating an official letter, they accompany the refugee to interviews at the job centre, help the refugee find a job through personal networks and/or teach German, Dutch or Danish. These practical activities leave less time and space for social interaction, where the refugee also gets the opportunity to support the volunteer in a more meaningful way. For example, sharing food and talking about cultural differences can be a great way to have contact on a more equal footing. This type of contact helps the relationship to deepen, which creates the possibility for refugees and volunteers to support each other beyond the practical aspects, for example by doing activities together and providing a listening ear.

When setting up a buddy system for refugees, what should one keep in mind? An important recommendation following from the above is to try to establish the relationship on a more equal basis. This can be done by emphasising the importance of the buddy also learning about the culture of the refugee, for example by sharing food and other cultural activities, and generally creating space for more than just the practical matters. This can be sometimes difficult if the official system is falling short, as was the case in the Belgian study, where social workers were supposed to do much of what the buddies ended up helping the refugees with. It might also help to establish the relationship with the view of it being a long-term one, so that refugees would be able to repay the favours they received at the beginning. This is another difference between expats and refugees; where expats are leaving again after a few years, refugees often intend to stay. Many of the refugees in the German study were committed to the relationship – the buddy had become family – and planned to repay the favours in the future. Buddy systems should also try to increase communication between the volunteers, to help them share how they deal with various issues as well as how they establish reciprocity in the relationship.

Setting up and running a buddy system for refugees is not necessarily easy and takes up a lot of time. Hanne Lee has several years of experience running the Red Cross buddy system for refugees in Slagelse Municipality as well as being a buddy herself. For example, matching refugees to volunteers can be difficult because there often is no common language and not much is known about the refugee before matching them. Another difficulty is that many potential volunteers work full-time. "Then it's hard to help with things which has to do with bank and hospital and doctor and dentist." Matching is often done by chance, and this actually works out rather well in about two-thirds of the cases – and many of these connections keep for many years. And if it does not work out, a new match is made. Hanne emphasises that this asks something of the coordinator, in terms of communicating with both parties and resolving potential conflict. "You can't be afraid of conflicts, because you have to go in and deal with that." Being a coordinator takes a lot of time, and one might also run into pushback from other people about such a system, because not everyone will think it is a good idea. She also advocates for organising a regular activity to bring volunteers and refugees together. In Slagelse, this has the form of a weekly Café where any volunteer and refugee can meet each other and get help, if needed.

Hanne Lee has also been a buddy herself and she recognises how many refugees see the connection as a family relationship that goes both ways: "I had a period where I was ill, and they were really caring for me. We are caring for them, but they are also caring for us. [...] Some people call us grandfather and grandmother." Even though many connections work really well, there are also specific difficulties that arise. In some cases, language keeps being a barrier, when the refugee has difficulty learning the host language. It can also be difficult when the refugee has not been able to meet their own expectations of having a permanent job in their profession of choice after a few years. Unfortunately, many refugees face barriers for being able to do the job they were educated for and worked in for many years in their home country. In some cases, refugees decide to try their luck in a different country, and disappear from one day to the next, which can be very difficult for the buddy to make peace with, having invested much in the relationship.

## Notes

1 Breitenmoser, A., & Bader, A. K. (2019). Retaining repatriates – The role of career derailment upon repatriation and how it can be mitigated. *International Journal of Human Resource Management*, 1–28.
2 Dang, Q. T., Rammal, H. G., & Michailova, S. (2021). Expatriates' families: A systematic literature review and research agenda. *Human Resource Management Review*, 100877.
3 The BuddySystem is used in about 30 European countries with around 300,000 students expected to subscribe to the system: https://buddysystem.eu/en/the-project (accessed on 21 August 2023).

4   Hale, R. (2000). To match or mis-match? The dynamics of mentoring as a route to personal and organisational learning. *Career Development International, 5*(4/5), 223–234.

5   Wycherley, I. M., & Cox, E. (2008). Factors in the selection and matching of executive coaches in organisations. *Coaching: An International Journal of Theory, Research and Practice, 1*(1), 39–53.

6   Brafman, R., & Brafman, O. (2010). *The magic of instant connections.* New York: Random House.

7   Cox, E. (2005). For better, for worse: The matching process in formal mentoring schemes. *Mentoring & Tutoring: Partnership in Learning, 13*(3), 403–414.

8   Karcher, M. J., Nakkula, M. J., & Harris, J. (2005). Developmental mentoring match characteristics: Correspondence between mentors' and mentees' assessments of relationship quality. *Journal of Primary Prevention, 26*(2), 93–110.

9   Stock, I. (2019). Buddy schemes between refugees and volunteers in Germany: Transformative potential in an unequal relationship? *Social Inclusion, 7*(2), 128–138.

10  Vescan, I. A., Van Keer, R.-L., Politi, E., Roblain, A., & Phalet, K. (2023). Dyadic relations between refugees and volunteers: Support exchange and reciprocity experienced in buddy projects in Flanders, Belgium. *Current Research in Ecological and Social Psychology, 5,* 100132.

11  https://redcross.eu/projects/friends-show-the-way (accessed on 9 August 2023).

# Experience

DOI: 10.4324/9781003246855-24

A Pakistani expat in Turkey – "The only challenge is the language"

*Syed is a Pakistani chartered accountant working for an NGO helping Syrian refugees in Turkey. He has been living there for 3.5 years now, and has worked for various NGOs in countries such as Liberia and Sierra Leone. His wife and three kids have joined him in Turkey.*

### What were your expectations in terms of making contacts in Turkey?

It's not difficult, people are very lovely. People are warm and they respect foreigners. [...] they have been taught for very long that Turkey does not have friends. But now when they see people coming from outside Turkey, they are happy to receive them, and they are happy to offer them very cordial relations. So, there is no problem in contacting the locals. [...] The only challenge is the language. [...] the places where I am in the south, it's hard to find English speaking people. [...] If someone wants to come to Turkey and really wants to have some good social network, better is that you learn Turkish.

### When you arrived in Turkey, how did you start to make contacts in general?

In general, I mean my first source of contact were my colleagues. Usually, you get to know your colleagues and you start talking and working and get to know the city. The first thing I had to do was issuance of my work permit and residency, and to find a better apartment for myself and my family. [...] They took me around, they showed me the city and so that was my first source of contact. Now I have a bit bigger social network, because I mean, the work is more stable [especially after the first year

when the Syrian war was at the very peak and work demands were high].
I met some friends of friends. [My friends are] either working with me or
they are living next doors.

**So how did you get in contact with your neighbours?**

That's very interesting. We have neighbours and they don't speak English.
We don't speak Turkish. Actually, my kids speak Turkish now, so they
make some conversation but it's actually a lovely conversation. We use our
mobiles, hand gestures and try to explain. Just last night, we had a coffee
with them. And we had almost an hour chat; I was speaking in English.
They were speaking Turkish. We were understanding us very well.

**Now in your current situation in Turkey, how many
people would you call a friend?**

Look in Turkey. I mean, there are situations where you definitely need
some help from the local people, for example, visiting public offices. It's
not easy to get around and get the work done from the public offices. [...]
So, you definitely need someone. A person, I mean, 'a friend in need is a
friend indeed.' So, my son had an accident [...] and we run to the hospital
and the hospital at first thought that I am a Syrian refugee. So, they actually asked me, show us your refugee card. And I was already in a panic.
And luckily, a Turkish friend was there with me. And he sorted that issue
for me. And he and his family just stood beside me all the time we were in
the hospital for a weeklong. Then the family visited to check on us, they
actually extended lots of help.

**And with your new friends now in Turkey, do you see
any impact of cultural differences?**

I mean, not very much, not very much. The culture of Turkey and Pakistan
is very similar. [...] I don't drink alcohol but at one place, I was at one
place for a couple of times. They have a unique drink called Raqqa. It's a
local beer. And they offered me a couple of times and I refused. And then
I said 'Come on man, I don't drink, but why you keep insisting?' And he
said 'No in Turkey, we find that it's a must to drink a drink and if you will
drink, we'll be happy to see that you're having it and you're enjoying it.'
So, I tried it once. And I said 'Come on, the taste is really bizarre. It's very
salty.' [...] And they said, 'Yes, finally!'. They love to share their history
and culture and they speak high about all the things they do. They are
great hosts. In [city] they have a culture of having big gatherings of elders
of the family and then in the middle there is a shisha which you smoke,

and then the cashews and nuts and dried fruits around. So, you eat that and exchange views and discuss all sorts of topics.

## What was your best strategy in Turkey to meet local people?

Best strategy? I never had a strategy to be honest. It was just by default, because you would experience this wherever you will work outside of your home country. The most immediate circle of the people you're working with, you will be close to them first. And then you will find the common interest and then gradually, your circle will keep increasing. And that's what I always do [...] So, it's the same group of people of your work and actually in the neighbourhood you are living in. So, you introduce yourself, you say okay, we are here. I'm here from Pakistan and working here. [...] in the very beginning I went with some other expats to some, clubs or all these pubs, but [...] I didn't find much use of it.

# Recommendations for expats, organisations and societies

## Introduction

Living and working abroad can be a great adventure with many advantages. Meeting and experiencing other cultures can be inspirational and enriching. It is also a way to test and increase your intercultural sensitivity and openmindedness,[1] and it offers plenty of opportunities to develop your intercultural competence. Working abroad generally has a positive influence on one's career, and living abroad also can make one more creative.[2] This book highlights the social aspect of living and working abroad and gives advice on how to best manage this particular challenge. In this final chapter, I will discuss what expats and their partners should consider when moving abroad, and how organisations can support them with making new social connections in the host country. I also take a look at how governments and municipalities can facilitate social integration to encourage international talent to stay in the country.

## Moving abroad as an expat

Many expats and partners don't really think about the social aspect of their new life abroad. Most of the expats that were interviewed for this book said that they didn't really have any expectations with regard to making friends before arriving in the host country. Many assumed it would just naturally develop, but, as we've seen in Chapter 1 (p. 27), this is not always the case, which can be very frustrating. My research emphasises that one should be aware of how important it is for feeling well in the host country to have a social network. Having people with whom one can do activities and who could offer support in what is often a stressful time can really help deal with challenges. It is worthwhile to put an effort into building new friendships, so one can make the most of living and working abroad.

DOI: 10.4324/9781003246855-25

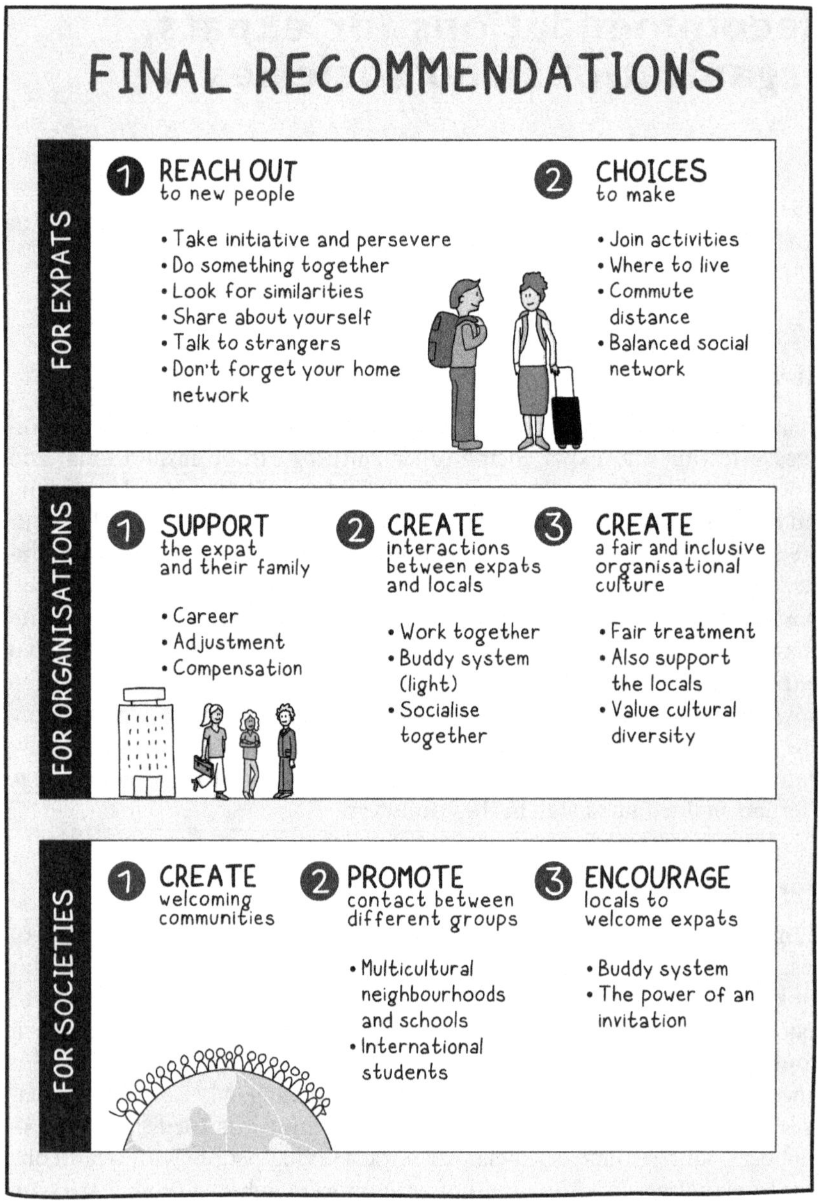

# FINAL RECOMMENDATIONS

**FOR EXPATS**

**① REACH OUT** to new people
- Take initiative and persevere
- Do something together
- Look for similarities
- Share about yourself
- Talk to strangers
- Don't forget your home network

**② CHOICES** to make
- Join activities
- Where to live
- Commute distance
- Balanced social network

**FOR ORGANISATIONS**

**① SUPPORT** the expat and their family
- Career
- Adjustment
- Compensation

**② CREATE** interactions between expats and locals
- Work together
- Buddy system (light)
- Socialise together

**③ CREATE** a fair and inclusive organisational culture
- Fair treatment
- Also support the locals
- Value cultural diversity

**FOR SOCIETIES**

**① CREATE** welcoming communities

**② PROMOTE** contact between different groups
- Multicultural neighbourhoods and schools
- International students

**③ ENCOURAGE** locals to welcome expats
- Buddy system
- The power of an invitation

*Figure 10.1* Final recommendations for expats, organisations and societies. Illustration by Heldermaker.

## Connecting with new people

The starting point for expats, partners and their children is making that first connection with new people. A good way to do this is to join activities where you can meet new people and do something together. Having fun together and enjoying each other's company by participating in a joint activity is a great way to start a friendship.[3] To further develop the contact, it can really help to look for what you have in common with the other, and to share information about yourself. In Chapter 1, I talked more about the role of similarities and how self-disclosure can help develop a friendship. One should be careful, however, that one is not the only one to share things about themselves, and that intimacy gradually increases, because this is associated with closeness and liking.[4]

Another way to make new contacts is to talk to strangers, for example when you are waiting for the train. Research has shown that connecting with others make people happier, yet strangers often ignore each other. Many do this because they underestimate how pleasant these conversations could be, and fear that the other is not interested in talking. In Chapter 1 (p. 23), I mentioned the study among commuters in London and Chicago, where some commuters were instructed to strike up a conversation with a fellow commuter. They could talk about anything, for example, they could ask where they live, how long they've lived there, what they do for a living or what they think about a particular news story. The commuters were also instructed to give some background information about themselves, and to try to continue the conversation for as long as the conversation naturally allows. These commuters had a much more positive experience and also thought they would be more likely to talk to a stranger again. So, next time you are commuting to the office or waiting in a queue, why not strike up a conversation with the person next to you? It's a great way to get out of your comfort zone, and who knows what it might lead to.

As an expat, it also is good to realise you should make an effort to create new connections in the host country, and that this might not always be easy. In Chapter 2 (p. 45), I discussed how the motivation to make new friends in the host country is a key factor, and that this can change over time as the network grows. This also goes for locals from the host country and expats who have been there for a long time – they have already a well-established social network and are not necessarily up for making new friends. This doesn't mean they might not be interested in meeting with you, but you will have to take the initiative and persevere. If you wait for an invitation, you might have to wait for a long time. It is also good to realise that people who have an established social network might not so easily reciprocate with invitations each time you invite them, simply because they don't really have the time and energy to take the initiative for a new friendship. Don't take this lack of invitations as a sure sign that they don't want to meet with you; it might be worthwhile to still persist and try to gradually build the friendship anyway.

Expats also should not forget their network back in the home country, especially if they plan to return home again at some point. While the internet has made it much easier to keep in touch online, the geographical distance and the fact that it is more difficult to meet face-to-face may weaken the friendship. Long-distance friends can still be very close,[5] but it is important to remember to invest in these relationships as well. After having lived in Denmark for 10 years now, I still am in contact with most of my good friends from when I lived in the Netherlands. This does take an effort – on both sides – but is well worth it.

### Shaping one's social network

Expats can influence to some extent what their social network will look like in the host country. A key mechanism highlighted in Chapter 1 is proximity (p. 32). You are more likely to develop friendships with people you meet more often. By seeking out specific activities, one can influence who one might make friends with. For example, you can make sure to always join in with the lunch and other activities at work, the summer barbecue in your street, or join a club where you might meet like-minded people. You will be most likely to create new connections with people you see often.

Another way in which the expat can shape their social network is by deciding where to live. You are more likely to develop friendships with people who live close to you, simply because you meet them more often. When making this decision, expats often think about their jobs and availability of good schools, but I also would recommend including social life in these considerations, especially if one would like to get to know the locals of the host country. One aspect is how far one decides to live from work. Spending time on a commute means the time can't be spent on socialising (unless you start talking to strangers!). It also puts you at a larger geographical distance from colleagues from work, who might be potential friends. Another aspect is the city or neighbourhood one decides to live in, or if one decides to share accommodation. Choosing a neighbourhood with a lot of other expats will limit the possibility for creating friendships with locals. I once visited a Dutch expat just outside London for an interview, and they told me they chose to not to live in the 'Shell street' with only Dutch families and a Dutch primary school, simply because they wanted their family to have more local network. Of course, sometimes the expat does not really have a choice where to live, for example when the safety of the expat and their family requires them living in an expat compound (see Box 2.1 on p. 51). Living in a city might seem obvious as an expat because of the many other expats and specific services that are available, but it might actually be more difficult to connect with locals there. Locals might become tired of the ever-changing expat population, which may reduce their willingness to connect with another new expat unless it is very clear the expat is planning to stay long term.

While it might be difficult to connect with locals, it is important to have a balanced social network that includes both expats and locals in the host country. Contact with other expats can offer a lot of valuable support especially in the beginning of the stay, and expats can learn a lot about the host culture from locals (see also Chapter 4). It is important to also connect with locals because those who do are more satisfied with the stay in the long run.[6] This is, however, not always easy, and depends on the culture of the host country. As mentioned in Chapter 1 (p. 27), in some countries it can be difficult for expats to connect with locals. It can be very helpful to find out the best strategy for making local friends for a particular country. For example, in some countries such as Denmark and the Netherlands, there is more of a division between work and private life, and it is less likely you will build a friendship with colleagues where you also meet outside of the workplace (that is not to say they will not be friendly to you!). In such countries, a good strategy is to join one of the many associations where the locals meet in their free time (see also Box 2.2 on p. 57 about making friends with Danes). When working and living abroad, it is important to keep an open mind and be curious about what could explain a puzzling situation. Developing your intercultural competence, for example by doing the exercises in Chapter 3, will help you deal with challenges in both work and private life.

## What can organisations do?

Many organisations nowadays have employees with a different nationality than that of the host country. In the past, it was mainly multinational corporations that were sending expats to their subsidiaries around the world, but now it has become rather common for any organisation – also the medium-sized and small ones – to hire internationals. This has led to an increasingly international workplace, and organisations need to manage this well to be able to retain this global talent, with the HR department playing an important role.

## How can organisations support expats?

The belief that the organisation values one's contribution and cares about one's well-being has been long recognised as important for both the employee (e.g. job satisfaction) and the organisation itself (e.g. commitment to the organisation, job performance).[7] This perceived organisational support (POS) is also as crucial for the success of international assignments. Organisations can support their assigned expats in three different areas.[8] First, the organisation can show the expat that they care about their career, for example by providing them with a mentor (see Chapter 6) and have regular talks about what the next career step would be, and how the expat assignment fits in. This type of career support helps the expat adjust and be committed to the organisation and to complete the assignment. The second area where an organisation can support the expat and their family is the adjustment to the host country, for example through cross-cultural training, relocation support, spouse career support and language training before and during the assignment. Relocation support with visa, housing, schools, taxes etc. is very beneficial at the start of the stay. It also is important to support the partner and children because the family experiencing difficulties is one of the main reasons for expats to return home early.[9] Third, the organisation can show they care about the expat's financial needs by offering a good compensation package that reward the expat for their contribution. This can include incentives to accept an assignment, especially if it is a dangerous location, and other benefits such as a cost-of-living allowance and rest and relaxation leave time. Such benefits and perks influence expat's job performance and satisfaction. These financial benefits also make it easier for the organisation to retain the expat because they increase their commitment to the organisation.

When organising the support for expats, it is both headquarters and the local subsidiary who play a role in the support.[9] The source of the support has often not been distinguished in research on organisational support of expats, but headquarters will probably take the lead with offering career and financial support – unless the expat is hired on a local contract – and adjustment support before the expat departs. The local subsidiary can further support the expat and their partner in their adjustment during the assignment, in dialogue with headquarters who can ensure that support structures are indeed in place in the local subsidiary. Research does tell us that support from headquarters is crucial for retaining the expat.[9] Many expats leave the organisation after returning from their international assignment, with all the subsequent costs of loss of valuable knowledge and international experience. Making sure that the expat is supported by headquarters, and that a clear repatriation policy is discussed, will be very helpful in keeping the expat in the organisation after the international assignment is completed.

Many more organisations now employ expats who took their own initiative to find a job abroad. It is important to realise that these self-initiated expats also could use some support in settling into the host country, especially when one wants to retain them in the long term. Often, there is no structure or unit in place, like in multinational corporations, who support these expats. They are just another regular employee – except they are not because they face specific challenges in terms of settling into a new host country, of which they might also not (yet) speak the language. It is recommended that the HR department also considers this group of employees and support them. In addition to more formal HR practices as mentioned earlier, supervisors and other colleagues are an important source of support. Support from supervisors has a positive impact on how satisfied the expat is with the job, and how much they want to stay with the organisation and complete the assignment.[9] Colleagues can also support expats, for example, as we have seen in Chapter 4, local colleagues from the host country can have a positive effect on the expat's performance. The HR department can play an important role in facilitating the supportive role of the expat's colleagues, for example by informing the managers of expats about how they can support the expat, and by appointing one or more local colleagues as a Host Country Liaison (Chapter 5) or buddy (Chapter 9).

### Creating interactions between expats and locals

Many expats will find themselves surrounded by local colleagues, so organisations should encourage positive interactions between expats and local colleagues to ensure that they work well together. According to intergroup contact theory, frequent interactions between members of different cultural groups can lead to more positive attitudes towards each other when certain conditions have been met.[10] Intergroup contact is more effective if the groups have equal status, if they work together to achieve common goals and if there is institutional support – such as from an organisation or institution – for the interactions between the two groups.

A first step is to make sure the interactions actually take place. Mere exposure to each other is not enough: organisations need to do something because simply sitting at the same lunch table does not mean there will be any interactions between expats and locals. As one expat in Denmark said:

You cannot begin to imagine how many times I've sat on a table with 5–6 other Danes, who have COMPLETELY ignored me and gone on with their Danish conversations, knowing well I couldn't understand a thing. I was invisible. Even after I said hi and took a seat, they would just continue with what they were saying and doing, without ever trying to include me.

A great way to stimulate interactions between expats and locals is to have them work together. Organisations can create global teams or projects where employees of different cultural backgrounds work together towards a clear common goal. Such intercultural cooperation is also a great way to develop the intercultural competence of employees, which is very important in today's globalised workplace (see also Chapter 3). A study on Australian NGO expats who were in Vietnam to develop the capacities of the locals[11] showed how important it was for expats to work closely together with the locals because this offered a good platform for informal learning, also for the expat. The study also showed that spending time together socially to build a friendship outside of the work role was important for successful capacity building, especially since Vietnamese culture puts a lot of emphasis on relationship building. In addition, when expats and locals work together on a task, group-based pay could be considered to increase the cooperation.[12]

Another way of making sure expats connect with locals is by setting up a buddy system within the organisation – in Chapter 9 I discussed how an organisation can do this. A related idea is to set up a conversation programme for expats and locals within the organisation, which can be seen as a 'buddy light' system. A U.S. American university experimented with this idea as a way to stimulate the intercultural interaction that is the basis for intercultural friendships and networking.[13] They asked students to meet up for an hour at least six times in a semester and organised an orientation at the start, several social events, and a handbook with suggestions for conversation topics and management. They also had someone design a computerised partner-matching programme to make it much less time-consuming. Such a programme could easily be applied to employees, for example through a 3-month cycle in spring and/or fall where expats and locals meet about twice a month for an hour. In light of intergroup contact theory, it is important to communicate that the expats and locals are equal partners and that both can get something out of the contact (e.g. improved language skills).

Organisations could also encourage social contact between expats and locals, for example by making sure that the expat is not isolated in an office away from the locals and that there are common spaces to meet.[14] Another way is to organise social events where employees get the opportunity to chat. Since people often have the tendency to stick to those they know, it is recommended to do something during the event that makes expats and locals interact, for example a team building activity. Another option to encourage interactions between expats and locals is to take the opportunity to get input from everyone on a particular topic through setting up a World Café.[15] A World Café is a method to host a large group dialogue, where people are spread over several tables to discuss a topic. The groups rotate and add to the previous discussion that is recorded on the paper at the new table, and ultimately, the input is shared in the larger group. This is a great way to get input on a topic of interest from employees, and organisations can simply make sure that the groups at the table are composed of both expats and locals. Such events also make expats and locals connect more afterwards, since they have something to talk about.[16] Organisations can also make an inventory of possible activities outside of the workplace where an expat could meet locals of the host country, such as a buddy system organised by the local municipality, and encourage the expats to participate (see Box 10.1 about the foundation *Eet Mee* that brings people together through dinners).

---

### Box 10.1   Eet Mee: A remarkable instrument for social integration

Annelies Kastein, Director, Foundation Eet Mee

In today's diverse and dynamic societies, the challenge of social integration is a recurring theme. Addressing this challenge head-on is the innovative concept of *Eet Mee* (Dutch for "Join me/us for dinner"). Successfully implemented in the Netherlands, this award-winning initiative brings together people of various backgrounds and ages through intimate home-cooked meals. Beyond merely sharing stories and exploring cultures, these gatherings have the potential to foster new friendships, acting as a vital bridge between generations and cultures.

#### Connecting through the dining table

Eet Mee orchestrates informal dining encounters between local residents and also newcomers, including expats and refugees, such as Syrians and, more recently, Ukrainians. These meetings take place around the dining table, allowing participants to share not only flavours and recipes but also narratives, experiences and a profound sense of connection. For newcomers struggling with language barriers, cultural differences and feelings of isolation, this informal setting provides a comfortable space to build relationships and integrate into the social fabric of their new environment.

## From modest beginnings to nationwide impact

Originating as a small project in Utrecht in 2009, Eet Mee has since evolved into a nationwide effort, resulting in over 12,000 matches (with each match referring to a participant at a dinner). Using various formats, including a matching platform with diverse theme groups, Eet Mee pairs hosts and guests based on shared preferences and availabilities. These interactions culminate in dinners that break down biases, enhancing mutual respect and appreciation.

## Cultivating personal relationships

At the heart of Eet Mee is the cultivation of personal relationships. Hosts and guests often form lasting connections that extend beyond mealtime. These relationships can even develop into friendships that offer practical support, counteracting the isolation often felt by newcomers and contributing to their overall well-being. A pivotal aspect of Eet Mee is its facilitation of intercultural connections. Regardless of whether expats and refugees participate as hosts or guests, sharing traditional dishes and customs creates a universal means to access each other's cultures.

## Beyond food: supporting language and communication

Beyond cultural exchange, Eet Mee also supports language acquisition and communication. Through the themed *Taal Aan Tafel* (language at the table) group on the platform, individuals seeking to improve their Dutch language skills are matched with hosts who assist them. These mealtime conversations empower newcomers to enhance their language abilities and bolster their confidence in using the local tongue. This not only contributes to their daily functioning but also to education and employment.

## Building bridges through shared experiences

Participants hold these dining experiences in high regard. "Having dinner brings people together. It was important for us to learn more about life in the Netherlands. Communication with local residents helps in this. And we also introduced our culture to them. We had a lot of common topics, like daily family life, education, work, travelling, culinary topics. These meetings help us understand the Dutch better and vice versa. We will stay in touch with the family." Also for refugees, these dinners can break down a wall: "Having a homemade dinner with welcoming people really made us feel the rare feeling of being normal again. Since we fled our country, we are constantly under stress and pressure. But such a simple thing as meeting new people and being welcome to their home really was heartwarming."

### A multifaceted exchange

Encouraging expats to step outside their social circles, Eet Mee invites them to participate in these inclusive initiatives. In essence, Eet Mee has evolved into a potent instrument for the social integration of expats and refugees. Through home-cooked dinners, informal interactions, intercultural exchanges and the fostering of enduring relationships, this initiative provides an authentic and welcoming environment for mutual understanding and contributes to successful integration in diverse societies.

### Create a fair and inclusive organisational culture

For the contact between expats and locals to be successful, it is important that organisations create the right conditions. Intergroup contact has more positive effects when the groups have equal status, and the contact is supported by the organisation.

First, organisations should make sure that expats and locals are treated fairly. One important aspect is the fairness of the expat's compensation with regard to the locals. If local colleagues do not feel the expat's compensation is relatively fair, they will be unwilling to support the expat. A large compensation gap will not lead to a constructive environment for interactions between expats and locals. Organisations should also reduce ethnocentric policies such as always sending parent country national expats from headquarters to local subsidiaries,[17] which suggests that expats are more valued than locals. As also mentioned in Chapter 6 on intercultural mentoring, the locals of the host country subsidiary are an important source of global talent and also play an important role in knowledge management, so it makes sense that they should also be treated fairly.

The organisation can also make sure to support expats as well as locals. We have seen how important perceived organisational support is for expats, and the same is the case for the locals. If they perceive the organisation as supportive and caring for them, they are more likely to be helpful to their colleagues, whether they are an expat or not.[18] Especially career development support, such as formal programmes and policies that help locals from the host country develop managerial skills and advance, can be a great way to signal to the locals that they are valued and part of the global network of the organisation, and locals might reciprocate by helping expats.[19] Organisations should also make sure it is clear to the locals if they are expected to help the expat, and they could also reward them for their efforts.

The HR department can also help in creating a culture in the organisation where cultural diversity is seen positively, as a source of learning and innovation. Cultural diversity is just another aspect of the diversity of the workforce in an organisation, and valuing the differences between employees can have benefits in terms of attracting, retaining and motivating talent, as well as enhancing creativity and innovation in responding to a more diverse range of clients. A truly inclusive organisation encourages a sense of belongingness and uniqueness among all employees, where people feel valued for who they are and what they bring to the organisation.[20] Earlier mentioned aspects such as fair treatment of all employees is an important ingredient for an inclusive culture. The leaders of the organisation can also help create an inclusive culture through showing appreciation for others' contributions and inviting all group members to give input. Another way to create an inclusive culture is to make sure that all groups have access to information (this is very relevant in the case of expats who might not speak the local language), can participate in decision making and that there are procedures for resolving conflicts.

### Health and safety

Expats face unique demands and pressures and organisations should provide a healthy workplace for all their employees. Such a workplace not only includes physical aspects but also psychological factors such as stress and mental health, and social factors such as social support and relationships in the workplace.[21] To ensure well-being of all employees, it is important that organisations also take the social aspect into account of the expat's working life abroad, as has been discussed in this book. Furthermore, general practitioners and other health professionals should also recognise the importance of social networks for the expat's health and be aware that a lack of social connections in the host country can lead to health issues (see also Box 10.2). The psychiatrist Carlos Sluzki offers a mapping tool that can be used to determine strengths and weaknesses in a patient's social network[22] and suggests interventions which can be as simple as telling the patient to call someone they haven't seen in two weeks, 'just to chat.' Also, expats can be encouraged to simply talk to a 'stranger' when commuting or standing in a queue, or make an effort to greet one's neighbours because this improves well-being.[23]

---

**Box 10.2   Social connections as a 'need-to-have'**

Signe Biering, former diplomat and leadership coach, advises companies on how to onboard internationals

Our work at Project Onboard Denmark[24] and my work as a coach of international leaders in Denmark have shown just how crucial social relationships are for people from diverse backgrounds. The COVID-19 pandemic put a spotlight on the huge significance of these connections, revealing clear differences in how isolation affected internationals compared to Danes.

For internationals, social relationships act as a lifeline, especially when they are in a new place. Being away from home means they rely heavily on bonding with fellow expats, getting to know Danes and connecting with colleagues. These connections offer them emotional support, help them deal with feelings of loneliness and guide them as they adapt to a different culture, language and lifestyle. By having a mix of social contacts, internationals find the confidence to shape a meaningful life in Denmark.

Interestingly, many of my clients are surprised by how much their emotional well-being impacts their work dynamics. This underlines how intertwined our personal and professional lives are, affecting not only our interactions with others but also our overall sense of belonging. Ignoring these connections can lead to feeling detached from our surroundings.

When the COVID-19 pandemic hit, it really emphasised the importance of these relationships. As lockdowns and social distancing measures took hold, we realised just how vital even the smallest social ties were. But, the impact of being isolated was quite different for internationals compared to Danes. During the lockdown, I spoke with more than a dozen internationals, and all but one of them felt incredibly socially isolated. The lack of in-person interactions left them without the emotional and practical support they usually got from their social networks. Interestingly, they hesitated to reach out to Danish colleagues for a chat or a walk, feeling like they were on their own in feeling this way. They struggled to admit to their colleagues that they were lonely and needed connections.

While the pandemic was an extreme situation, it definitely showed us how fundamental social relationships are for internationals. These connections provide a sense of belonging, both in Danish society and within their work environments. They give emotional support, aid in adjusting to a new culture and help with personal growth – qualities that we used to see as just "nice to have." Now, we know they are a "need to have." The pandemic highlighted just how vital these social contacts are and reinforced the need for welcoming and supportive communities, especially for internationals. As we move forward, it's crucial to recognise these differences and make sure we nurture diverse social networks for internationals, making sure they stay connected, engaged and strong.

## Attracting and retaining talent as a society

Many countries struggle to attract and retain international talent in the face of increasing labour shortages. Governments at both the national and local levels can do much to create a welcoming environment which helps to retain this valuable human talent. A good example of what a society can do is Canada, where immigrants make up about a quarter of the population. Canada is very welcoming to immigrants, even topping the Gallup's Migration Acceptance Index in 2019. Pathways of Prosperity, an alliance of university, community and government partners dedicated to fostering welcoming communities and promoting the integration of immigrants and minorities across Canada, have done some research on what makes a community welcoming.[25] The most important characteristics are about access to affordable and suitable housing, healthcare and immigrant-serving agencies that can help them when needed. Canada offers free services to newcomers, for example for help with looking for a job, finding a place to live, registering for language classes and learning about community services. Having opportunities to find a job or start a company are important too, as are positive attitudes towards immigrants of all racial, cultural and religious background.

Such positive attitudes can be stimulated from a young age. People who have contact with other racial groups as a child – for example in their neighbourhood or at school – are more likely to have more racially diverse social groups as an adult.[26] Societies can implement policies that increase intercultural contact in neighbourhoods and at schools, and universities can increase the contact between international and local students. Having intercultural friendships also is something students take with them to life after university.[27] Universities can play an important role in creating a welcoming environment for international talent by making it normal for local students to work together and interact with students from different cultural backgrounds. The local students then take these positive attitudes and intercultural skills into the labour market, where they are more likely to better work with newly arrived expats and welcome them to the community.

A welcoming environment for international students may also help retaining this source of global talent to the host country. Several countries such as Australia, Canada, Finland, France, New Zealand and Norway have eased their immigration policies to encourage the immigration of international students.[28] Universities should encourage and facilitate contact between international and local students because such contact may lead to intercultural friendships, embedding the international students in the host country. They then might want to stay for a job. This intercultural contact also is a great opportunity for the development of intercultural competence – not only of the international students but also the locals. Workplaces are internationalising and many people do business beyond geographical borders. Internationalisation at Home[29] is increasingly emphasised in universities in Europe to help non-mobile students gain international experience and intercultural skills. It is crucial, however, that contact between international and local students is encouraged because mere exposure to someone of another culture in the classroom is not enough. Intercultural interaction needs to be stimulated, for example through a buddy system or activities where students have to work together.

Canada also emphasises the importance of welcoming communities where policymakers at all levels of government, service providers and the general public all have an important role to play. They have set up the buddy system, Canada Connects, which helps newcomers settle by matching them with Canadian citizens or long-time community members[30] because: "Integration is a two-way street and everyone can get involved to build welcoming communities." This does not have to be at the national level, but can be locally organised as well, as for example in Denmark, where some cities (e.g. Copenhagen and Odense) have buddy systems where the expat or partner is connected to a host volunteer. Locals play an important role in being welcoming to newcomers. For example, people often underestimate the power of an invitation. Locals have their established social network and don't necessarily have the time and space to invite an expat for something, so if they are able to do this – for example, extend an invite to an expat for a party you are organising anyway – this can really help the expat feel more welcome and part of a social network. One Indian expat said about her Danish local colleague:

> She was just very welcoming in many ways. Inviting me to her house I think was a pretty significant step because she didn't know me that well and she still did it. I'm very grateful she did! That was very nice!

Such welcoming communities offer a lot of scope for new friendships. Expats who are able to create a new social network in the host country are more locally embedded and less likely to leave the country again.[31]

Living and working abroad can indeed be a great adventure. Making new friends is essential for having a good time in the new host country, and organisations and societies can do much to encourage positive relationships between expats and locals, to the benefit of everyone involved. It might not always be easy, but as Ilse, the German expat in the Netherlands, said:

> I think every country, every place you go has a place where you can meet people easily – it might be a bar – it might be, if you have children, a crèche or day care… It can be even a very silent place like a library, but when you get your coffee, you stand in the line, and you talk with someone.

## Notes

1  Caligiuri, P. M., & Hippler, T. (2010). Maximizing the success and retention of international assignees. In K. Lundby & J. Jolton (Eds.), *Going global. Practical applications and recommendations for HR and OD professionals in the global workplace* (pp. 333–376). San Francisco, CA: Jossey-Bass.
2  Maddux, W. W., & Galinsky, A. D. (2009). Cultural borders and mental barriers: The relationship between living abroad and creativity. *Journal of Personality and Social Psychology, 96*(5), 1047.
3  Hall, J. A. (2018). How many hours does it take to make a friend? *Journal of Social and Personal Relationships, 36*(4), 1278–1296.
4  Fehr, B. (2008). Friendship formation. In S. Sprecher, A. Wenzel, & J. Harvey (Eds.), *Handbook of relationship initiation* (pp. 29–54). New York, NY: Psychology Press.
5  Becker, J. A., Johnson, A. J., Craig, E. A., Gilchrist, E. S., Haigh, M. M., & Lane, L. T. (2009). Friendships are flexible, not fragile: Turning points in geographically-close and long-distance friendships. *Journal of Social and Personal Relationships, 26*(4), 347–369.
6  Podsiadlowski, A., Vauclair, C.-M., Spiess, E., & Stroppa, C. (2013). Social support on international assignments: The relevance of socioemotional support from locals. *International Journal of Psychology, 48*(4), 563–573.

7  Rhoades, L., & Eisenberger, R. (2002). Perceived organizational support: A review of the literature. *Journal of Applied Psychology, 87*(4), 698–714.

8  van der Laken, P., van Engen, M., van Veldhoven, M., & Paauwe, J. (2016). Expatriate support and success: A systematic review of organization-based sources of social support. *Journal of Global Mobility: The Home of Expatriate Management Research, 4*(4), 408–431.

9  Goede, J., & Berg, N. (2018). The family in the center of international assignments: A systematic review and future research agenda. *Management Review Quarterly, 68*, 77–102.

10  Pettigrew, T. F., & Tropp, L. R. (2006). A meta-analytic test of intergroup contact theory. *Journal of Personality and Social Psychology, 90*(5), 751–783.

11  Fee, A., Heizmann, H., & Gray, S. J. (2015). Towards a theory of effective cross-cultural capacity development: The experiences of Australian international NGO expatriates in Vietnam. *International Journal of Human Resource Management, 28*(14), 2036–2061.

12  Wang, C.-H., & Varma, A. (2018). A process model of how interpersonal interaction leads to effectiveness of the expatriate-host country national relationship: An intergroup contact perspective. *Cross Cultural and Strategic Management, 25*(4), 670–689.

13  Aaron, R., Cedeño, C., Gareis, E., Kumar, L., & Swaminathan, A. (2018). Peers to peers: Developing a student-coordinated conversation partner program. *Journal of International Students, 8*(3), 1316–1327.

14  Shimoda, Y. (2013). Talk, trust and information flow: Work relationships between Japanese expatriate and host national employees in Indonesia. *International Journal of Human Resource Management, 24*(20), 3853.

15  https://theworldcafe.com/key-concepts-resources/world-cafe-method/ (accessed on 23 August 2023).

16  Shimoda (2013).

17  Wang and Varma (2018).

18  Toh, S. M., & DeNisi, A. (2007). Host country nationals as socializing agents: A social identity approach. *Journal of Organizational Behavior, 28*(3), 281–301.

19  Yamao, S., Yoshikawa, T., Choi, D., & Toh, S. M. (2020). When do host country nationals help expatriates? The roles of identification with the multinational enterprise and career development support by the subsidiary. *Journal of International Management, 26*(3), 100778.

20  Shore, L. M., Randel, A. E., Chung, B. G., Dean, M. A., Holcombe Ehrhart, K., & Singh, G. (2011). Inclusion and diversity in work groups: A review and model for future research. *Journal of Management, 37*(4), 1262–1289.

21  De Cieri, H., & Lazarova, M. (2021). "Your health and safety is of utmost importance to us": A review of research on the occupational health and safety of international employees. *Human Resource Management Review, 31*(4), 100790.

22  https://sluzki.com/publications/articles/129/personal-social-networks-and-health-conceptual-and-clinical-implications-of-their-reciprocal-impact (accessed on 23 August 2023).

23  www.goodnewsnetwork.org/mister-rogers-had-a-point-routinely-greeting-six-neighbors-maximizes-wellbeing-outcomes/ (accessed on 23 August 2023).

24  www.onboarddenmark.dk (accessed 23 August 2023).

25  https://theconversation.com/as-canada-welcomes-historic-numbers-of-imm igrants-how-can-communities-be-more-welcoming-206054 (accessed 23 August 2023).

26  Emerson, M. O., Kimbro, R. T., & Yancey, G. (2002). Contact theory extended: The effects of prior racial contact on current social ties. *Social Science Quarterly, 83*(3), 745–761.

27  McCabe, J. M. (2016). *Connecting in college*. Chicago, IL: University of Chicago Press, p. 160.

28  www.oecd-ilibrary.org/docserver/eag_highlights-2011-14-en.pdf (accessed on 23 August 2023).

29  www.eaie.org/blog/internationalisation-at-home-practice.html (accessed on 23 August 2023).

30  www.canada.ca/en/immigration-refugees-citizenship/campaigns/canada-conne cts.html (accessed 23 August 2023)

31  Yunlu, D. G., Ren, H., Fodchuk, K. M., & Shaffer, M. (2018). Home away from home: Community embeddedness and expatriate retention cognitions. *Journal of Global Mobility: The Home of Expatriate Management Research, 6*(2), 194–208.

# Index

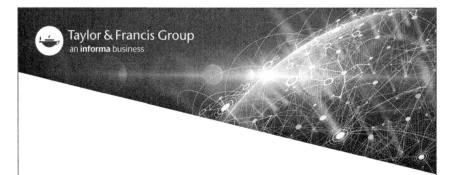

Printed in the United States
by Baker & Taylor Publisher Services